THE REGIONS OF BRITAIN

The Cotswolds

THE REGIONS OF BRITAIN
Previous and forthcoming titles in the series include:

The Pennine Dales	Arthur Raistrick
The Upper Thames	J. R. L. Anderson
The Lake District	Roy Millward and Adrian Robinson
The Scottish Border and Northumberland	John Talbot White
The Islands of Western Scotland	W. H. Murray
The Peak District	Roy Millward and Adrian Robinson
The South-East	John Talbot White
East Anglia	Norman Scarfe
Cornwall	W. G. Hoskins
The Welsh Marches	Roy Millward and Adrian Robinson
The Central Midlands	Victor Skipp

JOSCELINE FINBERG

The Cotswolds

EYRE METHUEN · LONDON

First published 1977

Printed in Great Britain for
Eyre Methuen Ltd
11 New Fetter Lane, London EC4P 4EE
by Cox & Wyman Ltd
Fakenham, Norfolk

ISBN 0 413 28500 6 (hardback)
ISBN 0 413 37330 4 (paperback)

The Cotswolds

Contents

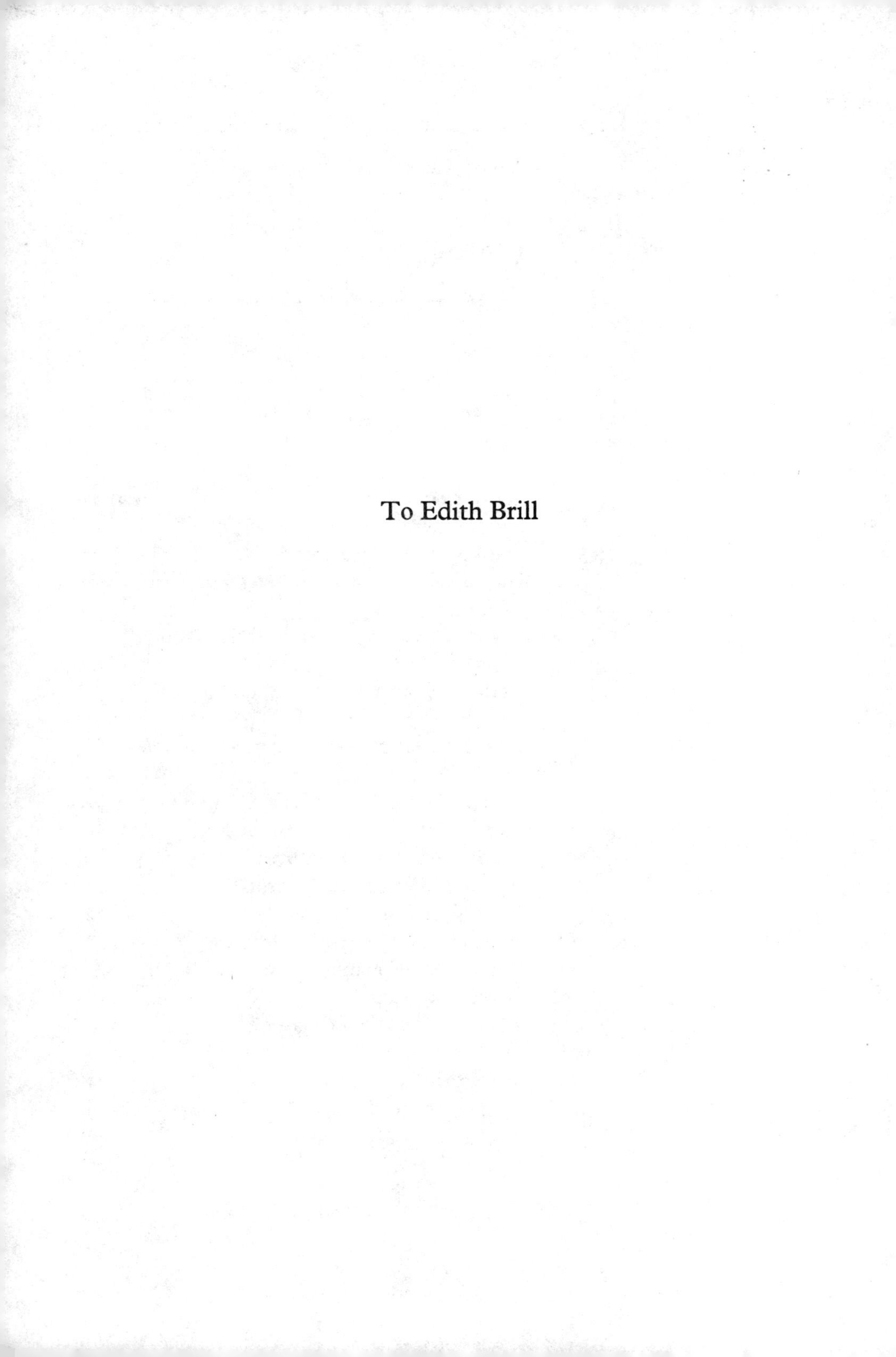

To Edith Brill

The Cotswolds

Illustrations

MAPS

Acknowledgements

Without the help of my late husband, Professor H. P. R. Finberg, this book would never have been written.

My thanks are also due to Professor R. Millward for help with chapters 1 and 2; to Mr Ogilvy of the Slimbridge Wildfowl Trust in connection with chapter 2; to Professor Stuart Piggott in connection with chapter 3; to Mr J. M. Giles of Messrs Strachan of Lodgemore, and the staff of Messrs Marling and Evans of Kings Stanley, in connection with chapter 11.

I should also like to thank Mr Peter Turner for taking many photographs specially for the illustrations and for a number of helpful suggestions.

Acknowledgement and thanks for permission to reproduce the illustrations are due to P. D. Turner for plates 2, 3, 4, 5, 6, 7, 11, 12, 13, 16, 17, 18, 20, 21, 23, 24, 26, 27, 28, 29, 33, 34, 35, 38 and 39; to the Controller of Her Majesty's Stationery Office, Crown Copyright, for plates 8, 9 and 10; to Aerofilms Ltd for plate 14; to Mrs F. L. Griggs for plates 15 and 31; to the National Monuments Record for plates 19, 22, 32 and 36; to English Life Publications Ltd for plate 25; to Reece Winstone for plate 30; and to Eagle Photos for plate 37. The maps were drawn from the author's roughs by Neil Hyslop.

The Cotswolds

Introduction

A band of golden limestone known as oolite lies across the breast of England from the Humber to the Dorset coast; it creates a gently flowing landscape and provides marvellous building stones which make its presence immediately recognizable. This formation is at its widest, and reaches its highest levels and its most attractive and distinctive character, in the upland country called the Cotswolds.

The Cotswolds lie mainly in Gloucestershire, but the south-western fringe extends into Avon and Wiltshire, and rather over a fifth to the east lies in Oxfordshire and takes in a few square miles of Warwickshire. Old maps, indeed, show extensive islands belonging to Worcestershire, but these ancient anomalies were removed in 1931. At the Four Shire Stone near Moreton-in-Marsh, only Oxfordshire, Gloucestershire and Warwickshire now meet.

No two Cotswold lovers will agree about the precise limits of the Cotswolds. For the purposes of this book, therefore, they are defined by easily recognized boundaries which enclose a region with a fundamental unity in geological structure, history, and economic development. This region forms a roughly lozenge-shaped territory, lying between Banbury (north-east), Bradford-on-Avon (south west), Cheltenham (north) and Malmesbury (south). From Banbury to Bradford-on-Avon is about sixty miles, from Cheltenham to Malmesbury about thirty. Approximately half the land lies between the 400 and 600-ft contours, the rest mostly between 600 and 900 feet, forming a scarp at the northern and western edges with heights above 1,000 feet here and there. On Haresfield Beacon the view from the scarp embraces the Severn estuary, the river a silvery sash in the middle distance, with the mountains of Wales and Dean Forest in the

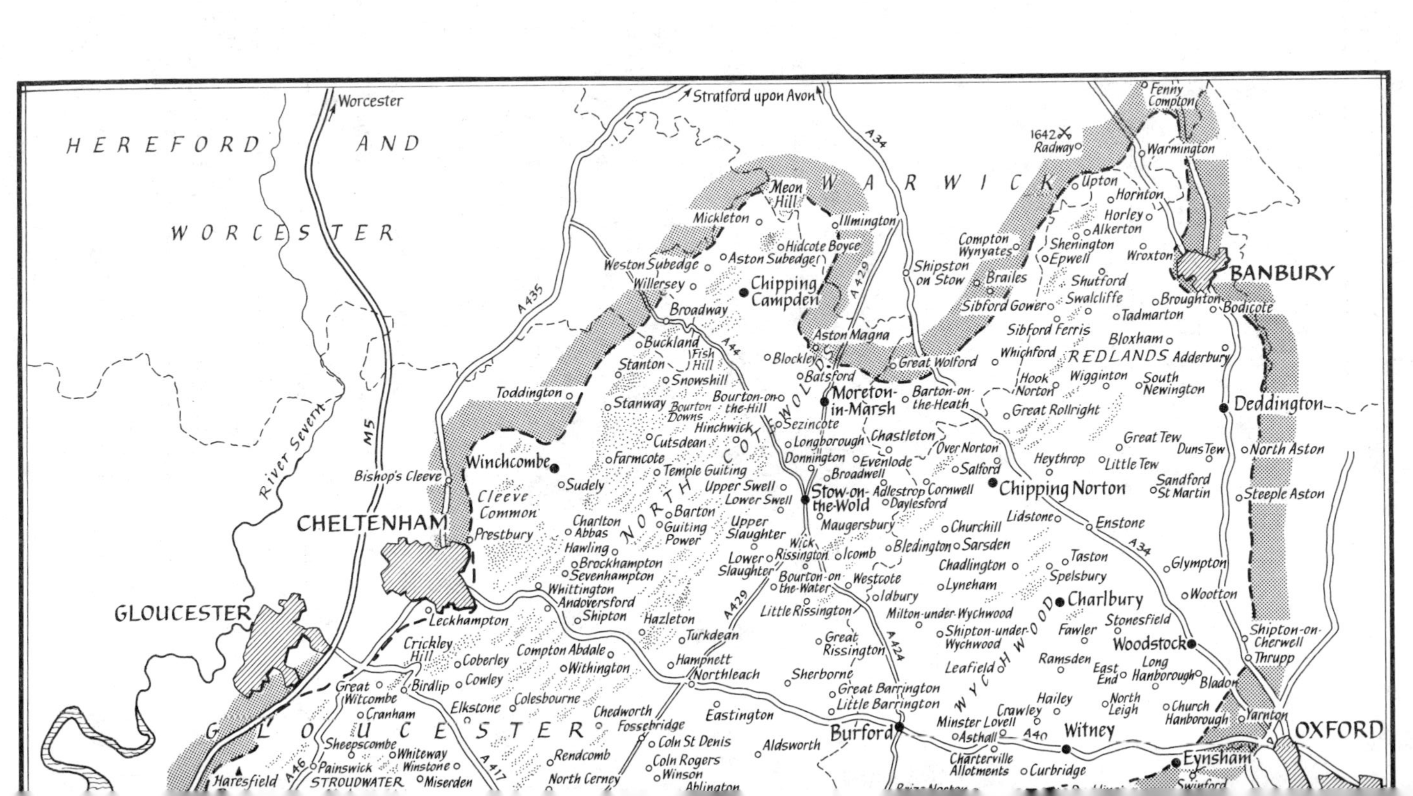

HEREFORD AND WORCESTER
WARWICK
NORTH COTSWOLDS
REDLANDS
WYCHWOOD
GLOUCESTER
Worcester
Stratford upon Avon
BANBURY
OXFORD
CHELTENHAM
GLOUCESTER
Fenny Compton
Warmington
1642 Radway
Upton
Hornton
Horley
Alkerton
Wroxton
Shenington
Epwell
Shutford
Swalcliffe
Tadmarton
Broughton
Bodicote
Bloxham
Adderbury
Compton Wynyates
Brailes
Sibford Gower
Sibford Ferris
Whichford
Hook Norton
Wigginton
South Newington
Great Rollright
Deddington
North Aston
Steeple Aston
Great Tew
Little Tew
Duns Tew
Sandford St Martin
Chipping Norton
Heythrop
Enstone
Glympton
Wootton
Shipton-on-Cherwell
Thrupp
Yarnton
Bladon
Woodstock
Church Hanborough
Long Hanborough
North Leigh
East End
Stonesfield
Eynsham
Swinford
Taston
Spelsbury
Charlbury
Fawler
Ramsden
Hailey
Witney
Crawley
Curbridge
Minster Lovell
Asthall
Charterville Allotments
Leafield
Shipton-under-Wychwood
Milton-under-Wychwood
Lyneham
Chadlington
Sarsden
Churchill
Lidstone
Salford
Over Norton
Cornwell
Daylesford
Adlestrop
Evenlode
Chastleton
Barton-on-the-Heath
Great Wolford
Shipston on Stow
Ilmington
Hidcote Boyce
Aston Subedge
Aston Magna
Blockley
Batsford
Moreton-in-Marsh
Longborough
Donnington
Broadwell
Stow-on-the-Wold
Maugersbury
Icomb
Bledington
Westcote
Idbury
Wick Rissington
Great Rissington
Little Rissington
Bourton-on-the-Water
Sherborne
Great Barrington
Little Barrington
Burford
Aldsworth
Eastington
Northleach
Hampnett
Turkdean
Lower Slaughter
Upper Slaughter
Lower Swell
Upper Swell
Sezincote
Bourton-on-the-Hill
Chipping Campden
Meon Hill
Mickleton
Weston Subedge
Willersey
Broadway
Buckland
Fish Hill
Snowshill
Stanton
Stanway
Bourton Downs
Hinchwick
Cutsdean
Temple Guiting
Farmcote
Guiting Power
Barton
Hazleton
Brockhampton
Sevenhampton
Charlton Abbas
Hawling
Whittington
Andoversford
Shipton
Compton Abdale
Withington
Chedworth
Fossebridge
Coln St Denis
Coln Rogers
Winson
Ablington
Rendcomb
North Cerney
Colesbourne
Cowley
Coberley
Elkstone
Leckhampton
Crickley Hill
Birdlip
Great Witcombe
Cranham
Sheepscombe
Whiteway
Winstone
Miserden
Painswick
STROUDWATER
Haresfield
Toddington
Winchcombe
Sudely
Cleeve Common
Prestbury
Bishop's Cleeve
River Severn
A34
A429
A44
A435
M5
A40
A424
A417
A46

Map 1 *The Cotswolds.*

background and Dunkery Beacon on Exmoor a shadow on the sky to the south-west; from Cleeve Cloud the Severn Plain melts into the sky with the outline of the Malverns forming a romantic side-screen; from Dover's Hill the spires of Coventry can sometimes be glimpsed in the purplish distance beyond the shoulder of Meon Hill, the long bulk of Bredon, the Cotswold outlier from which Housman gazed at the same 'coloured counties', interposing on the west.

It is said that rain falling on the narrow road along Edgehill will drain on one side into the Thames, on the other into the Severn; the source of the little river Churn at Seven Springs, which a Latin inscription carved on stone claims as the source of the Thames, is less than a mile from the Edge above Cheltenham. The scarp is the watershed between the Thames and the Midland river systems, and in spite of their very modest elevation the Cotswolds constitute a real barrier, a border country with a very clearly defined character. In the river basins on either side, man has dominated the landscape in the most obvious way, felling the forests and draining the marshes, and covering the whole with his prairie corn-fields, anonymous houses, acres of grass, brassica, and regimented fruit trees. In the hills an immemorial cooperation between man and nature still determines the appearance of the landscape. The beech has been naturalized here at least since Roman times and probably much longer: it still clothes as a valuable crop the steep slopes of the scarp and the southern valleys, where planting and replanting through the centuries have preserved and improved the natural woodland; it is used to provide a beautiful windbreak for exposed farmsteads and villages, to grace a gentleman's park. Fields are still divided by low walls laid without mortar or earth to bind them, weaving over the humps and hollows of the barely covered rock, their flowing lines still broken here and there with great bushes of white thorn and elder. These walls wear a dressing of infinitesimal silver, brown or yellow lichens, and the granulation of the stone itself catches and holds the light, as if the unfailing sunshine in the millennial seas where it was formed had been permanently entrapped; church, manor house, cottage and barn, though they appear in the distance as a grey mass, on closer looking glow with the same quiet radiance, and fit into the hillsides almost like natural outcrops of the under lying stone. Every structure, in whatever style, on which the stone is used in the course of a few years is well assimilated, and adds to the harmonious variety.

Here and there a bit of new work will display the colour of the stone when fresh from the quarries, in the south Cotswolds a delicate creamy grey, over most of the area a pale buff, in the east a rich orange-brown. That this marvellous material created the finest vernacular building in the country can be seen in even

1. *A view from the South Cotswold Edge.*

the smallest Cotswold villages and towns. The Cotswold style, as it has come to be called, is a variation of the building fashions of the late sixteenth century, identified by prominent gables, low roofs with dormers, casement windows with stone mullions and transoms, and moulded dripstones and doorcases. In the Cotswolds, gables are numerous; on all the more important houses, and often on cottages, dormers in the roof take the form of small flat gables, and the flat gable is a regular feature. The chief glory of Cotswold building, however, is the stone-tiled roof, steeply pitched and slightly concave, swept without flashing or gutter round the angles of gables and wings, finished with beautifully dressed ridges and carved finials, and crowned by simple chimney stacks of smooth ashlar. This is not an arbitrary convention: the porous quality of oolite demands a steep pitch to allow the water to run off quickly; the concave slope helps to prevent the tiles from shifting. Exceptionally heavy timbers are needed to carry the great weight of a stone roof, and the high price of long members in a country early denuded of woodland probably encouraged the use of a flat gable as a means of reducing the number of full-length timbers required. The fame of Cotswold freestone meant that ornamental detail was usually carved by masons trained in quarries able to produce work of the highest quality, for dispatch to churches and public buildings all over the south of England. Greater height and symmetry in the design of elevations were in due course introduced to comply with current fashion, and windows were modified and improved, but for over two hundred years the Tudor forms, so well suited to the material, remained standard in the Cotswolds for all building below the rank of mansion, and survive in profusion in town and village, farmstead and barn. It is a style well adapted to modern living, and was successfully revived in the early years of the present century.

Although there are many slopes too steep for cultivation, it is easy to see that these favoured uplands are being prosperously farmed. There is nothing new in this. Already four thousand years ago Neolithic culture flourished on the shallow, but well-drained and relatively fertile soils. In Roman Britain this district, though it was at the very edge of the well-populated and thoroughly colonized southern province, was one of the most favoured. Large-scale sheep-rearing in the Old English period is suggested by the numerous Shiptons (= sheep farm) and kindred names. In the middle ages Cotswold was a name well-known far beyond the national frontiers; it appears in the fifteenth-century records of Italian merchants as Chiondisgualdo, and Burford, Northleach and Cirencester were given equally outlandish transliterations. The Cotswold sheep brought the towns and villages wealth which founded the local building style, and developed the local character. This is not a landscape for romantics who think that people are pollution; it is a land of old settlement, gentle with long civilization, with an unsurpassed tradition of continuity and excellence.

The landscape offers two principal types of scenery. From the Iron Age fort on the Edge above Old Sodbury, north-eastward to the Cherwell and south-east to Malmesbury and Burford, the wall-chequered wolds curve and sweep in bare graceful lines, with rare plantations of beech and conifer, with isolated farm-

2. *A modern stone mason building a traditional drystone wall.*

steads and separate farm-buildings sparsely sprinkled over them. The network of roads is somewhat sparse too, but even lanes have a generous width, often with wide grassy verges on which bloom limestone-loving flowers in great profusion – until the County Council arrives with its pot of poison. Traveller's joy, the wild clematis, ramps over the wayside walls and self-sown saplings. Steep turf slopes are decked with white thorn and elder. Most of the villages lie hidden from the main roads in the valleys which intersect the plateau. The Churn, the Coln, the Leech, the Windrush, the Evenlode and their feeders have each a string of stone-built, stone-tiled villages shaded by groups of fine beech and chestnut trees, along the course of their limpid, flower-strewn waters. The Coln is notable for trout, and formerly local people used to hunt all the Cotswold streams at night for crayfish. In the Oxfordshire Cotswolds the bare sweep of the wolds is fragmented by much deeper valleys, though the streams are insignificant; drystone walls, where they exist, are buried in vegetation; the villages perch high on the valley sides, and thatch rivals stone slate as a roofing material.

This is a sparsely populated land where agriculture is still the dominant industry, and towns are all very small with most of their traditional building as yet unspoilt. Only Cirencester has a population over 10,000.

The western fringe of the Cotswolds has a dramatic landscape. The Edge, as it is called, runs south-west in an unbroken line for fifty-two miles from Dover's Hill, then due south to Bath, with summits above Broadway and Cheltenham reaching over 1,000 feet above sea level. North-east from Dover's Hill the scarp continues as a geographical feature to another fine climax on Edgehill, but is much broken by streams and wind gaps. Steep valleys bite deep into the Edge, clothed in woods of beech near the summit with a more varied woodland below, and with small fast-flowing streams in their narrow bottoms. These features are most marked in the Stroudwater Hills, where the Frome, or Stroudwater, is fed by a complex of valleys deeply intersecting the wolds where they are highest. The neighbouring streams, the Cam, the Little Avon, the Bristol Avon and their feeders, as they emerge, create bays and amphitheatres in the scarp, with wooded promontories between them such as Cam Long Down, Stinchcombe Hill, Haresfield and Painswick Beacon; from their bare summits marvellous views are to be had of the Vales of Gloucester and Severn. Here almost every short valley has its small town, and the grey villages gathered about ancient mills and warehouses along the valley-floor are extended by terraces of cottages climbing up towards the woods. This is an industrial district of which the chief product was historically a famous broadcloth, with ancillary manufactures of pins, needles and machine parts; the harvest of the woodlands was turned into bobbins, reels, sticks, canes and umbrella handles. The cloth industry survives only on a small scale, and although supporting industries have shown themselves more flexible, keeping the little towns busy and fairly prosperous, the landscape is still that of domestic industry as it was before the final and most catastrophic stage of the industrial revolution, and therefore of extreme historical interest as well as of great natural beauty. The towns, however, are not all so comely as those with a purely agricultural hinterland, because for more than a century their position on the edge of the barrier scarp, and the canals and railways which have supported their industry, have rendered them accessible to cheap and alien building materials.

It is allowed
That Stroud
Holds naught that's pretty,
Wise or witty.

In respect of prettiness, the local rhyme is perfectly justified for the Stroud valley, but the others have been more fortunate.

The Cotswolds are well served by their road system. All the streams rise near to the scarp and drain south-eastwards into the Thames. Between each small basin run long undulating plateaux, roughly on the same axis, rising gently from the Thames valley. These sweeps of high ground carry most of the main roads. In a region so much favoured by primitive man, who was obliged to settle and move about on high ground above the dangerous marshes and forests below, the alignments of these roads are mostly of extreme antiquity. Later settlers, however, preferred the valleys, and to settle away from roads down which nothing but trouble was likely to come. Thus the uplands are crossed every few miles by direct routes relatively free from twisting village streets, narrow bridges and other obstacles. Insignificant lanes serve the villages, so that, except for cruising tourists on a Sunday afternoon, most of them are quiet places, at all times free from the pollution of heavy traffic.

Two principal routes intersect with these north-west-to-south-east lines of communication. A prehistoric trackway, sometimes called the Great Cotswold Ridgeways, over much of its course is still followed by classified roads. This is part of a route from the Bristol Channel to the Humber known as the Jurassic Way. It enters the region by way of Lansdown outside Bath, and underlies A46 for about twelve miles; further east B4070 and A426 follow the line across the head of the Coln valley at Andoversford to a point just short of Naunton, where the prehistoric route crosses the infant Windrush and goes over the next plateau to Stow-on-the-Wold. From Stow, A436 follows it as far as the Cross-Hands on the junction with A44. Thence unclassified roads follow it past the Rollright stones, round the head of the Swere valley to join A361 within a few miles of Banbury where it crosses the Cherwell. The whole of this course is dotted with prehistoric sites, but passes through only two villages, Lower Swell and Great Rollright.

A more important and intelligible line of communication, indeed to some extent a substitute for the older route, is the Roman Fosse Way (A429 in Gloucestershire) which traverses the wolds from Bath via Cirencester, Northleach,

Stow-on-the-Wold and Moreton-in-Marsh without any of the meanderings imposed on primitive people by the need to keep out of waterlogged valleys. This is still the best and most direct route from the east Midlands to the Bristol Channel and the south-west. Just south of Cirencester the road has for many centuries departed from the line of the Fosse to follow the older route, so that the modern traveller can easily reach M5 by way of M4.

The lay-out of roads in the central and northern Cotswolds is so convenient that very little beyond widening, for which the traditional broad verges have normally provided sufficient scope, has so far been required. Although traffic on A40 has multiplied about six times in the last twenty years, two by-passes, one for the five-way meeting at Andoversford and the other for Witney, have so far been thought necessary.

Access from the rich and civilization-bearing south-east has thus always been easy. From the midland plain the scarp, when it was penetrated by relatively few, extremely precipitous and stony roads, must have been a formidable barrier, but perhaps already a promise of delight. Shakespeare must often have made the slow and chilly passage of its 'high wild hills and rough uneven ways' on his way to London. But he seems also to have been familiar with the coursing on the sheep-walks. He makes Falstaff, on his way to the wars, turn aside on pretence of recruiting, to pay a visit in Gloucestershire. Surely he must have had in mind the neighbourhood of Chipping Campden, only twelve miles from Stratford. In my mind's eye I see Master Shallow's garden in certain orchards in Saintbury or Aston-sub-Edge.

The Bath Hills were happily explored by visitors to the Spa, but to the eyes of the men of the world who came down from London to the spa at Cheltenham, the central Cotswolds made no appeal – 'a region of stone and sorrow', Sidney Smith called them, and the agricultural experts of the period were hardly less scathing about the landscape. But since the twentieth century loomed up, a procession of artists and craftsmen, of which William Morris and Ernest Gimson were pioneers, has recognized its beauty and moved in to work and settle, closely followed by country-lovers generally. A tour through the villages has long been a favourite outing for Midland motorists, and lately the Cotswolds have been recognized as a holiday area to a limited extent. Moreover, since the last war farms have prospered exceedingly, and a little light industry has been introduced in some of the run-down towns on the wolds. These developments have profoundly modified the simple poverty-haunted traditions of the villagers, but at the same time guaranteed for their lovely background a measure of protection.

I

The Physical Structure: Stone

The geological formation of the Cotswold Hills is a relatively simple one. They consist of bands of clays, sands and limestones superimposed upon one another, and gently tilted by the earth movements that shaped the London Basin in Tertiary times.

The rocks were deposited between 100 and 170 million years ago during the Jurassic period, at the time when the Jura mountains were formed. In those remote ages the centre of what is now England was submerged by a vast but relatively shallow and tranquil ocean, and the climate was sub-tropical. Our region was surrounded by large islands, among them what is now Devon and Cornwall, with the Mendips as an offshore island, what are now Wales, the Pennines, and a land-mass which linked the London area and East Anglia to a larger continent which has become the mainland of Europe. This ocean, a greatly enlarged Mediterranean, has been given the name Tethys, and the continent Hyrcinia; the Cotswolds were developed in what geologists have called the Oxford Shallows.

In these warm, sunny waters deposits of mud, pebbles, broken shells and fossilized tissue were laid down over millions of years to form an elaborate series of beds of clay or limestone. Subsidence had let in the sea, and under the accumulating weight of sediment part of the sea-bed sagged still further, so that at Stowell Park near Northleach the lowest beds of the Jurassic formation lie about a thousand feet below the surface, while only a few miles away they appear on the surface in the Windrush basin about Bourton-on-the-Water and in the Stour and Evenlode valleys. They are again encountered in the dramatic valleys at the

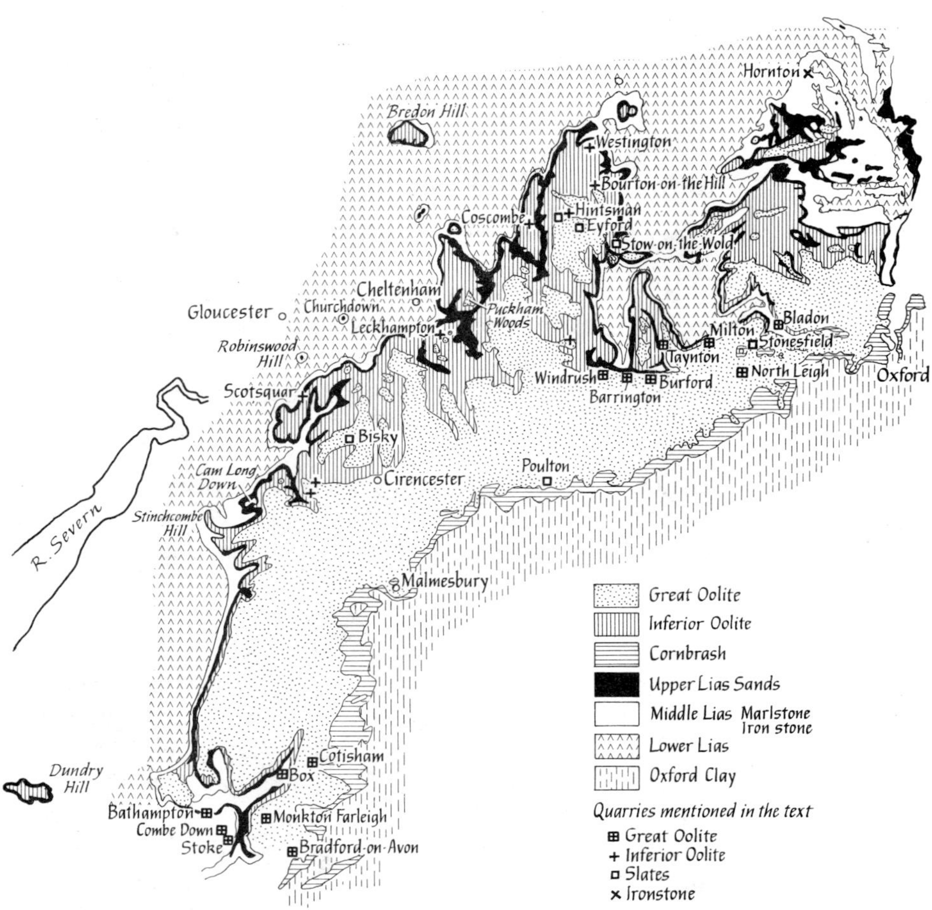

Map 2 *The geology of the Cotswolds showing the principal quarries.*

southern end of the Cotswold range where the sea-bed sloped down from the older carboniferous limestones of the Mendips.

The lower beds of the Cotswolds belong to the Liassic series. They are full of fossilized molluscs, especially ammonites, and the bones of primitive marine creatures and amphibians. The clays of the Lower Lias offer good material for brick-making which was formerly carried on at Aston Magna, Paxford, and elsewhere in the Stour basin, and at Wotton-under-Edge, Winchcombe and elsewhere at the foot of the scarp. They also proved invaluable for lining the floors of mill-dams in the clothing districts. On the other hand, the soils of the Lower Lias are heavy, cold, intractable and frequently water-logged. Their presence may often be inferred from such names as Coldpark Farm, Broadwater Bottom and Fulbrook.

The name 'Lias' was given to the series by William Smith, the father of British geology, born at Churchill in the Oxfordshire Cotswolds. He was an engineer and canal builder by profession, and borrowed the terms he used from the expressive vocabulary of working farmers, builders and quarrymen. The lias rock occurs in thin bands among the clays and in his day the *layers* or *liers* were quarried for flagstones and memorial tablets. Blocks of lias were the appropriate material for the delightful clapper bridges at Bourton-on-the-Water, Lower Slaughter and other villages; many of the houses in the neighbourhood had, or still have, floors of this material, especially the blue lias, a smooth stone admirably fitted for this purpose, but rather liable to flake if exposed to the weather. In a small quarry-pit in the surface of a field above Upper Swell near Flagstone Farm, for example, there remains a gallery in which the blue lias was mined for the floors in the village below, and the Hornton quarry near Banbury still offers it for sale.

The clays of the Lower Lias were succeeded in the Middle Lias series by lighter sandy or micacious clays, loams and sandstones, which again are rich in fossils. In the disused Tuffley Brickworks on the flank of Robinswood Hill, a Cotswold outlier near Gloucester, an exposed rockface displays the Lias series from the blue-grey stone of the Lower Lias up through the Marlstone to a narrow ferruginous band of the Middle Lias. The soil of the Middle Lias reveals its presence on the floor or sides of many of the valleys within the plateau as lush meadowland. Apart from fragments of fossils, the stone consists of pebbles, pellets and broken crystals of carbonate of lime, probably deposited as a shoal or ridge in the shifting sea-bed. Each layer again must be thought of as taking millions of years to accumulate.

The marlstone of the Middle Lias determines the character of the Oxfordshire Cotswolds east of the Evenlode. North from Bloxham it is rich in limonite, and has long been mined for iron ore in opencast mines. It is generally called ironstone. The soil is a light loam and excellent corn-land. The iron gives the buildings of the area, including the crowning glory of Bloxham church, their characteristic hot brown colour, varied here and there by dark olive and purple stones, and by a frosting of white lichen. This excellent building stone goes by the name of Hornton stone from a famous quarry in the village of that name.

The modern workings on the summit within sight of Edgehill Tower still provide material for memorial tablets and other decorative purposes. South of Bloxham, limonite is not present in workable quantities, but the building stone is still ochreous in colour. Apart from this, ironstone villages resemble those of the oolite.

The marlstone of the Middle Lias forms a terrace on the Cotswold escarpment throughout its length, often heavily wooded. Iron is said to have been worked on Robinswood Hill, and the name Iron Acton near Chipping Sodbury speaks for itself. The marlstone also makes a slight impression on the contours in the valleys which intersect the plateau, often carrying the valley road. The road from Stroud to Painswick (A46) offers an interesting example: it runs along this terrace above a deep combe on the other side of which, as a result of a fault, the old road to Painswick follows the same terrace on a higher level.

Since the clays of the Lias series form an impermeable layer, the Cotswold or Midford Sands associated with the marlstone act as a reservoir for surface water seeping through from above, and springs are forced out at this level. This spring-line is marked by a string of towns and villages – Dodington, Horton, Wotton-under-Edge, Stinchcombe and Dursley are sited on the marlstone terrace of the scarp, Uley in the upper Cam valley, Dudbridge and the older parts of Stroud in the Frome or Stroudwater valley, with Painswick on a marlstone spur between two side valleys. Reservoirs for Gloucester draw water from this layer at Great Witcombe and on Robinswood Hill, for Cheltenham from the Chelt valley below Dowdeswell and Whittington. In the north Cotswolds the same spring-line determines the site of the Hidcotes, Ebrington and Campden, of Bourton-on-the-Hill, Longborough, Oddington and Maugersbury on the slopes of the Evenlode valley, and Upper Slaughter, Naunton, Sherborne, Great Barrington and Great and Little Rissington in the Windrush basin are on or a little above the same feature. Andoversford, Withington, Whittington, Brockhampton, the Swells, Westcott and Adlestrop are built on the Upper Lias, obtaining their water (before mains were laid) from wells tapping the sands below. A sudden change from drystone walls to quickset hedge betrays the presence of the clay, and shows how, traditionally, the material for the walls was usually picked up off the surface, or quarried on the spot, leaving the dips and hollows which often increase the interest of the wide Cotswold verges.

Above the lias comes the oolite. Oolite (egg-stone or roestone to the quarryman) is a deposition of grains of carbonate of lime about minute specks of sand. The calcareous material is largely formed of crushed shells, decayed fish and other living bone and tissue, and partly of pebbles washed off from the lias formations, all swilled about together in very shallow waters. In Sapperton churchyard several flat tombstones are cut from slabs of oolite encrusted with fossilized shells of the commonest kind. A hill in the neighbourhood of Cricklade is called Cockleborough on account of the fossils found there.

3. *A slab of fossiliferous oolite in Sapperton churchyard bearing a characteristic engraved brass inscription plate.*

The layers of the Inferior Oolite cover the Cotswold plateau above the 800-foot contour line, and all the highest hills – Ham Hill, Cleeve Cloud and Charlton Kings Common, Belas Knap and Broadway Hill, the great promontories such as Nottingham Hill and Haresfield Beacon – are capped with the Inferior Oolite. Owing to the gradual up-tilting of the area to the east in the Jurassic period, the deposits have been almost completely worn away east of a line drawn from Chipping Norton to Woodstock, leaving rare patches on Madmarston Hill and a few others. The stone has a creamy buff colour when quarried, and weathers to an indescribable mixture of gold and grey with a mottling of white and yellow lichens.

Among the beds of the Inferior Oolite the poorer material has been much used for lime-burning and road metal. Among the ragstones, of which homestead and barn are built, Trygonia Grit is interesting for the fossils, notably oyster beds, which it contains. Hill Barn quarry in Sherborne parish offers a fine display of these. These freestones and peagrits provide the fine building stone throughout the north Cotswolds, especially the Yellow Guiting stone, which weathers to a rich golden colour. Coscombe Quarry above Stanway, which is still in production, displays the varieties of this stone in a splendid amphitheatre. Yellow Guiting is not confined to that neighbourhood; quarries on Bourton Hill, between Bourton-on-the-Water and Clapton, supplied it for the building of that beautiful but too famous village, and the stone from Campden's quarry at Westington, also still in use, is the associated White Guiting.

4. *Coscombe Quarry – note the tilted bedding planes left-centre.*

Freestone is the quarryman's name for stone which can be finely dressed, and is therefore suitable for smooth ashlar or decorative detail. The oolitic freestones are closely bedded and free from shell-fragments, and can easily be sawn or carved when fresh. When weathered they become hard and immensely durable, though if carelessly dressed or laid some are subject to the flaking called by masons spalling or onion-weathering, a disaster which has overtaken many Oxford facades dressed with Cotswold stone. It is the abundance of freestone which makes the beauty of Cotswold towns and villages. The golden ragstone, even the characteristic stone slates, are common to neighbouring parts of the Jurassic limestone belt. Only in the Cotswolds do cottage, barn and even pigstye show finely worked dripstones, ridges and gable ends, and towns such an efflorescence of attractive detail. Every town, and probably almost every village, had formerly a quarry of its own in which some freestone was present, quarries which can often be found quite easily on the adjacent slopes. The Edge, especially, is pock-marked with quarries. At Northleach, the market place itself is said to occupy the site from which much of the building stone, beginning with that for the church, was taken.

The most famous Cotswold quarry on the Inferior Oolite is at Leckhampton above Cheltenham. Here the outcrop is 138 feet thick. This face was already being quarried in the reign of Edward III, when a mason from Leckhampton found employment in the building of Vale Royal Abbey far away in Cheshire. It supplied stone for the medieval parish church at Cheltenham, and the face which students of geology come from all over England to visit was officially opened in 1793 to provide material for the Royal Crescent, the Montpelier Rotunda, the Queens Hotel and other famous buildings belonging to the Spa. The towering cliff-face displays a cross-section of the bedding-planes from the peagrit up to the ragstone. A free-standing spike of stone known as the Devil's Chimney, which is a prominent landmark from the town, is a residue of unserviceable rock left untouched by seventeenth- or eighteenth-century quarrymen.

The soil of the oolite is a delicate brown, a thin, light calcareous loam, full of stones. It was given by eighteenth-century agricultural specialists the contemptuous name of stone brash, which does it less than justice. 'As late coming as Cotswold barley' is a local saying, but when it comes it is a splendid crop. A very high proportion of the wolds is now under corn, mostly barley.

Between the Inferior and the Great Oolite lies a thin layer of clay known as fuller's earth, since it is the material traditionally used in cleansing wool and felting cloth. However the layer is not thick enough for industrial extraction except to a limited extent near Bath. Its importance is rather that the associated Cotswold sands form a reservoir to feed the springs which supply the villages of the upper valeys, and can be reached by wells from still higher settlements like Elkstone and Brimpsfield so that the plateaux are never barren and uninhabited wastes. At the top of Compton Abdale one of these abundant springs has been given a fine stone spout in the form of a crocodile's jaws. The soil is a sticky blue clay, often marked by patches of woodland.

Originally the Great Oolite probably overlay the whole of the Cotswolds, but the tilting of the whole mass left the western flank exposed to severe denudation. The series still occupies an extensive area of the dip slope between the 600 and 800-foot contours. Marshfield, Minchinhampton, Tetbury, Cirencester, Stow-on-the-Wold, Burford, Witney, Charlbury, Chipping Norton and part of

Woodstock, the most attractive market towns of the Cotswolds, as well as the magic valley villages of Churn, Coln, Leach and Windrush all belong to the series.

The Great Oolite has the colour of silver-guilt when quarried. When mature there is some variety: at Painswick a silvery moonlit quality, at Minchinhampton and Bradford rather a cold grey. The creamy orange which in some paint-makers' catalogues still goes by the traditionl name of 'stone' is derived from the Regency fashion for stucco painted and marked to resemble the honey-coloured Bath stone, which came from the Cotswold quarries of the Great Oolite.

It is never necessary to go far afield for fine freestone on the Great Oolite. Even for Dodington Park, the mansion of a nabob on which no expense was spared, the stone came from Toll Down, only a mile or so away. However, Box Ground Stone is the best and most sought after of all Bath stones, and probably the one that was first quarried extensively. According to legend, St Aldhelm (d. 709) visited Hazelbury, the parent settlement of Box, and throwing down his glove declared that where it fell they would find great treasure if they would dig for it. This story may be interpreted as evidence that Box stone was used for the first church at Malmesbury of which Aldhelm was abbot; it is certain that the freestone for Malmesbury's great mutilated abbey church came from the Hazelbury quarries, and the splendid romanesque south porch testifies to its enduring qualities. Extensive ancient workings are to be found alongside Quarry Hill, an unclassified road leading out of Box, and along the steep side of the By Brook valley alongside and above A4; somewhat later quarries on the level plateau above, on the ancient open fields of Hazelbury known as Box Grounds (*grounds* is the regional name for open fields). Other important Cotswold quarries in the Bath Hills were at Farleigh Down in Monkton Farleigh, Bradford-on-Avon, Monkton Down and Corsham. The blind arcades on the Saxon church of St Laurence at Bradford, still almost as sharp as on the day they were cut, testify to the virtue of the local quarries, one of which has recently been re-opened to provide stone for decorative purposes. Ralph Allen, the creator of eighteenth-century Bath, opened the quarries on Monkton Down, and his tramway for bringing down the stone was an innovation which offered an interesting spectacle to fashionable visitors. Later a line was made to link the quarry with the Kennet and Avon canal at Limpley Stoke.

By the seventeenth century the Great Oolite was almost always mined in inclined shafts driven into the hillsides. The removal of the considerable overburden was thus eliminated, and moreover the freestone is so soft and vulnerable to frost when fresh that, unless it could be stacked underground to mature, it could not be cut in winter. There are said to be upwards of sixty miles of underground galleries between Box and Corsham alone. The Corsham Down quarries, which are adjacent to Box Grounds, were the largest of all. In 1893 one quarry employed 1,025 quarrymen and 350 masons. Galleries run for miles in all directions from a vast excavation forming a bottle-shaped cavern 100 feet deep, locally known as the Cathedral, the scene from time to time of celebratory dinners, Methodist meetings and gatherings of quarrymen during industrial disputes. A vast reserve of maturing stone was kept there as a cushion against strikes or a sudden rush of business. The Cathedral itself was closed in 1850, and thereafter quarrymen used to bring their wives and sweethearts courting and picnicking in its twilit depths. After about 1900 many galleries were taken over for industrial purposes of a different kind, notably mushroom-farming. They have been progressively absorbed through two great wars by the Ministry of Defence, and are now occupied as naval stores and called H.M.S. *Royal Arthur*.

Around Minchinhampton there are many quary shafts, well-known to young people in search of adventure, bat fanciers and courting couples. Most of them have been sealed recently by the County Council on account of the incidence of serious accidents to unwary explorers. Stone from Balls Green quarries was used for the Houses of Parliament. Stone from Burleigh is still used for repair work on Gloucester cathedral and one of the quarries there is sometimes called the Dean and Chapter.

Freestone from Box was very widely used in the south of England and went even as far as Winchester in the Middle Ages. The superior attraction of Caen stone and later Portland stone lay chiefly in the ease of transport by sea. By 1800 Bath stone, as it came to be called, could be carried by canal, and was much used at Oxford. Stone from the Great Oolite, latterly called the Bathonian beds, was obtained by the university from 1280 onwards from the neighbourhood of Burford. The Taynton quarries, indeed, were already a source of profit when Domesday Book was made. The tower of Merton chapel (c. 1310) was built of Taynton stone, and it appears on most of the surviving medieval buildings in the university. William of Wykeham, founder of Winchester and New College, and Overseer at Windsor under Edward III, had as his Clerk of the Works one Richard Taynton, who no doubt learnt his trade in the quarries of his native village, and much Taynton stone was used in the castle, especially for St George's chapel. Stone from nearby Sherborne was used for the royal lodging. Taynton stone also appears at Eton in the beautiful chapel and other college buildings, and Taynton masons, working on the new St Pauls, are said to have found the familiar stone among the fire-stained ruins. The stones of Blenheim Palace, clean and sharp, and still showing the marks of the quarrymen's tools, came from Taynton, Stations and bridges on the Oxford–Worcester line come from part of the Taynton workings known ever since as the Railway or Rally Quar. (*Quar* is a dialect word used all over the Cotswolds.) Taynton stone was used in the vestibule and stairs of the Bodleian library extension built in 1939 as a veneer only $\frac{3}{4}$ inch thick and polished, a fine illustration of its beauty and tractability.

About two miles north of Burford along the Stow road (A424) there stands unobtrusively by the hedge a stone inscribed with pointing hand and the legend 'To Taynton Quarries'. A grassy trackway deeply hollowed out leads down to the workings, which almost alone among the Bathonian beds, are on the surface. To the right the Rally Quar presents a cliff forty feet high, and a fern-masked loading stage. The older workings are much overgrown. The quarries can also be reached by a track up from the village (a pearl among villages even by Cotswold standards), but the owner's permission must be obtained to visit them. In Idbury church, not three miles from the quarries, a memorial brass to Thomas Hautin, yeoman, shows a mason's axe and bolster.

The fine quality of Taynton stone brought the neighbouring quarries at Windrush, Sherborne, Barrington, Burford (Upton) and Milton into widespread use, though the stone is not equal to that of Taynton. Christopher Wren was induced by his master mason, Christopher Kempster, a Burford man, to use stone from his quarry at Upton, which has been known since his day as Kit's Quarry. This quarry had been in use for buildings in Burford at least since the fourteenth century; it appears in the building accounts of All Souls College, Oxford, in 1441, and it was used in the building of Cardinal College (Christchurch) in 1526, together with Barrington stone. Wren used both for Tom Tower, and probably also for some of the City churches. The town hall at Abingdon is thought to be Kempster's own masterpiece, and is probably of Burford stone. Kempster built himself a pleasant house at Upton (1698), with traditional Cotswold roof and chimneys, but with the then very new sash windows.

Barrington and Windrush both produced good durable freestones, though not quite equal to that of Taynton. Both were used at Windsor, and extensively in Oxford, and the Royal Commission appointed to select stone for the new Houses of Parliament in 1839 considered the stone of Windrush church the best preserved in the county. Unlike Taynton, both Windrush and Barrington freestone were mined in level shafts driven into the ridge along which A40 runs, and the innkeeper's wife at the New Inn at the cross-roads in Little Barrington parish, used to knock on the floor to call the quarrymen to their dinner. Milton stone was inferior, very subject to onion-weathering. The quarries are alongside an unclassified road from Burford to Milton-under-Wychwood. During the seventeenth and eighteenth centuries stone from Milton, the nearest source to Taynton, was probably dishonestly substituted in some cases, accepted as equivalent when demand exceeded supply in others, and by some ignorant architects even chosen, with disastrous results. There was, indeed, a perverse fashion for Milton stone among leading architects at Oxford in the latter part of the nineteenth century. Sir George Gilbert Scott, specified Milton stone for the new buildings at New College in 1875. Other unhappy examples were St Swithun's buildings at Magdalen and the Principal's Lodging at Jesus. Repair work carried out on St Mary's tower, spire, and nave and aisle parapets in the 1860s had to be redone in the 1890s, and thereafter no more Milton stone was used in Oxford, Magdalen Bridge (1882–3) is built of true Taynton stone.

The deserted quarries of the Cotswolds make charming haunts for botanists, geologists or mere ramblers looking for blackberries, but today many of them are being reopened to provide cement or material for the stone composition extensively used all over the region now that true masonry is prohibitively expensive. The material looks well when fresh; time alone will show how it weathers.

The stone tiles of the Jurassic limestone country come from the thin fissile limestones at the base of the Great Oolite series. They are not slates in the geological sense, but are always so-called. In Northamptonshire they are known as Colly Weston slates from the name of the most famous quarries, in Oxfordshire Stonesfield slates for the same reason; in Gloucestershire they could be obtained in so many places on the ragged fringes of the Great Oolite that they are known simply as Cotswold slates. Some stone can be used as it comes from the workings, and is called 'presents'. Presents are said to be the most durable of all, but are somewhat coarse-grained. They were used by the Romans and throughout the Middle Ages. Since the sixteenth century the associated 'pendle' stone which is much more plentiful, has supplied most of the roofs.

Pendle is dug in autumn and spread out upon the ground for the winter frosts to invade the thin film of water lying within the stone; when spring comes a blow with a mallet is sufficient to split it into slates. If the stone is allowed to dry out, however, it becomes 'bound', and nothing will restore its fissile properties. The stone may therefore be covered as soon as it is brought to the surface to keep in the quarry-sap until the onset of a hard frost. At Stonesfield, where the village is honeycombed with pit-shafts, at a given signal everybody turned out to help in uncovering and spreading out the stone, and if the frost came suddenly after dark, the church bells would be rung to call out the people. If a sufficient frost failed to materialize, the stone would be thoroughly soaked and built into clamps, thickly covered with earth and sown with vetches to keep the sun off, in order to preserve the quarry-sap during the summer.

Slate-quarrying was thus a seasonal occupation lasting from Michaelmas to January, and was popular work among labourers, keeping them warm and dry underground, and gainfully employed when there was not enough work for all on the farms. In spring and summer the mines were deserted and highly skilled slatters were at work above ground finishing the slates. Around Stonesfield many

5. *Cotswold roofs at South Cerney.*

of their little sheds and refuse-tips remain, buried in mounds of travellers' joy and bramble. The Stonesfield mines were for the most part small enterprises, engaged in fierce competition, and by the end of the nineteenth century they had strangled each other. According to local people the increasing mildness of the winters helped to kill the industry. The Duke of Marlborough's mine at Spratt's Barn, with a regular demand for slates used on his estates, remained open until 1909. Most of the shafts were filled in, but one was only covered, and conducted visits by students are now allowed under the administration of the Oxfordshire County Council Education Department.

For over three hundred years the Stonesfield district had supplied the roofs of Oxford, as well as the towns, villages and mansions of the Oxfordshire Cotswolds. Cheaper materials had become available for ordinary use, but slates were still wanted after the mines were closed for repairs, for alterations to Cotswold houses by people of taste, and for new buildings in traditional style on both sides of the Atlantic. To meet this demand, farmsteads, cottages and barns all over the Cotswolds were ruthlessly stripped between the wars, notably in Stonesfield itself.

The quarries of the Stonesfield district yield, besides vertebrate and invertebrate marine fossils, the remains of tiny primitive mammals, insects and flying repitles, and even the giant carnivorous dinosaur (megalosaurus), as well as fossil plants, the gingko, cycads and conifers. The surface quarry at Fawler is particularly rich in these remains. When the mines were open, quarrymen used carefully to watch for fossils in the course of their work and display them in their cottage windows for sale to scientists and amateur geologists. The fossilized remains of tiny mammals are extremely rare, and specimens from the Stonesfield mines are among the prized possessions of the university museum at Oxford.

During the Middle Ages the Oxford colleges seem to have obtained their 'presents' from Gloucestershire. Quarries at Stow, Guiting, Slaughter and Rissington appear in the building accounts. A quarry at Eyford Hill, about three miles west of Stow, is still producing slates, and from time to time small workings have been re-opened in the neighbourhood of Hawling and Salperton. The Cotswold Farm Park at Bemborough above Temple Guiting occupies fields much pitted by slate-quarrying, and this may be the Guiting quarry referred to in the Oxford accounts. A mile or so away, Huntsman Quarry was still producing slates after the last war. On Sevenhampton Common, high on the great ridge of the Inferior Oolite which culminates in Cleeve Cloud, old slate quarries are to be found in Puckham Wood, where a fault preserved a few acres of the Great Oolite from erosion. The builders of the Stroudwater Hills got their slates from quarries near Bisley and Througham. These are only a few of the many slate quarries on fringes of the Great Oolite in Gloucestershire, where the beds were often more accessible, and the weathering process simpler, than in the Stonesfield district. In Gloucestershire the pendle was never covered after quarrying, but stacked in rows or spread out on the ground at once.

Occupying a wide strip on the southern slopes of the Cotswolds from Badminton round to the Evenlode valley, an upper bed of the Great Oolite was christened by William Smith Forest Marble, because the Forest of Wychwood formerly covered a large part of the deposit. It is a very hard freestone suitable for sculpture. The well-preserved tympanum of the north door of St Peter and Paul at Church Hanborough is an example. The woods between the Roman villa by the Evenlode and North Leigh East End conceal old quarries of Northleigh Hardstone which is a Forest Marble much used at Oxford for plinths and cornices. The quarry at Hanborough still supplies material for repair and maintenance in the University. There are several outstanding villages on or near the Forest Marble beds, notably Ashton Keynes, Poulton, Filkins and Eastleach. In many villages in this district cottage gardens are fenced with thin flags of Forest Marble set on end, and nearly all the roofs are presents from the same series; there were large slate quarries at Poulton.

At a lower level on this south-eastern flank, one more thin bed of the Great Oolite consists of a rubbly, shelly limestone covered by a brown marl which is so fine for arable farming that it has been known since the eighteenth century as Cornbrash.

After the last of the Great Oolite series had been laid down, the receding sea and the slowly rising crust of the earth began to expose them as a giant shoal above the surface, a low whale-back formation much wider than it is now, fretted by runnels and wavemarks, and these wave or current marks remain on some of the stones lying about in the fields and incorporated into the dry-stone walls. Either before or during that upheaval, or in the following millennia, this whale-back was slightly tilted in a south-easterly direction, so that the northern flank sloped down rather steeply, and a much gentler dip-slope was left on the southern flank. This tilt can often be observed in the strata of a quarry; it shows well at Coscombe and Leckhampton. Here and there, however, as a result of local pressures leading to folding and faulting, the beds may appear horizontal, or even tilted in some other direction. This also can be seen at Coscombe, and more dramatically in the small Catsbrain quarry beneath the summit of Painswick Beacon.

On either side of this formation, the building of England continued in a further cycle of inundation, deposition and erosion. The Jurassic hills, indeed, are believed to have been for a time submerged again, but finally in the Miocene period the Cotswolds were uplifted clear of all future inundations. In the process, numerous faults developed on a north-west to south-east axis, but, except for the great ridge on which Stow-in-the-Wold stands, with little effect on the appearance of the landscape.

The Jurassic mass was now fully exposed to the operation of the wind and the rain. Surface water, absorbed by the porous rock and extruded at the spring-lines, began the formation of the rivers. Those streams flowing south-east down the gentle dip-slope formed long, spacious valleys; those flowing north and west

6. *Sheepscombe.*

followed much steeper courses down the face of the main escarpment, and in consequence carved out deep channels, their headwaters cutting back into the plateau. Thus were formed the network of deep combes, their sides clothed in woodland, their narrow floors emerald with meadow grass, which intersect the Stroudwater Hills, the dramatic gorge of the Bristol Avon and the secret bottoms where flow its feeders, notably the By Brook and the Somersetshire Frome, and similar features on the Cam, the Little Avon, the Chelt, the Isburne and the Stour. Here and there streams rising close to each other but flowing in opposite directions were pushed back until the neck of land between them was worn away, leaving detached portions as outliers. Cam Long Down perhaps best displays this development; it is easy to foresee that at some future time the same thing will happen to Stinchcombe Hill. Dundry Hill, south of Bristol, Robinswood Hill and Churchdown, Dumbleton and Bredon, now isolated far out in the Severn Plain, and Meon Hill in Warwickshire were originally united with the Cotswold mass. All these processes were greatly reinforced by the onset, about a million years ago, of the Ice Age.

2

The Physical Structure: Vegetation and Climate

Four successive advances and recessions of ice spanned a period of about half a million years with long intervals of milder climate, and during the period as a whole the evolution of reptile, bird, mammal and plant continued. Glaciers never overran the Cotswold Hills, but in so severe a climate the region must have been deeply covered with snow and can have supported only a tundra vegetation of lichens, sedges and perhaps a few dwarf birches. At times, fierce beasts such as bison, mammoth, rhinocerus, wolf and wild horse roamed the uplands, whose fossilized remains are found in the valley clays and gravels whither they were washed by the violent streams of the thaws when they came.

Today's gentle streams are misfits in the spacious valleys carved out by these waters, and above many of them hang dry valleys (locally called slads or slades) which were probably scoured out by melting snow during the Ice Age. The torrents in the vales of Severn and Thames cut into the flanks of the uplands. Enormous quantities of water, trapped by a wall of ice in the Severn valley, were pent up in what is now the Vale of Evesham, and formed a huge lake to which geologists have recently given the name Lake Harrison. Later this lake itself was frozen and the ice advanced into the Stour valley to within a mile of Moreton-in Marsh, bringing with it deposits of boulder clay or *till* to form a moraine. This is the broken, hummocky ridge, rising to little more than 400 feet O.D., running from the foot of the oolite at Dorn to Barton-on-the-Heath, and carrying the great watershed between Thames and Severn across the Moreton gap. Moreton itself stands in the flat, featureless plain created by the outwash fan of sands and gravels from this moraine.

When the ice retreated, Lake Harrison naturally filled up again. It was quite

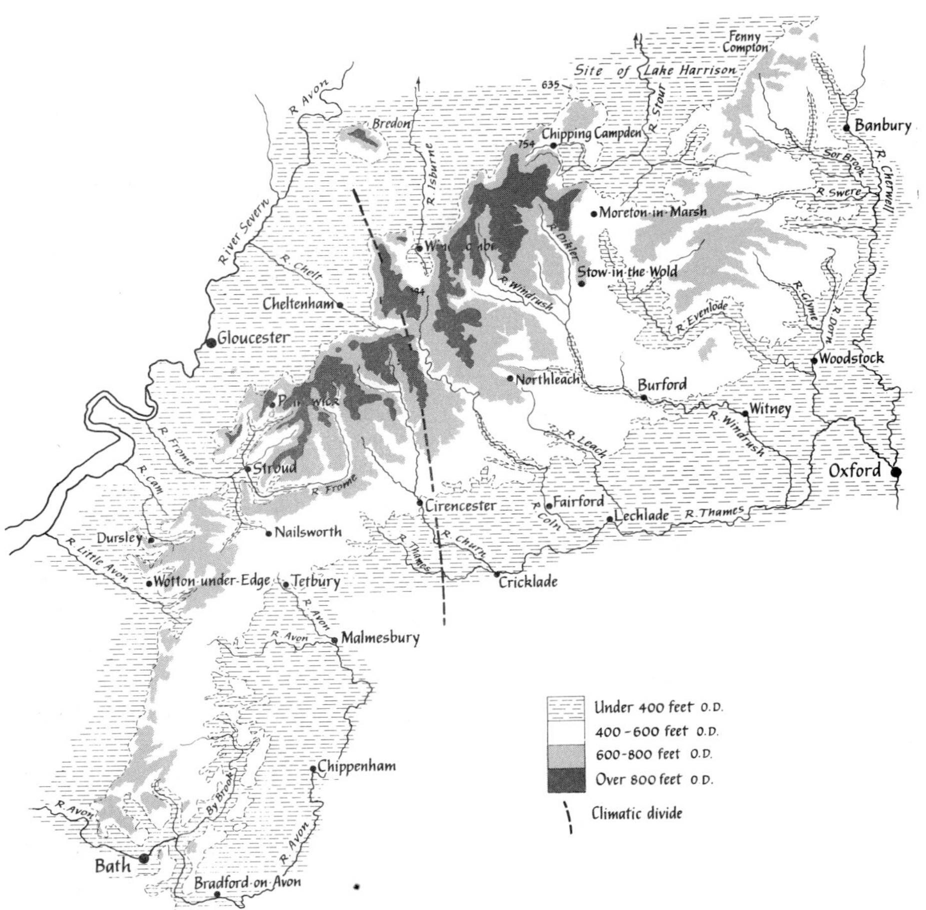

Map 3 *Relief map showing climatic divide.*

extensive enough for waves to develop, which have cut a bench all along the base of the scarp from Moreton up to Fenny Compton and beyond at a level of about 400 feet O.D. At the Fenny Compton gap it is likely that overflow water found its way into the Cherwell valley, which, like other Cotswold streams, is too wide and open to have been shaped by the modest stream which now flows through it. When at last the ice melted, Lake Harrison drained away, largely down the new bed of the Warwickshire Avon. This happened perhaps 10,000 years ago.

The Ice Age had left the highest parts of the plateau with a thin covering of soil capable of developing only scrub and light woodland, but over most of the Cotswolds forest was soon established with the return of a milder climate. In a peat-bed near Cheltenham dating from about 6000 B.C. an enormous preponderance of hazel, with pine and elm, were the principal pollen grains present, with oak, birch, alder and willow in small quantities. This is thought to suggest that hazel scrub was then turning to forest, with pine giving way to trees of a wetter and warmer climate, generally referred to as Atlantic. Oak, alder, elm, willow, and hazel are still the commonest trees at the foot of the scarp valleys with sycamore which was then absent. Charcoal taken from a Neolithic long barrow near Notgrove dated about 2000 B.C. revealed on analysis the presence of ash, cherry, hazel and elm. Charcoal taken from another near Nympsfield, dated about two hundred years later, yielded hawthorn, hazel, beech, ash, horse chestnut, cherry, oak, yew, elder and alder, the trees of the modern Cotswolds. Although no scrub or woodland existing today in England can be called natural vegetation, botanists consider that some in the Cotswolds may be regarded as semi-natural, that is, consisting mainly of native species or naturally introduced immigrants.

Ash-oakwood would have been the first to develop in the post-glacial clothing of the Cotswolds. Ash trees are common and grow to a considerable height, but pure ashwood is now only present as strips of wood or coppice on the thin brashy edges of the valleys. Ash-oakwoods are now chiefly found on the Upper Lias clays: the remains of Wychwood Forest in Cornbury Park, Guiting and Withington Woods are the chief examples. Woodland clothing the scarp and the combes generally shows an upward succession from ash-oak or even pure oak at the bottom, where the elm *Ulmus glabra* will also be fairly common, through ash-oak-sycamore to ash-oak-beech, with beechwood proper at the edge of agricultural land at the top, which in a natural state would have been occupied merely by hawthorn, hazel, elder, birch, dogwood and brambles.

The beech has been so successful in colonizing the best soils and aspects that ash-oak-beech is by far the most common woodland of the Cotswolds, though elm, birch, sycamore and the occasional horse chestnut are likely to be represented. It is interesting to observe at Little Hill near Dursley, where leaching has deprived isolated patches of lime, how the primeval oak remains dominant, and in Witcomb Wood, where the soil was too shallow, the ash has remained in possession. However, the beech is always remembered as the characteristic Cotswold tree, and indeed has been called 'the weed of the oolite'. When established, it grows to a height and size unsurpassed even in its natural home on the chalk. Like the ash, isolated trees in parks and field boundaries attain great size and splendour but are very vulnerable to the wind. On the Cotswold plateau there is seldom sufficient depth of soil for self-sown saplings, and apart from small beechwoods possibly of semi-natural origin at Eyford and Adlestrop, almost all beechwood is known to have been planted during the last hundred years or so. Oakley Wood in Cirencester Park may be the result of natural colonization, but the name shows it was an oak wood when the Saxons knew it. In the western hills,

7. *A Cotswold rarity* – Pulsatilla vulgaris (*the Pasque Flower*) *growing wild.*

on the other hand, the high rainfall encourages a growth of humus on the shallow limey soil which offers an ideal habitat, and here the beechwoods are undoubtedly of natural origin.

These magnificent beechwoods begin west of Ermine Street with the Buckholt and Cranham group, perhaps the finest of all. Maitland Wood, and Stockend Wood between Painswick and Haresfield Beacon, Randwick, Standish and Pitchcombe Woods near Stroud, the glorious screen of beech above Dursley, notably Folly Wood; Westridge Wood sheltering Wotton-under-Edge and Midger Wood in Hillsley are the most notable among the others. The wet climate gives Cranham Woods especially a wonderful floristic richness compared with the poorly covered wood-floors in the parent chalk country. The list includes the green hellebore, three kinds of violet, sweet woodruff, sanicula, the Lesser Wintergreen *Pyrola minor*, *Daphne laureola* and *mezereon*, Yellow Archangel and a number of orchids, for example the broad and common helleborines, Tway-blade *Listera ovata* Birds Nest *Neottia nidus avia*, and the rare Yellow Birds Nest.

A still richer herb carpet may be expected in the ash-oak-beechwoods, including the green-flowered Common Helleborine *Epipactis* and *Epipactis leptochila* which is especially fond of Wychwood; the Large White Helleborine *Cephanthera alba* and *C. rubra*, and the very rare Red Helleborine now found only in a few Cotswold woods; the Green and Stinking Hellebores; Hounds Tongue *Cynoglossum montanum*, which is a rarity found only in Wychwood; Fragrant Solomon's Seal *Polygonatum fragrans*, which is scarce, and the parasitic Toothwort *Lathraea squamaria*, which are relatively uncommon outside the Cotswolds. Angular Solomon's Seal is found only here. Meadow Saffron *Colchicum autumnale*, (sometimes wrongly called Autumn Crocus), is still found in woods and meadows near the scarp and also around Wychwood. Lily-of-the-Valley was formerly common but may now be extinct. *Lilium martagon*, the Turks Cap Lily, grows in certain woods near Campden and Blockley. Grape Hyacinth *Muscari racemosum* and Columbine *Aquilegia vulgans* in certain Oxfordshire woods is thought to be native. Primroses are fairly common on the lias at the edge of woods, but are seldom found on the oolite.

With the possible exception of some very small areas, Cotswold grassland has developed by degeneration from woodland and scrub, but only a few high dry and steep valleys remain as old pasture. Downland is now confined to the edge of the plateau in its highest parts, the chief areas being Cleeve Common, Charlton Kings Common, Painswick Hill, Haresfield Beacon, Minchinhampton and Rodborough Commons, Selsley Common, Stinchcombe Hill, a few small areas near the western edge farther south, and Madmarston Hill and a few of the neighbouring summits in Oxfordshire. Downland now merges imperceptibly with rough grazing, which still occupies many of the steepest parts of the scarp, notably above Hailes, Broadway and on Dover's Hill. Many plant species are common to both. Where the surface has been grazed close by sheep or rabbits the herbage is dominated by the bents, notably *Festuca ovina*, and Wild Thyme, Rock Rose, Milkwort and Birds Foot Trefoil (known locally as Hens-and-Chickens or Butter-and-Eggs) decorate the turf. However, since myxamatosis decimated the rabbit population the coarse Tor Grass has gained a hold at the expense of the more decorative species. The scrubby terrain offers more variety, notably several orchids: the Bee and Fly Orchids, the rare Musk Orchid, Fragrant Orchid *Gymnadenia conopsea*, Burnt Stick Orchid *O. ustulata*, and Pyramid Orchids *Anacamptis pyramidalis*. The area west of A424, north of Hinchwick, formerly Bourton Downs, is especially rich in interesting plants.

The greatest rarities are Cotswold Pennycress, *Thlaspi perfoliatum*, an insignificant plant to be found in quarries and other stony places in the north Cotswolds, the Limestone Woundwort *Stachys alpina*, now almost confined to the Painswick neighbourhood, and Downy Sedge *Carex filiforma*. In a few places in the north Cotswolds the beautiful and comparatively rare Pasque Flower, *Anemone vulgaris pulsatilla* survives. The cowslips and violets which formerly starred the lower pastures are now chiefly to be found on rough grazing and on roadsides. Apart from the ubiquitous Rosebay Willowherb, the showiest plants of the roadside are the lovely blue Meadow Cranesbill, Moon Daisies, blue Scabious, pink Musk Mallow, and Traveller's Joy, but many of the species already mentioned can be found on the wide verges, together with the somewhat rare Black Mullein *Verbascum nigrum*.

Many of the plants which have been mentioned above are extremely rare, indeed vanishing species. Most people now know better than to dig up a rare plant, but do not always appreciate that by picking, and thus eliminating one season's reproduction, a whole community of the species, or worse still an isolated specimen, may be destroyed. Those interested are implored to seek them book in hand rather than to pick so much as a single flower for purposes of indentification.

Little requires to be said of Cotswold wild-life. Badger and fox are common; the rare yellow-necked mouse has been seen. There is a moderate population of wild fallow deer in the woods, and roe deer and muntjac have been seen. The quarry mines provide an excellent habitat for bats; the Lesser Horseshoe and the rarer Greater Horseshoe Bat are certainly in possession, but the presence of Pipistrelle, Noctule, Barbastelle, Common Long-eared and Whiskered bats is insufficiently recorded. The woods are full of the large white edible snails commonly supposed to have been introduced by the Romans and called Roman snails, though their presence seems to be attested in the Neolithic period. Bird-life has no unexpected features, though some uncharacteristic water birds are beginning to appear in the Cotswold Water Park. There are now thirty breeding pairs of Great Crested Grebe. The lakes have become among the most important in southern England for wintering duck, notably pochard, and there are about forty pairs of tufted duck. Best of all the Water Park has become a favoured haunt of the kingfisher.

One special feature of the Cotswold Hills is the effect of the ubiquitous loose stones. The film of water which the frost invades when slates are made from the pendle stone has already been mentioned. Under a microscope each granule of oolite may be seen to have a tiny hole. These so retain moisture that long after down and meadow elsewhere are cracked and yellow, the pastures of the Cotswolds retain a sort of greenness, and growth is not completely arrested on the arable. This was of immense importance on the historic sheep-walks, and remains most favourable to the barley. For the same reason Cotswold houses are very cold in winter, but deliciously cool in hot weather.

Conditions of drought would otherwise be by no means uncommon in the eastern Cotswolds. The climax of the scarp at Cleeve Cloud constitutes a marked climatic divide. Westwards the Edge encounters the full force of the rain-bearing winds funnelling up the Bristol Channel, and the southern end of the Cotswold range is very narrow. The whole area thus experiences a maritime climate, damp, but less cold than might be expected at such altitudes farther inland, receiving from 32 inches of rain a year to 37 inches in a few isolated and especially exposed areas. Eastward of Cleeve Cloud the high plateau has the same rainfall but loses the sea's tempering influence, while the lower slopes of the plateau on the south-eastern flank, well screened by such a rampart, have a relatively dry, chilly climate with an average of only 27 inches of rain, in places less; the same applies to sheltered parts of the north Cotswolds. In the eighteenth century when the climate of England was more severe than it is now, it used to be said of the Cotswolds: 'Eight months of winter and cold weather all the year besides,' and the local saying 'at Stow-on-the-Wold the devil caught cold' is frequently quoted on the northern plateau. The cold winds sweep almost unimpeded over the somewhat bare country, their gustiness only increased by the rare plantations. Ferocious gales are very rare, however.

The atmosphere above such porous soil is naturally relatively low in humidity. With an average of 5·1 hours of sunshine, the Cotswolds can well stand comparison with the south coast, and the dry and nimble air is as invigorating as sea-breezes. Sea mist does sometimes invade the western hills, but elsewhere there is seldom a blanket of fog by day, though the roadside plantations do favour the formation of disconcerting patches in winter, and in late evening cold air may gravitate into a deep valley when the resulting stagnant and freezing conditions can cause disastrous frosts in May and October. There are frosts most nights from December to March and often in April so that the growing season is a short one, but snowstorms are rarely heavy enough to interrupt the traffic.

Summer temperatures can rise to 27 °C or even 34 °C in a heatwave, but even then the heat is seldom sultry. April, June and September are the dryest months and the western hills experience as much rain in July and August as in November and December (an average of three inches), torrential rain falling hour after hour. October is a sunny month, but with heavy rain.

This is the climate at present, but it is considered to have been a good deal milder and dryer about 4000 B.C. when the first farmers are thought to have arrived in these hills.

3

From the Coming of Man to the Roman Conquest

The Cotswolds are extremely rich in antiquities. Paleolithic man first drifted into the Thames and Severn valleys during the last interglacial interlude. One of his scanty tools, an all-purpose weapon, called rather misleadingly by archaeologists a hand-axe has been found near Lechlade, and another specimen near Hanborough, but we have no evidence that they penetrated the Cotswold uplands.

After the departure of the ice, a period of about four thousand years elapsed during which the warm, wet Atlantic climate became established, and under its benign influence the Mesolithic peoples of northern Europe spread into Britain. The Maglemosians, sometimes called the Forest Folk, came from across the swamps and rivers which were soon to form the North Sea. They were hunter-gatherers with a much more varied repertory of tools than Paleolithic men, including boats, fish-hooks and improved flint tools, notably the tranchet-axe, capable of dealing with brushwood and saplings, and flint spear- and arrow-heads. They probably used fire to assist the process of forest clearance which they undertook to make glades attractive to deer and wild cattle, and may have used it also in driving game. These people have left some traces in the south Cotswold valleys. Other tribes came from farther south with dogs at their heels, and used tiny arrowheads (microliths), which are found in great quantity on the Cotswold plateau. These Mesolithic peoples are thought to have been of Nordic stock and fair colouring, a complexion very common among Cotswold natives still.

About 3500 B.C. a much warmer, drier climate set in, and with it came the first herdsmen and farmers. The Neolithic immigrants who settled on the chalk are thought to have crossed the Channel bringing with them both domesticated animals and seed-corn. Those who settled in the Cotswolds brought only animals. They had come ultimately from the Mediterranean, and are called Iberians. Possibly they came to our region from earlier settlements in Cornwall and Wales scouting for better pasture, and saw scrubland on the summit of the scarp. Perhaps they made use of a dry river-bed full of oolitic rubble near Frampton-on-Severn to afford a safe passage for their animals through the dense swampy forests of the Vale. We may imagine the indigenous Mesolithic folk watching from Haresfield Beacon the new arrivals borne in (and in some cases probably swallowed) by the treacherous Severn tides; perhaps they were peeping from the thickets as the swarthy strangers drove their beasts before them up the steep slope in search of dry camping ground. The docile beasts would have been surprising enough, but the mental equipment they could not see was far more shocking, for these people were the first builders, whose monuments are still a notable feature of the Cotswold landscape.

Our evidence for their way of life comes chiefly from the great mausoleums they built, probably for the families of their chiefs. They must have formed, like all subsequent incursions, only an 'upper crust' of the population. They were a pastoral people, rearing mainly cattle and pigs, and, like the natives, devoting much of their energy to hunting. They were able to overwinter some of their stock, probably with the aid of tree-loppings, for paleo-botanists notice a marked decrease in elm-pollen coinciding with their arrival in Britain. They are thought to have begun a process of selective breeding and they knew the advantages of castration. They knew how to make pottery, but probably not how to weave when they first arrived, since they seem to have had very few sheep; they must have dressed in skins. They knew enough about carpentry and wickerwork to make the hide-covered coracles in which they arrived. Fruits such as blackberries, crab apples, sloes and bullaces, hazel nuts and possibly acorns added variety to their diet, but what they brewed for consolation and rejoicing we do not know, nor how soon they began to cultivate corn for bread and drink. The tombs present only a generalized picture of an age nearly two thousand years long.

At least one hundred long barrows, as these monuments are always called, are known to have existed in the Cotswolds. Unfortunately, a considerable number have been wrecked by haphazard antiquarian digging and others by the plough, but many survive. The form is very distinctive. Marker stones show that the plan was carefully laid out beforehand; it has even been suggested that there were professional builders. The monument consists of a mound between 100 and 200 feet long, wider and higher at one end than the other; it may be as much as 18 feet high. This huge cairn of loose stones was left bare by the builders, but is now always covered with vegetation. It encloses a number of burial chambers constructed of shaped orthostats of oolite – invariably the Great Oolite, even where the Inferior was nearer to hand. In perhaps the majority of cases, those regarded as the older examples, the burial chambers are approached through a portal recessed to form two horns at the wider end of the mound, and these horns are a constant feature, even where the chambers are reached from the side of the cairn. The cairn is revetted, the portals faced, and gaps between the orthostats within filled with dry-stone walling. Evidently it was the long-barrow men who introduced this craft into the Cotswolds. It has been estimated that the stone used to raise one of these monuments would be more than enough to build a parish church, and that the building would have occupied about five thousand man-hours, including the quarrying of the stone with antler picks and shaping with stone mauls.

In the chambers a varying number of persons were interred, occasionally more than twenty. It has been possible to detect a family likeness in some cases, victims of osteo-arthritis in others. A few skeletons are found, but careful assessment has shown that what was interred was by no means always a recent corpse; important forbears may have been brought from humbler graves, but there may have been some ritual of secondary burial involved. Alternatively, the confusion in which the bones are often found may be due to the activities of later intruders, for apart from robbers, single burials of later cultures are sometimes found in the chambers as well as in and around the mound. Potsherds, flints and personal ornaments suggest that the dead were given food and equipment for some hereafter. Nearly all the tombs contain many animal bones: red deer, roe deer, horse, wild boar, wolf, wild cat and the occasional bird, cattle and pigs and occasionally a dog. These are nearly all partially burnt. Horses' bones are not found in the long barrows of kindred cultures, and since the horse is not a forest creature, this suggests either that the horses were domesticated, or, more probably, that some part of the hills had always been clear of heavy woodland.

Two long barrows are worth visiting. Belas Knap (the beacon), which is regarded as a late specimen on account of its side chambers and false portal, overlooks the edge behind Humblebee Wood above Winchcombe. Better still is Hetty Pegler's Tump, north of Uley village (reached from B4066). In this earlier specimen it is still possible, after more than four thousand years, to stand within the (now empty) burial chambers. Hester Pegler joined with her husband in 1677 to sell the piece of the open field on which the barrow stood. It was then known as Cold Harbour, a name generally given to a vagrants' refuge. It is not known why the barrow came to be given her name, but it may be noted that interest in antiquities began during her lifetime. Respect for the ancient dead

8. *Interior view of Hetty Pegler's Tump.*

came much later and did not last. In the nineteenth century, when the Hoar Stone long barrow in Duntisbourne Abbots parish was destroyed by ploughing and careless excavation, the bones were re-interred in the churchyard, and a cross carved from one of the orthostats of the nearby Jack Barrow raised over them. Several Neolithic monuments were spoiled by members of the Cotteswold Naturalists' Field Club in those days – they regarded the opening of a barrow as a suitable activity for a day's outing.

A barrow at Ascot-under-Wychwood in the Evenlode valley has recently been scientifically excavated and dated approximately 2800 B.C.; beneath it a Mesolithic settlement and a Neolithic settlement had each existed and been abandoned with intervening periods of forest and scrubland coverage. Very few stone axes have yet been found on the Cotswolds, and it is thought that this means either that the Neolithic people made little attempt to clear the forest, or that they found it largely cleared already. This excavation seems to refute both these ideas. The reduction of forest would have been absolutely necessary to improve grazing and to make it easier to protect the herds. Moreover, to overwinter only a few cattle on tree-loppings would require the young shoots from several acres of woodland. A Danish archaeologist has proved by practical experiment that it is perfectly possible to chop down mature trees with a Neolithic stone axe. The undergrowth might then be burnt, and the scrubland vegetation which would follow would provide new summer grazing. Alternatively, it could be broken up for cultivation; slash-and-burn is a primitive method of breaking new ground well attested in Neolithic sites elsewhere. The normal practice of primitive farmers is to allow each patch of arable to revert to scrub when after a few years the yield ceases to be worth having, and to open up new fields. Thus the forest would be cleared round successive transient settlements. Very few traces of habitation sites have come to light, but a surprisingly large number of parishes on the plateau each has its long barrow, so it is tempting to conjecture that the missing Neolithic sites may be buried under the villages themselves. The good supplies of water that herdsmen need are not to be had everywhere in these hills.

Although the Neolithic people had building stone to hand on the Cotswolds, tools had to be imported. The flint mines of the chalk were not the only sources of supply. At least equally efficient axes were made from some of the ancient rocks of the highlands of Britain, and one of the few axes which have come to light in the Cotswolds was made in Flintshire, another on the Langdale pikes in Cumbria, and a polished greenstone chip is thought to have been a broken axe from Cornwall. There is no doubt that even in Mesolithic times there were established trade-routes for pedlars both by sea and land. The Severn had led the long-barrow men to their homeland; they lived on that great highway which served the west of the country from the dawn of time until the railways were built. Their kindred were settled in Cornwall, on the coast of Wales, the west coast of Scotland and in Ireland. Archaeologists distinguish them as the Severn-Cotswold group, and their monuments, though spread all over the Cotswolds, are thickest on the ground above the Severn and along the course of the Jurassic highway.

Did those kindred people beyond the western sea always maintain contact with the Mediterranean? Did they send apprentices to smiths in Egypt, or were they able to capture Mediterranean metal-workers to teach their own people? Was the point of contact in the Cornish tin-mines? We do not know, but Ireland became a primary source of metal goods of copper, bronze and gold for the Bronze Age in northern Europe. About 1800 B.C., when the deteriorating climate began to make the long sea-passage from Ireland difficult, the tribes who acted as middlemen for these goods and themselves possessed metal-working skill began to take over the trade-routes of Britain. A bronze spearhead of Irish manufacture has been found on Rodborough Common near Stroud, and a hoard presumed to have belonged to a travelling smith turned up at Monkswood near Cold Ashton, where the Jurassic highway enters the Cotswolds. It contained bronze sickles, bracelets, necklets, spears and pins.

The chambered tombs of the Neolithic overlords reveal a process of adjustment to the customs of the newcomers, who buried their dead individually in modest round barrows. The Soldiers Grave at Nympsfield is a large *round* barrow with a single burial chamber of dry-stone walling containing fifteen skeletons. A few round mounds had the traditional Megalithic chamber within. Sometimes a body would be laid in the chamber of a long barrow or buried in the mound. Often barrows of both kinds come together, and this evidence of cultural sharing is peculiar to the Cotswolds.

The most important known Bronze-Age burial is one of a characteristic group consisting of five round barrows in close proximity to a long one, near Snowshill. In it were found beside the skeleton of the warrior, a stone battle-axe, a bronze dagger and a bronze pin all of continental origin, and a British-made bronze spear.

By far the most important monuments of the Bronze Age are the stone circles. Stonehenge, unique and startling in the grandeur of its conception and craftsmanship, belongs none-the-less to a group of circular and other arrangements of megaliths, generally called henge monuments and presumed to be temples, which are spread all over England, the largest being at Avebury. We have two of these in the Oxfordshire Cotswolds – the famous Rollright Stones and the almost unknown and well-concealed Cornwell Circles only a few miles off. The latter is much the smaller of the two, but consists apparently of no less than four complete rings and a single stone in a neighbouring field. There are remains close by of a possible long barrow.

Rollright is a much richer site. To the north-east of the circle lies a long barrow. The diameter of the circle itself varies between 100 and 113 feet and the stones are of varying heights. Local folklore insists that they cannot be counted, but there are now said to be over seventy, not including the adjacent monolith known as the King Stone, which, like the Hele Stone at Stonehenge, points the direction of the rising sun. This huge stone has a most curious shape, as if it were half of a porthole-type entrance such as was found at long barrows (Windmill Tump, Rodmarton, and Norn's Tump, Avening) and perhaps it was taken from the dismantled long barrow behind it. The stones all come from the Great Oolite, and are much eroded and damaged: a chip struck from any of them was formerly so widely regarded as a talisman that a single piece would sell for £1 at Faringdon Fair. Not far from the circle there is another Bronze-Age monument, possibly a denuded burial chamber, which is known as the Five Whispering Knights or the

9. *The Rollright circle (the King's Men).*

10. *A longstone – the King Stone at Rollright.*

Traitors. It consists of four orthostats with a single great capstone. The local maidens used to regard these stones as a kind of oracle: one old lady declared, 'Time and again I have heard them whisper – but perhaps after all it was only the wind.' The Three Shire Stones in Marshfield, three orthostats based in Somerset, Wiltshire and Gloucestershire respectively, with a capstone, have the appearance of a similar monument, but were erected in the eighteenth century.

Isolated Bronze-Age monoliths are widely scattered over the parts of Britain favoured by prehistoric man. The Cotswolds have their share: a Longstone on Minchinhamton Common, and the Tinglestone in Gatcombe Park, the grickstone in Old Sodbury parish, the Hangman's Stone where the parishes of Yanworth, Stowell and Hampnett meet, and another on the boundary between Siddington and Preston; the Hoar Stone at Enstone, and the Thor Stone at Taston nearby from which the hamlet takes its name.

The long barrows do not seem to have attracted much folklore, but it is far otherwise with standing stones. There is a fund of common tradition which is everywhere given a local twist. The Rollright stones are known as The King and The King's Men. Standing stones are generally believed to go down to a stream to drink, and the King and his Men do so when the clock strikes twelve. The journey to the river may have some reference to the stone avenues which are found connected with some circles, notably at Avebury. The most coherent legend attached to the Rollright Stones is woven into a rhyming tale: the King and his followers have set out to conquer England, but as he breasts the hill he encounters a witch.

'Seven long strides shalt thou take,' says she,
'If Long Compton thou canst see,
King of England thou shalt be.'

He thinks himself safe, but finds after his seven strides the view blocked by the long barrow behind the King Stone (it is now reduced by ploughing). Then says the witch:

'Thou and thy men hoar stones shall be,
And I myself an eldern tree.'

This catastrophe is also attributed to the treachery of the Whispering Knights. The neighbourhood abounds in elder bushes, and a ploughboy a hundred years ago would have been terrified to stick his knife into one of them. A village custom, now long abandoned, brought the people up to the Rollright Stones at midnight on Midsummer Eve when the elderbushes are in flower. They formed a circle about the King Stone, and when the elder was cut they believed that the King turned his head. The elder was supposed to bleed if stabbed and, according to another story, so would the King Stone if pricked at midnight. The elder was the centre of Anglo-Saxon rites which survived the coming of Christianity, and indeed remained in numerous local superstitions until the beginning of this century. Another custom was recorded by William Stukeley, the eighteenth-century antiquarian. There had existed, apparently, a plot or maze cut in the turf near the King Stone where the young people kept a festival with cakes and dancing, probably some kind of fertility rite, for it was stamped out by the Puritans. The tradition lingered very late that the circle was in some way 'holy ground'.

Longstones may go to drink and dance, but it is impossible to move them and unlucky to attempt it. This belief has saved some of them from serving as bridges or road metal. It is sometimes said that the stone is buried eight or ten feet deep, but in fact the monoliths generally have the shallowest possible socket. Roughly the same story is told of the two Hangman's Stones: a sheep stealer was strangled by the struggling creature whose legs he had tied together, as he rested on, or climbed over, the stone. It need hardly be said that none of these tales is likely to bear any relation to the rites for which the monuments were raised, which are still a matter of conjecture. However, at least until very recently longstones continued to be the object of superstitious practices connected with fertility.

Between 1800 and 1500 B.C. the climate is thought to have deteriorated steadily. The people of Britain gradually adopted a more settled mode of life. Traces of field boundaries can sometimes be seen from the air. A fine set on West Littleton Down a few miles north-east of Bath has long been known, but is now obliterated. In recent years crop-marks indicating burials and settlement presumed to relate to the succeeding period have been revealed by air photography along the south-eastern flanks of the Cotswolds, notably at Kempsford, Ampney, and Lechlade, and a few farther up the river valleys. Straddling the parish boundary between Eastleach and Aldsworth, over 70 acres of field boundaries have been identified.

With the introduction of iron about 800 B.C., our Cotswold people, from being a somewhat isolated, possibly even a backward community, found themselves surrounded with sources of the new, sought-after metal. The use of iron seems to have been introduced by Celtic people from the mainland of Europe, the forerunners of wave after wave of immigrants of the same stock but different tribes, each bringing a more advanced technology, and apparently a more aggressive life-style, culminating with the arrival of Roman arms and civilized institutions.

Even the first arrivals, known to archaeologists as Iron Age A, or Hallstadt (from their type-site) people, were able to support more trade in pottery, ornaments and other luxuries from the continent than any previous invaders, and they came to use as currency iron bars of a size and shape convenient for working into a sword. They introduced cremation, so we cannot tell to what extent they mixed with the native stock, but their culture thoroughly penetrated the Cotswolds. They were the makers of many unimpressive single-rampart 'camps', such as those at Norbury in Farmington, at Colesbourne, Ampney St Peter, Ablington, Windrush, Lyneham, Stow-on-the-Wold, Chastleton, Idbury, Tadmarton, Icomb Drum and Ranbury Ring. The scanty evidence so far collected has shown hardly any trace of settlement, so they were probably mere cattle-pounds or sheep-folds. Settlements at this period were very generally surrounded by a ditch and bank, and numerous small enclosures have left crop-marks visible from the air.

After 250 B.C., coastal Britain and the whole of Wessex presents a picture of conquest or of a prolonged struggle against better-armed invaders of the La Tène, or Iron Age B, culture, but for more than a century, shielded by the swampy forests of the upper Thames, the Cotswold people were immune from the strife which created the magnificent fortified camps of Wessex and the south-western peninsula, though they absorbed much of the incoming culture. Their weakest point was the high rampart of the western scarp adjoining the Severn highway. Here there is a series of forts, of which Horton and Beckbury still have only a single rampart, while at Sodbury, Leckhampton, Cleeve, Crickley and Shenberrow, the second is probably a later addition. Excavation at Crickley Hill between 1969 and 1973 revealed an early Iron-Age rampart of rubble laced with timber, to which were later added bastions at the gateway and an outer horn-work with a second gateway. Within was found a paved street much worn by traffic, lined with large rectangular timber houses 28–82 feet long and 23–25 feet wide (characteristic Bronze-Age or early Iron-Age long houses which would have accommodated both men and beasts). These houses had been burnt down and slightly later a very large round house had been built of a type found in Wessex.

About 100 B.C. strangers, who may have stemmed from a warrior tribe which dominated Cornwall and was conquering its way eastward, did gain a footing in some of these forts. The newcomers also occupied most of the Cotswold outliers such as Oxenton Hill and Bredon. After a time, however, their distinctive stamped pottery gives way to the bowls with beaded rims and linear engraved patterns used by the natives. The Cotswold people were evidently determined to protect their iron trade with the Forest of Dean, for they now established a fort on the west bank of the Severn at Lydney. They were also under threat from the east, especially from the new Belgic empire of the Catuvellauni, with its headquarters in Hertfordshire. These people were of mixed Celtic and Germanic stock, who had learnt much from their Roman enemies, and were hungry for further conquest. The Cotswold response is seen in the two forts on Meon and Madmarston Hills, and the linear earthworks in Wychwood. During this troubled period there was an important settlement at Salmonsbury, on the outskirts of

Bourton-on-the-Water, where a double rampart seals off a tongue of gravel defended on the remaining sides by the swampy confluence of the Dikler and Windrush. Here and on Meon large hoards of currency bars have been found.

Caesar's invasions can have been no more than exciting news-items brought by travelling pedlars in the Cotswolds, and the overthrow of the capital of the Catuvellauni a by no means unwelcome outcome.

Some time shortly before A.D. I, a fresh incursion of Belgic people swept northwards through Wessex and the rich, ill-defended Cotswold territory fell into their hands. Resistance in the outlying forts, for example on Bredon, resulted in a fearful massacre. The conquerors, who called themselves the Dobunni, established their *oppidum* or capital at Bagendon on a low-lying site in the Churn valley. Several sections of the huge defensive ditch remain just north of the village, and the excavations at this site have given us quite a well-filled picture of their life.

The ditch enclosed an area of about two hundred acres, large enough to provide protection for flocks and herds. The immense number of bones which have come to light suggest a mainly pastoral hinterland where large flocks of sheep were kept as well as cattle and pigs. However, the Dobunnic territory included the Cornbrash, and numerous querns and huge storage jars show that there was plenty of corn available. The principal activity of the inhabitants, however, seems to have been the manufacture of metal goods. The smiths of Bagendon were highly trained and skilful, some of them almost certainly native Cotswold men working for Belgic masters. They seem to have used coal as well as charcoal for smelting, a technique not rediscovered until the end of the seventeenth century. They knew how to use a touchstone to assay metals, how to de-silver lead and to manufacture plate, and used enamel for decoration; their wire was of high quality. Many of the wattle huts had well-laid stone floors and doors with iron latches. Their clothes were of wool or skins, which might be fastened with magnificent bronze or iron brooches and pins. Other ornaments included finger rings and bracelets of bronze or iron, sometimes with a stone inset, and glass beads, some of which had a twist of colour in them. The grave of a Celtic lady buried near Birdlip contained a round bronze mirror ornamented with symmetrically placed roundels incorporated in a free geometric pattern, the hallmark of the native tradition, touched with the red enamelwork introduced by the conquerors. One other mirror of closely similar design has come to light at Desborough, not far from the eastern end of the Cotswolds along the Jurassic way. The two are among the most prized treasures of Celtic art in Britain. Less richly ornamented round mirrors were quite common.

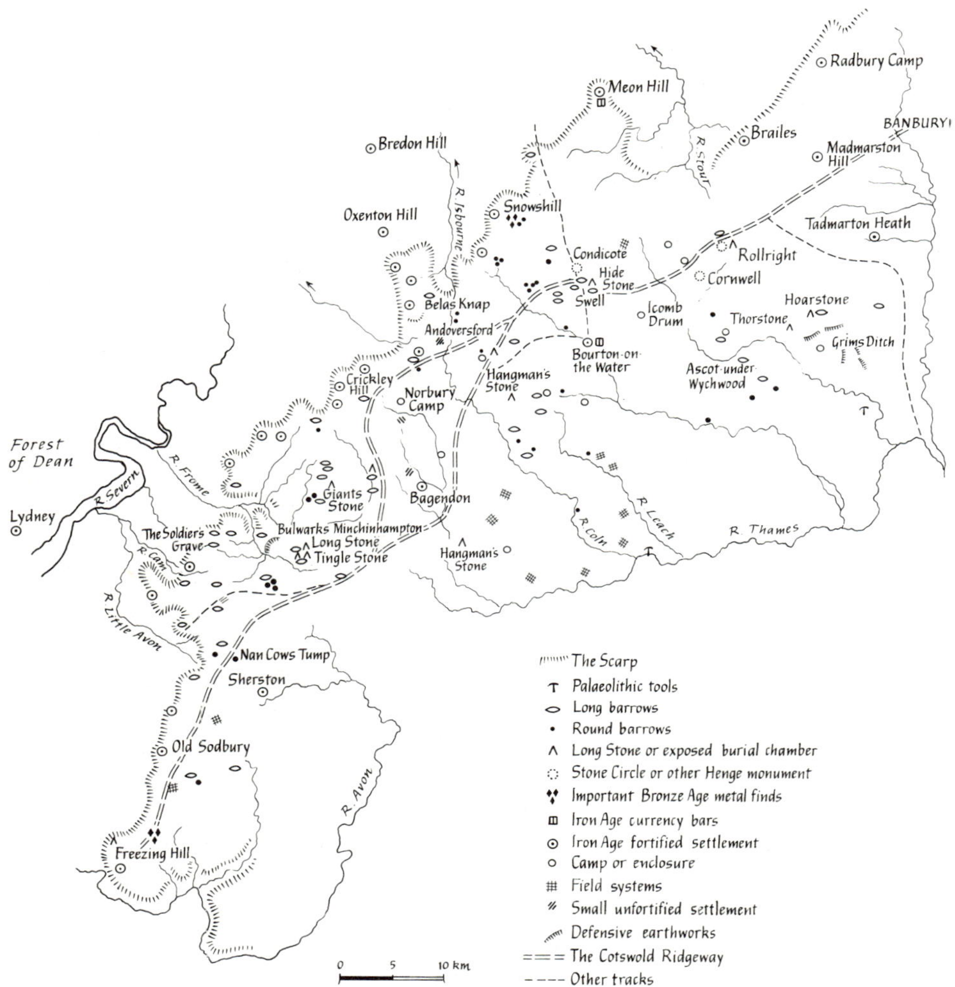

Map 4 *Principal prehistoric sites.*

There was a mint at Bagendon. Most Belgic peoples had a coinage based more or less remotely on Roman models; that of the Dobunni is distinguished by a tree device on the obverse of gold coins. The reverse of both silver and gold specimens shows a version of the triple-tailed horse, which is used by all the Belgic tribes of the last incursion. The earliest Dobunnic coins are uninscribed but before long a king's name began to appear above the horse's head. The distribution of these coins in Britain shows that the continental luxuries found in the huts at Bagendon came through the port of Colchester in the territory of the Catuvellauni. These included glass from the Mediterranean, many kinds of fine Gaulish and Italian wares, and wine imported in huge amphorae. They seem to have eaten plenty of meat, though little game, imported shellfish and fresh-water fish from local streams, and had some kind of home-brewed liquour. They used oxen for ploughing, and the rough native ponies served as pack-animals, but their chief office was to draw the war-chariots used by all Belgic peoples.

Some time before the Roman conquest, the Dobunni became tributaries of the Catuvellauni. Two kings were already simultaneously issuing coins bearing the tree of the Dobunni, and taking up opposite positions in regard to the menace of Rome, Catti, followed by Corio, held sway from the Stroud valley south into Somerset; they maintained the hostility traditional among most Belgic tribes and especially the Catuvellauni. The eastern Dobunni, in possession of Bagendon, perhaps hoped to recover their independence with the aid of a powerful ally. The silver coins of their king Bodvoc bear a classical profile clearly delineated, and when the Roman army reached the Medway in A.D. 46 his envoys were there to tender their submission. There is no sign of armed resistance at Bagendon, but on Minchinhampton and Rodborough Commons there are Belgic earthworks, presumably strongholds of the southern Dobunni. It may well have been through this friendly territory that Caratacus made his way to renew defiance from Wales.

The first stage of the Roman conquest established a frontier on the Jurassic uplands about A.D. 47, linked with the south-east by two trunk roads, Ermine Street (A417) which enters the Cotswolds between South Cerney and Down Ampney, and Akeman Street, which runs along the south-eastern flank from Cirencester a mile or two south of Bibury, Burford and Charlbury, of which only the first two miles is now a trunk road (A433). To these was added a military frontier road, the Fosse Way (A429), running from south-west to north-east right through the friendly territory of the Dobunni.

The Roman camp at Chesterton, on the outskirts of Cirencester, belongs to this period. What an opportunity for the smiths and cattle-dealers of Bagendon! The military base was soon moved forward to the site of Gloucester in preparation for further conquest, but Cirencester remained an important road-junction and a suitable place for the Romanized tribal capital of the Dobunni. Some time about A.D. 70 Bagendon seems to have been deserted.

4

From the Roman Conquest to Domesday Book

I

From a ruinous struggle with the Roman army the Dobunni had been preserved by the prudent diplomacy of King Bodvoc, whose coins are found in the earliest layers of the new town. Under Roman rule, the Belgic warlords continued to exercise power under the watchful eye of the provincial administration, as members of the governing body of their new *civitas* with its dependant territory, the old kingdom shorn of its southern conquests in what is now Somerset. However, they could no longer augment their resources by an onslaught on their neighbours; their taste for slaves, wine and other luxuries could only be satisfied by increasing the produce of their lands until there existed a surplus after the exactions of Roman tax-gatherers and army requisitions had been met, and the cost of public buildings in the tribal capital demanded by Roman provincial policy subscribed. They seem to have proved themselves efficient exploiters of their estates. By the second century, Corinium had been dignified with handsome public buildings, and under Diocletian it became the capital of Britannia Prima, one of the four sub-provinces of the British Isles, second only to London in size and opulence, and one of the largest comparable cities in the western empire, with 240 acres within the walls. The collonaded basilica (town hall) alongside the Forum was 320 feet long; it now lies beneath the Avenue. There were splendid public baths, probably a theatre, and an amphitheatre outside the walls. This is now called the bull-ring, and the stone-faced terraces, now thickly mantled with turf, still rise 27 feet above the level of the arena, which is an elipse 160 feet long and about 134 feet wide.

The massive defences seem originally to have consisted of a stone-faced earthen bank, part of which can still be seen at the Watermoor end of the town.

Later stone walls were added, and four massive gateways, and later still bastions which enabled an improved *ballista*, introduced in the fourth century, to rake the ditches. The Churn was diverted from within the town to flow down the western ditch (its present course).

In the admirable Corinium Museum in Park Street, funeral monuments to two cavalry officers recall the military station at Chesterton. A relief of three seated female figures represents the Three Mothers, Celtic goddesses of fertility, bearing loaves and fruit. The Roman Jupiter, the Sky-father, appears in Celtic form as a horseman or as a standing figure, trampling the giant Darkness, very much like St Michael or St George. An acrostic scratched in plaster hides the words 'Pater noster', perhaps from the age of persecution, while a majestic inscription records the re-erection of a religious monument by the governor of Britannia Prima, presumably under the pagan revival of Julian-the-Apostate (361–3).

There are several magnificent mosaic pavements dating from the fourth century, taken from various parts of the Roman town, on view in the museum. The work of the Corinium paviours at this period has been identified by stylistic features in the great villas at Woodchester, Chedworth, Withington, Witcomb, Tockington Park and at North Leigh in Oxfordshire. The materials used for the tesserae are blue and white lias, various shades of oolite, and for reds and purples baked tile and red sandstone brought from across the Severn. Tesserae from Cirencester have been found at East Grinstead in Sussex.

Corinium was not the only urban population for the Dobunnic countryman to feed and support. There was a military colony at Glevum (Gloucester) and a thriving spa, Aquae Sulis (Bath). The baths there are the best-preserved Roman remains in the country, built, like the rest of the city, of Cotswold stone. The ploughman may well have gone hungry to supply these cities with bread, but only a very prosperous territory could have supported them at all.

Most of this outstanding material prosperity must have come from the soil. The Cornbrash may already have produced a surplus of grain for export in the Iron Age; improvements in technique, and especially the introduction of corn-drying equipment, would have raised its potential and that of the Stonebrash. The evidence of Bagendon points to exports of hides and perhaps wool. British cloth and rugs are mentioned by classical writers, and the immense quantities of wool produced in Britain under Constantine (306–37) is on record. It seems safe to assume that wool was an important crop on the villa estates of the Dobunnic gentry.

The term *villa* is normally applied to any domestic building on stone foundations in a rural setting containing such unquestionably Roman features as baths and even a single mosaic floor. These are spread all over the Cotswolds, and more are constantly coming to light. A large number are still unexcavated. Most of them would have been modest farmhouses, but a substantial number, more than a dozen in Gloucestershire alone, were by the fourth century luxurious country houses whose owners farmed their own estates as large landowners do today. It is believed that most of them were natives, not immigrant officials or retired soldiers. The large villa estate may represent the possessions of a kinship group absorbed by the fourth century into the hands of one member richer or more able than his relatives, who became his tenants.

The following composite picture of a Romano-British villa will give a good idea of life on a Cotswold farm, and most of its elements are indeed confirmed by Cotswold excavations. The best of the Cotswold villas, unfortunately, were unscientifically dug over by antiquarians in times past.

> The dwelling is placed near light calcareous soil or medium loamy soils. . . . The dwelling house is sheltered on three sides by slopes, itself standing on a southward-facing swell. . . . It is joined by a dirt-track to the main road a few miles away. . . . The residence has been closed off by a wall from the farmyard. In the close is a garden planted with vine, fig, and box; on the west side sycamore, walnut, sweet chestnut, and holm oak have been set to form a windbreak. In the garden are beds of flowers amongst which are seen pansy, poppy, and lily, and various useful potherbs. Part is devoted to market gardening and here are planted the cabbage, carrot, parsnip, and celery.
>
> On the south side of the yard is an aisled building for the farmhands and bailiff; the latter lives in a heated room at the end. In the same part the women of the household live and work at spinning and weaving. . . . Originally livestock were housed in the aisles, but these have been shifted elsewhere and the aisles divided into rooms. Threshing used to be done here in wet weather, but now a circular threshing floor has been made in the yard, and a roomy barn has been built near it for the unthreshed grain. . . . In the yard poultry and geese are kept. . . .
>
> Byre and pigstye are ranged on each side of a barn where fodder and grain are stored. . . . The pigs are grain-fed for fattening, and the oxen get oats and barley in seasons of heavy labour, but also beanstraw, vetch, and hay. . . . Some of the farms . . . run large flocks of sheep.
>
> The pigs graze in the forest, but the sows are brought into the stye for farrowing, and selected young pigs for fattening. The dung is cleared into a pit, and taken to the fields in autumn and winter on stretchers . . . the heavy land is limed periodically, and the lighter loams marled to improve their texture. A good deal of farmyard manure, and the clearings from the latrines

> also, are kept for the roots. The farm is first and foremost a corn farm; wheat, spelt, emmer, and barley are the main crops, but the owner is experimenting with oats. . . .*

A group of villa sites of this type is associated with the Cornbrash between Burford, Woodstock, Charlbury and Chipping Norton. Three of them, at Northleigh, Stonesfield and Fawler, are known to have been luxurious houses. The name Fawler is derived from the Anglo-Saxon words *fagan flore*, meaning a coloured floor; magnificent pavements were destroyed at Stonesfield by a farmer annoyed by visitors from Blenheim Palace coming to view them. The site at Northleigh is open to the public. A large house built round four sides of a courtyard has been excavated, and a single pavement of the Corinium saltire pattern is preserved. The farm buildings have not yet been uncovered, but were evidently extensive. The site of a rather more modest farm has been excavated in Ditchley Park, but from the size of the barn it has been estimated that there might have been about 1,000 acres under plough. The farm-slaves' quarters, eliminated in the fourth century, have also been uncovered, and a circular threshing floor (which suggests that oxen were used to tread out the corn) but no corn-drying equipment. In the face of the imperial government's insatiable demand for wheat, many owners at this time found it more profitable to set up their farm-slaves as *coloni*, that is serfs, with a hut and an acre or so of land each on which to feed themselves as best they could. Alternatively, the owner might rely on tenants to work the estate. The first house at Ditchley, a Celtic longhouse, had been rebuilt in the second century as a single range of rooms with two wings linked by a wooden veranda, and roofed with baked tiles. This was destroyed by fire, and after a long interval a new house was built with a stone collonade round it, and possibly a second story. The new roof was of Stonesfield slates. Surprisingly in a house of this quality, there was no central heating.

Another group of similar size and sophistication lies scattered along the lower slopes of the scarp. There were large villas, for example, at Frocester, Woodchester and Witcomb, and slightly smaller establishments at Whittington and in the Isburne valley. At Witcomb has been found the coulter of the heavy plough introduced by the Belgic conquerors, which first made possible the cultivation of the heavier lias soils. This villa is approached through orchards, and it is not impossible that fruit-farming may have been carried on there in Roman times, though these were probably mainly corn-farms. These villas certainly had their

* Quoted by S. Applebaum in *The Agrarian History of England*, Vol. I, pt 2 (Cambridge University Press, 1972), pp. 220–1.

vineyards on sheltered slopes. The site at Witcomb can be visited; some stone walls still stand six feet high and there is one fine pavement on view. Frocester is now in process of excavation. The remains of a formal garden have been identified, and the presence of fuller's earth in the soakways suggests that there may have been an establishment there for processing cloth. The villa at Woodchester was undoubtedly the most magnificent on the Cotswolds. It was built round two courtyards, one for the dwelling and one for the farm, and entered through a domed gatehouse. Every room in the inner courtyard appears to have had underfloor heating, and there were spelndid floors in the rooms and corridors. The house lies under the village churchyard, and one superb example of the Corinium paviours' art representing Orpheus surrounded by wild beasts and birds, among them bear, lion, tiger, elephant, ox, hare, and peacock is occasionally uncovered for public viewing. The farm courtyard contained a granary added in the fourth century, and possibly a brewery.

Another group of rich villas lying in the valleys of the upper Coln and Churn are most likely to have been centres of sheep-rearing enterprise. To this group belongs the famous villa a mile or two from the village of Chedworth, one of the best preserved villa-sites in the country in a most beautiful setting on the edge of Chedworth Woods. Here some of the walls are still standing to a height of two or three feet, and the hypocaust, or underfloor hot-air heating system, is partly exposed. Several mosaic floors of the fifteen which are known to have existed are still in good condition. One splendid example of the Corinium school depicts satyrs and nymphs within a square border, the corners filled with figures symbolizing the four seasons. Spring and summer are lively though somewhat conventional figures, but winter, a man in a cloth cap, tunic and breeches, with an ample muffler round his neck, carrying a dead hare in one hand and a branch in the other, looks like a true Briton dressed in the produce of his own Cotswold sheep. The residence was of two stories, and roofed with Cotswold slate.

The villa's water was channelled in the fourth century into a new stone cistern (nymphaeum) approached through a pillared portico. Three stones from the wall of this tank bore the Christian Ch-Rho monogram, suggesting that at the time of the rebuilding the owners of this luxurious house were Christians. The farm-buildings have not been clearly identified.

A few miles upstream, just outside the village of Withington, was another large villa, of which nothing now remains but a single fine pavement, now in the British Museum, depicting the Corinium school's favourite Orpheus theme. It has been estimated that the Romano-British Withington estate, if it marched with those of the nearest known sites of comparable houses, of which there are four in the

TO/

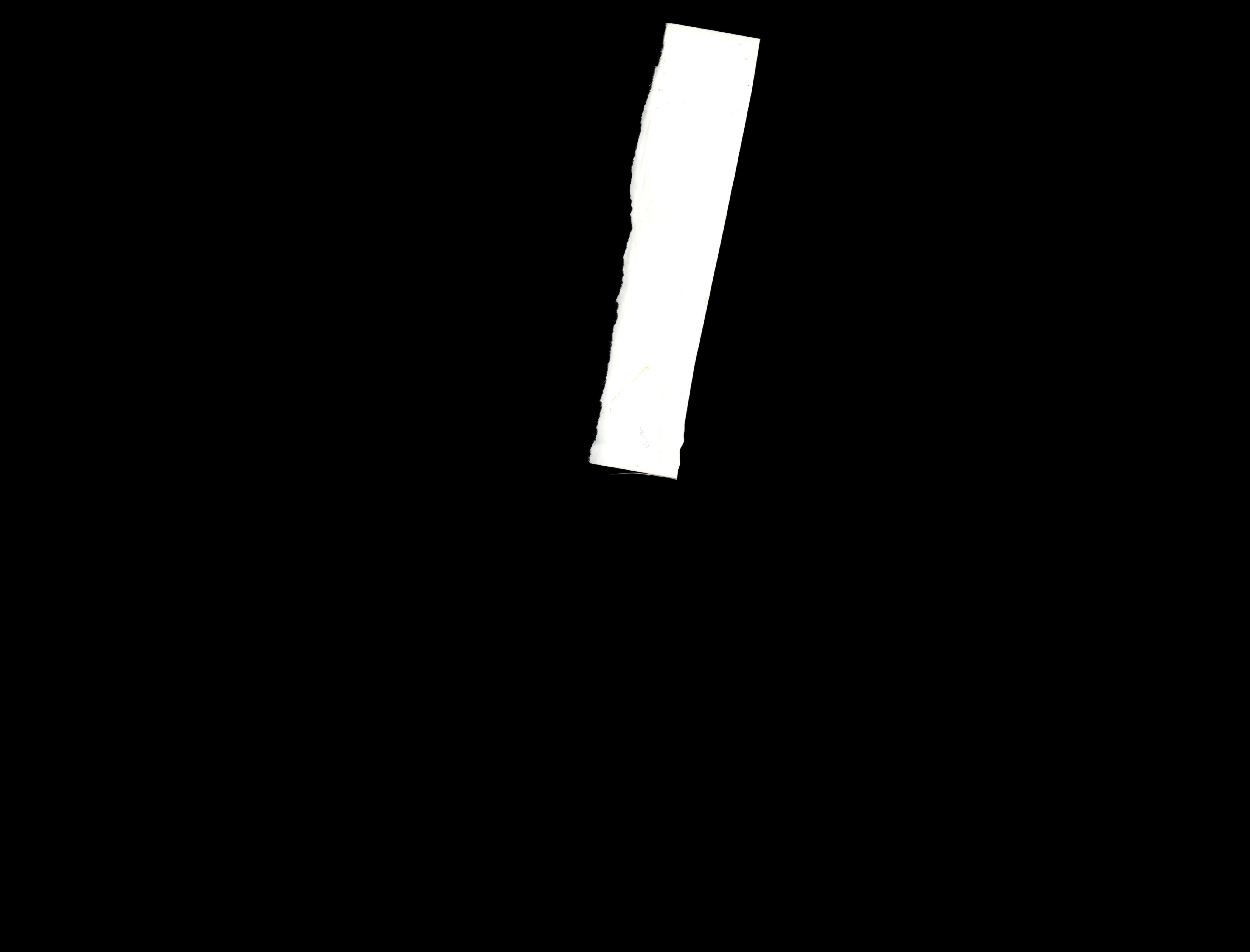

immediate neighbourhood, would have been about 4,000 acres, much of it hill-pasture. The whole of this district seems to be strewn with traces of Romano-British occupation, including the site of Chedworth village itself.

Another group of Roman sites is found between Castle Combe and Bath. If the substantial villa at North Wraxall was characteristic, these were mainly corn farms. At North Wraxall mixed farming gave way to arable in the late third century, and pig fattening was introduced. By the fourth century slaves had been set up as *coloni* and the graveyard of the community took the place of one of the large farm buildings.

The characteristic find on the Cotswold ironstone suggests villages or small towns perhaps to be associated with mineral exploitation, though there is a villa site at Wigginton. A settlement site has been identified in Bloxham Grove, and traces of houses have been noted at Adderbury, Deddington, Hanwell, Wigginton, Drayton, and in Wykeham Park two miles outside Banbury. There was a large settlement covering fifty acres at Lower Lea in Swallcliffe, perhaps a migration from Madmarston Hill; the foundations of important buildings have been found, and a quantity of black earth with stones red from burning which suggests the presence of furnaces for extracting ore. Finds of coins in Banbury itself have been numerous, and an ancient inn called The Altar Stone used to display a Roman carving representing 'a ram and fire'; no trace of Roman occupation, however, came to light when the sewers were laid. Coins have also been found under the market-place in Chipping Norton in sufficient quantity to suggest a roadside settlement on an ancient ridgeway leading southwards through the Stonesfield area, which was used by salt-dealers in the Middle Ages.

Such roadside market-centres in the Cotswolds were never fortified as those nearer the coasts generally were in the fourth century, and the absence of ruined walls or ramparts has preserved their remains from the destructive attentions of antiquarians. They are found on all the main arteries belonging both to pre-Roman and Roman road-systems.

In the Cotswolds such sites are often distinguished by the field-name Chessels. There is a Chessels in the parish of Kingscote where the built-up area covered at least fifty acres, and outdoor paving, squared ashlar, tiles and flues, a mosaic pavement, and much other Roman building material, as well as masses of coins and other small finds, indicate a well-built and prosperous market town lying on a ridgeway which runs along the crest from the neighbourhood of Wotton-under-Edge, and intersects with the Jurassic way about two miles east of this site. This ridgeway served the villas of Rodmarton and Cherington, and another site in Tetbury Upton, and connected with Corinium. Most of the finds are in the

Map 5 *The Roman Cotswolds.*

museum at Gloucester, but a head of Minerva is at Cirencester. Another site, directly on the alignment of the Jurassic way, lies partly under the Andoversford by-pass (A40) and goes by the name of Wycomb. This field-name, originally spelt Wyckham, shows that it has long been recognized as a Roman site (*cf.* Wykeham Park outside Banbury). The excavators have found paved streets, the foundations of a temple and another important public building, and many houses, besides thousands of coins and brooches, a bronze statuette of Mars and other votive carvings, and of course much pottery. The villa at Whittington was almost in the suburbs, and may well have been built by a successful tradesman. This town would have been the normal market centre for the important group of villas in the upper Coln valley.

On the Fosse Way there is a site of fifty acres, known as White Walls, in the parish of Easton Grey, about half-way between Bath and Cirencester, presumed to have been a market and posting station. No station is known to have existed on the fifteen steep miles between Cirencester and Bourton-on-the-Water, but there, across the Windrush ford whose flagged and pebbled surface can be seen beneath the modern bridge, the traveller came to a large posting inn, whose forge and stables have been examined by modern excavators. The main street of quite a large, straggling town ran all the way from the river-crossing to the pre-Roman stronghold of Salmonsbury, still inhabited during much of the Roman period. Many buildings also lie beneath the present centre of the village, and traces of a suburb at Whiteshoot Hill. Only two miles beyond Bourton there was another largish settlement, the Chessels in Lower Slaughter parish, where Ryknield Street, a prehistoric track straightened and surfaced by the Romans, intersects with the Fosse Way. In this neighbourhood Roman coins were once so plentiful that they used to be taken to Stow market and sold by the peck. The villas in Stow, Oddington, Longborough and Rissington parishes would have been within a market journey of either of these settlements.

The next posting station northwards along the Fosse Way was either at Dunstall, a mile short of Moreton-in-Marsh, where there was a largish settlement, or at Dorn, three miles beyond it, where the great road passes out of the territory of the Dobunni. Here the bank of a ten-acre enclosure is still identifiable, and carved altars and funerary stones, stone foundations and coins in plenty have been found about the unexcavated site. The name is undoubtedly British, and probably refers to a gated stronghold, perhaps a military post. Both of these settlements would have had a market.

On Akeman Street eastward from Corinium the traveller came first to a small town at Coln St Aldwyn; a Chessells on the east bank of the Coln is matched by Coin Slade on the west and marks the site of a sizeable settlement. The next station seems to have been at Asthall, where a bath house later converted into a dwelling has been found by the river, and the outline of foundations used to be clearly visible in dry weather. There was a village between Barrington and Taynton, and villas at Widford and between Asthall and Minister Lovell. Only five miles farther east of Asthall along Akeman Street came a settlement covering fifty acres near Wilcote (another Wyckham), which would have been the market centre on the edge of Wychwood forest for the Stonesfield group of villas. There have also been finds suggestive of settlement at Charlbury.

Little can be known of life in the Romano-British countryside. Remains are found scattered in the majority of Cotswold parishes, more often than is realized within or very close to existing villages, notable examples being Poulton, Chedworth, Notgrove and Lower Swell. The large villa within 100 yards of Box church is significant in this respect.

St Patrick and Gildas, the two Roman Britons whose extant writings are our chief sources of information on fifth-century Britain, take it for granted that their fellow-countrymen are all Christians. In all likelihood there was a bishop in Corinium by the end of the fourth century, but remarkably little obvious trace of British Christianity remains in the Cotswolds. The Chi-Rho monograms at Chedworth and the pagan-revival column at Corinium are significant, however, and it has been suggested that certain alterations at Witcomb, and the creation of a large hall at Whittington, may possibly have been made in this connection. The church at Woodchester standing on the site of a great villa; the finds associated with the churchyard at Bisley, Poulton, Bitton and Lower Swell; the mosaic pavement exposed in the chancel at Widford; the foundations of a Roman building directly below the now-demolished church of St Peter at Frocester may not be coincidences. Perhaps the mounds in Bisley parish full of pagan altars represent the apparatus of paganism turned out of a local temple but diplomatically given decent burial at a safe distance. An altar of equestrian Mars and one to Silvanus or his native counterpart, together with calcined stone, were dug from beneath Bisley church tower, and in the graveyard a good deal of Roman pottery has turned up. Another site within the parish yielded three votive carvings, including a ram-headed serpent (*cf.* the 'ram and fire' at Banbury), a third site six altars, four of them to equestrian Mars, as well as small finds. Christianity had apparently as yet made little impact in remote farms and upland villages, but it was as Romans and Christians that the Dobunni would presently confront the barbarian invader.

II

The protracted collapse of the Roman province began towards the close of the fourth century, but for well over a hundred and fifty years no serious heathen incursion seems to have infiltrated the Dobunnic territory.

In the first half of the sixth century West Saxons from the Thames valley made a large cemetery at Fairford, and another only a little later at Poulton; a few isolated burials are found farther up the Cotswold valleys. The barrow of some nameless Saxon leader in Asthall parish, now marked with pine trees, can be seen to the south of A40, and at Shakenoake Farm south-east of Wilcote early-Saxon and late-Roman pottery are found together. Akeman Street was probably a frontier in this area, and the settlements at Asthall, Coln St Aldwyn and Wilcote would have been wiped out in the struggle. The road has never recovered its position as a trunk route. People of Anglian origin now began to establish themselves in the remoter northern Cotswold valleys, leaving another cemetery at Ebrington, and Irish raiders made frequent descents on the Severn shores. Villa-owners migrated to the cities for safety, and these came to be dominated by their armies. Corinium, Glevum and Bath fell under the sway of three different 'kings'. An increasingly primitive kind of life might be carried on for a time in the villas, probably by a bailiff or tenant farmer, and sometimes squatters camped out in abandoned mansions and eventually set them on fire.

In 577 the dreaded onslaught came. Ceawlin and Cuthwine, confederate Saxon leaders, stormed into the south Cotswolds, no doubt by-passing the impregnable defences of Corinium. The three kings joined forces to oppose them, but were overwhelmed at Dyrham on the Edge a few miles from Bath. The Saxons have left traces of this early occupation in pagan cemeteries at Avening and Andoversford, and of their long-term occupation in the place names of the south and central Cotswolds. *Dun* (= down) may mean specifically hill-pasture, so that Withington's Saxon name *Widiandun* suggests that the spoils of war had included some of the Romano-British sheep-farms.

In 628 Ceawlin's successor Cynegils was forced to come to terms at Cirencester with Penda, a powerful and aggressive warlord of Mercia, who proceeded to allot Gloucestershire and the Oxfordshire Cotswolds, together with Worcestershire and part of Warwickshire, to two Northumbrian princes who with their war-bands had fought under his banner. For five generations of their descendants the region was known as the principality of the Hwicce, a satellite of Mercia. The name appears in modern form in Wychwood and Whichford, but its meaning is obscure, since the population of the principality was of mixed Saxon, Anglian, Northumbrian and British stock.

The Saxons continued to infiltrate the Evenlode and Windrush valleys leaving pagan cemeteries at Oddington and Hampnett. A sufficient number of British tillers of the soil remained to teach the invaders their names for most of the rivers; Thames, Severn, Avon, Frome, Churn, Coln and Windrush are all British names, and the British name for the Evenlode survives at Bladon. Churchdown, Churchill and Crouch Hill are bi-lingual, Nympsfield refers to a

British shrine, and the common suffixes *comb* and *don* have British roots. A Saxon personal name need imply no more than a Saxon landlord.

Saxon and Anglian settlers were pagans, but the Northumbrian princes were Christians, and no doubt most of their followers also. No place-name in the Cotswolds carries a suggestion of a heathen shrine, except possibly Taston, where the megalith was called Thor's or Thunor's Stone. When St Augustine

11. *St Mary's, Bibury – the Saxon east wall of the nave.*

sought to make contact with the bishops of the nearest British province, the meeting, Bede tells us, took place on the frontier between the West Saxons and the Hwicce, which at that time must have run along the south-eastern flank of the Cotswolds. A very weak tradition refers to Ampney (others claim Cricklade), and an old local legend tells how St Augustine visited Long Compton to settle a dispute between the Church and a British prince in a story full of anachronistic and marvellous embellishments. Another century was to pass before a bishop was sent from Canterbury to form a diocese for the principality and convert the heathen remnant.

Throughout most of the Old English period, many country people would have heard mass outdoors in places of traditional sanctity. The sites of Bisley and

Nympsfield churches were probably such. Ozleworth church stands within an earthwork which was probably a 'henge' monument of the Bronze Age, and there is another of these not far from Condicote church. Priests would have come from local centres. By the end of the seventh century, ministers, or monasteries, had been founded at Bath, Gloucester, Tetbury and Withington, and the eighth century added foundations at Malmesbury, Bibury and Hawkesbury. The abbeys of Tetbury, Withington and Bibury disappeared within the Saxon period, butt he church at Bibury is an enlarged and much-altered Anglo-Saxon minster church, in which the most notable Saxon features date from the late tenth or early eleventh centuries. The nave was more than sixty feet long, without aisles, and there were shallow transepts now incorporated in the north and south aisles, and a central tower replaced by the present one in the Norman period. The east wall of the nave is the most interesting relic of the Saxon building: the early English chancel arch rests on carved Saxon imposts and pierces the string course which originally supported a great stone rood. The faint outline of one of the figures may be seen on the left side. Inside the church are casts of two finely carved Saxon gravestones, and built into the north wall of the chancel are pieces of a sculptured cross-shaft, decorated with interlacing circles and pellets showing Scandinavian influence.

Four miles away at Coln Rogers the Saxon nave and chancel of a much smaller church have survived almost intact. The nave, chancel and south porch at Daglingworth are Saxon, including the sundial over the south door within the porch, a circular face within a raised roll-moulding on which the markings have been well preserved by the protection of the porch. Within the church are three contemporary carvings – a crucifixion, Christ in Majesty, and St Peter with keys and book. At Duntisbourne Rous the nave of the simple little church is probably Saxon. Foundations of a Saxon church have been excavated at Cirencester and the church at Somerford Keynes contains many Saxon features. Outside this favoured district Saxon relics are scanty. In the Oxfordshire Cotswolds the handsome Saxon tower at North Leigh was situated at the crossing of the original church, clearly an important one. At Swallcliffe the walls of the three western bays of the nave are of Saxon workmanship, and suggest a building of some size.

By far the most important Saxon relic in the Cotswolds is the chapel of St Laurence at Bradford-on-Avon, founded by St Aldhelm. The main fabric up to about half the total height dates from St Aldhelm's time (*c.* A.D. 800), the upper half from the late tenth century. It is only 38 feet long including the tiny chancel, with two side chapels or porches (of which only one remains). High up on the east wall of the nave, carved slabs representing angels were originally placed

12. *The Saxon tower at North Leigh.*

lower as part of a vanished rood. In the ten-century rebuilding the exterior walls were faced with dressed stone decorated by pilaster strips on the four corners, with three additional reeded pilasters up the east gable of the nave and with a broad frieze running all round which consists of a blind arcade flush with the wall supporting a double string-course.

Two Cotswold foundations of the Old English period were of outstanding importance. Malmesbury, traditionally founded by an Irish scholar named Maildubh, was endowed by King Ethelred of Mercia and his kinsmen, but its first abbot was St Aldhelm, a relative of King Ine of Mercia. Adhelm was a man of great learning and charm, the author of both learned treatises and poetry, who according to legend used to play his harp and sing on the bridge below the abbey to attract and convert passers-by. The abbey acted as a powerhouse of learning during the westward expansion of Wessex, and also perhaps as a sort of buffer between the two thrusting rivals, Wessex and Mercia. This abbey adopted the Benedictine rule in the tenth century, and later produced another outstanding personality, the historian William of Malmesbury.

The abbey of Winchcombe produced no such characters of national importance, and nothing now remains of its buildings, but it was one of the largest landowners in the Cotswolds. It was founded in 798 by King Kenwulf of Mercia, and housed the archives of the Mercian royal house as long as Mercia remained an independant kingdom. Soon after the year 1000 the Mercian districts administered from such royal manors as Cirencester, Bradford, Winchcombe, Shipton-under-Wychwood, Charlbury, Wootton, Bloxham and Deddington, were reorganized as shires on the Wessex model, and Winchcombeshire was created, consisting of the Gloucestershire Cotswolds east of Cleeve Hill and the great ridge between the Coln and Churn valleys, with Gloucestershire adjoining it on the south-west. Less than twenty years later, however, the two were amalgamated, but the forgotten boundary still notionally divided the central and south Cotswolds.

The English lost little time in restoring most of the land that had gone to waste during the years of conquest, and continually extended the area of cultivation, so that at the Norman Conquest there was little but marginal land left to reclaim. This was done principally at the expense of woodland, as a high percentage of place-names in the south Cotswolds and the neighbourhood of Wychwood testify, the absence of such names on the central plateau indicating that scrub and down land was already clear. Names including ash, oak, hazel, box and alder, and the common suffix *leigh* or *ley* denote woodland clearings. One bizarre name, St Chloe, traced to its earliest appearance in the records as *Sengedleag*, indicates a clearing made by the traditional method of slashing and burning widely used by primitive farmers in the unending struggle. About a hundred years before Domesday Book the boundaries of the woods and *feld* (downland) of Hawling were recorded. The woodland was a vast expanse beginning about a quarter of a mile from this tiny upland village, extending over the summit of the scarp and down to its foot. By the time Domesday Book was made, this forest in which a man might lose himself had been reduced to a small wood of unspecified size, and two new settlements, Roel and Sudeley, had been created. Except for a few industrial settlements in the south Cotswolds, nearly every existing village is recorded in the survey, as well as some which have since disappeared such as Roel, Pinnock, Harford in Naunton and Upton in Blockley, as well as a larger number in Oxfordshire, though Coln Roger and Coln St Denis and similar pairs have only a single entry.

During the Old English period a change, possibly begun in Roman times, came in the pattern of the arable fields which cannot be even approximately dated. A standard plough-team of eight oxen was introduced, and the awkwardness of turning such a team at the furrow's end probably suggested the making of a longer furrow. All newly reclaimed land, and soon old cultivation as well, was laid out in long furrows. Villagers may have cooperated to make up full teams among them, and thus developed, probably, 'share-lands', of which we begin to hear in the eighth century. The arable was laid out in blocks which came to be known as furlongs, in which individual holdings were intermixed. Such 'open fields' lasted in the Cotswolds until the nineteenth century in many parishes. The last remnant of them may still be seen at the time of writing at Westcote near Stow, where the individual strips are divided from each other by baulks of old tussocky grass scattered with thorn saplings, wild rose and weeds.

The practice of laying the arable up in ridge-and-furrow does not certainly date from the Old English period, but it is certainly ancient. Beginning in the middle of each land (a section of the ground to be ploughed in one piece) by laying two slices one upon another, the ploughman turns his furrows towards the same centre year by year, so that each land builds up after a few years into a ridge varying from two feet to over four feet high. No baulk was then necessary to mark off one man's property from another's. Cotswold farmers believed that ridging was indispensable for their wheat, and the practice continued long after the open fields had been enclosed. Thus the ridges sometimes fit within the post-enclosure fields, but often the pattern of the open-field furlongs is preserved, and in spite of modern efforts to eliminate the ridges by cross-ploughing, they can often still be seen.

There is enough evidence to show that Mercian landowners exploited the incomparable sheep-pastures. For example, Eafe, abbess of Gloucester in the eighth century, acquired a sheep-walk between Coberley and Withington, and the abbess of Withington extended her property to the east bank of the Coln to take in pastures up towards the Shiptons, themselves sheep-farms. There were royal sheep-farms at Shipton-under-Wychwood and Shipton-on-Cherwell, and others at Shipton Moyne and Shipston-on-Stour. Other significant names are

Sheepscombe and Yanworth (a farm for breeding ewes) and several Washbrooks. King Offa made a trade agreement with Charlemagne on a standard size of English cloths for export.

The Cotswold flocks must have suffered heavily during the two black years after the Danish army descended on Gloucester in 877. The army crossed the wolds to Chippenham 'slaying and burning whatever was in their path as is their custom'. After Alfred's resounding victory at Eddington the following spring, they retreated to Cirencester and remained there a twelvemonth. Tar Barrow (Tori's barrow) is perhaps a relic of this dire episode; it is one of the few Scandinavian personal names found in the Cotswolds, which were outside the mainstream of a conflict which continued intermittently for two hundred years. (Dane in several Cotswold names such as Woeful Danes Valley is always in origin *dene* = valley). Gloucester, Bath, Malmesbury, Cricklade and Oxford were the strong points (A.S. *burh*) in Alfred's system of defence against the Vikings. The remains of the Saxon rampart at Cricklade can be seen to the right of B4041 as it leaves the town; at Winchcombe there are some traces of Mercian defensive work, though the town is not recorded as a *burh*. In spite of the Danish menace it was a period of high artistic and intellectual achievement in Wessex. One of the finest examples of contempoary craftsmanship was found at Minster Lovel in 1860, and is proudly exhibited in the Ashmolean Museum at Oxford, together with the more famous Alfred Jewel. Both are probably from the same workshop and are thought to be ferrules used to preserve the pages of manuscripts from fingermarks. The Minster Lovel Jewel is a small socketed disc of chased gold richly decorated with gold filigree and cloisonné enamel.

In the year 1001 King Ethelred II granted the royal manor of Bradford-on-Avon to the nuns of Shaftesbury, that they might find 'an impenetrable refuge from the treachery of the heathen'. Domesday (1086) records that the abbess had then at Bradford a market and thirty-three burgesses, as well as a rich manor with over a hundred humble tenants. Twenty-two of these were swineherds, keeping the monastic pigs in a wood half a league long; there was arable 'land for forty ploughs', and a vineyard. Woodland swine-pastures were evidently a feature of the south Cotswolds still. Bisley parish was probably then a series of clearings, and some of the tenants paid part of their dues in honey, almost certainly wild honey gathered in the woods. The village of Cranham is not even mentioned. The steep woods along the scarp slopes from Cleeve Hill northwards were then much larger, as were Chedworth and Guiting woods; Wychwood still covered an enormous tract of country and was a favoured hunting resort of the Saxon kings. In the north and central Cotswolds, however, apart from these, no more woodland remained than was required by villages and hamlets for fuel, building and winter fodder.

Downland pasture is excluded from the Gloucestershire survey, so we cannot tell just how important were the sheep-runs at the time, but Chedworth in the heart of the wolds was a large rich manor, and contained, apart from the arable, fifteen hides of wood, pasture and meadow. Many villages are only rated at five hides in all, with no separate assessment for wood etc.; the Chedworth assessment therefore surely points to pastoral enterprise on a considerable scale. The tenants at Shipton-under-Wychwood had no ploughs at all, and may be supposed to have been almost entirely occupied with sheep, apart from labour-services on the lord's demesne farm. The survey records that the wool of the Cirencester flock is reserved for the queen. The unusually high number of slaves on Gloucestershire manors may represent shepherds, cowmen and swineherds. Alternatively, it may be attributable to the high proportion of estates already in the hands of the Church.

The rich cornland in the triangle between Banbury, Heyford and Rollright was well populated, most of the wood had been eliminated, and there was a fair amount of good meadowland along the Cherwell and its feeders. There were also a number of fisheries yielding revenue along the Cherwell.

Some Cotswold manors had their own salt-workings at Droitwich, notably Sodbury, Chedworth, Guiting and Stanway. Pack-horses carrying this essential commodity were sufficiently numerous to leave an ineradicable mark on the landscape. Some of the old saltways are marked on the Ordnance map, and names such as Salters Hill above Hailes, where one of these routes climbed up the Edge into the Cotswolds, Saltways Farm and Salterley Grange mark out their course. One route passes Hawling, Salperton, Chedworth and follows the side of the Coln valley down to Lechlade. Another route led through the Guitings, Sherborne and Eastleach; a third entered the north Cotswolds after passing Salford, and went by Chipping Norton and Stonesfield towards the Thames. Although Sodbury was near the salt-pans on the Severn, the far purer Droitwich salt came by way of Cheltenham, Leckhampton and Painswick into the south Cotswolds.

Although a hundred years of civil strife and foreign invasions had done a certain amount of damage which is reflected in the Survey, the picture of the Cotswolds that Domesday gives us is on the whole of a prosperous countryside, comfortably full of folk.

5

From Domesday Book to the Dissolution of the Monasteries

After the Norman Conquest, strong castles rose along the Severn shore, but within the Cotswolds these relics of an alien aristocracy are rather thin on the ground. Bishop Alexander of Lincoln (1123–45) built a castle at Banbury which remained a formidable stronghold and prison throughout the Middle Ages, but at Malmesbury the abbot obtained permission from King John (no doubt in return for some financial consideration) to pull down Bishop Roger of Salisbury's castle. Enough of it seems to have remained standing, however, to be of some use in the Civil War. The Bell Inn, formerly the Castle Inn, stands on the site. A castle at Cirencester was sacked during the disorders of King Stephen's reign and never rebuilt, though Castle Street still records its existence. Castles at Tetbury and Chipping Norton have left only a few insignificant earthworks.

A substantial mound next to the church at Upper Slaughter has yielded material from the eleventh to the thirteenth centuries, but the castle has virtually no history. Considerable earthworks remain of the stronghold which gave its name to the lovely village of Castle Combe, but they are inaccessible in the park about a mile north of the village. That of the Musards, from whom Miserden takes its name, also lies hidden in private woodland. At Brimpsfield a thicket next to the entrance to the churchyard conceals a deep ditch and a formidable motte (mound), and a few fragments of stonework remain among the nettles and saplings. The Giffards were given Brimpsfield by the Conqueror, and their castle was demolished about 1322, after one of them had joined the Berkeleys' unsuccessful rebellion against Edward II and lost his head at Gloucester. The castle at Deddington also makes one brief appearance in history, for it was there that the earl of Warwick captured Edward's favourite Piers Gaveston, who had called him a 'black dog'. Declaring that 'the witch's son shall feel the black dog's teeth', the earl took him to Warwick, and executed him without further formality. The castle was demolished soon after, but large mounds remain south-east of the town, surrounded by a bank and ditch made before 1100. An inner bailey containing a small keep, hall and chapel was formed perhaps a hundred years later. At Ascot-under-Wychwood there are earthworks of two castles, one a simple motte-and-bailey fortification of the early period at the west end of the village known as Ascot Earl, the other a mile and a quarter from the church in Ascot Doyley representing the bailey of the Doyley's castle built 1129–50. Excavations show that there was a stone keep thirty-five feet square here and several houses within the bailey. The Manor House which stands within the latter contains thirteenth-century features, though it was largely built in the sixteenth and seventeenth centuries. There was a castle at Kempsford, standing upon a Saxon earthwork, but nothing now remains of it. The vicarage garden occupies part of the precincts and the outer rampart, known as Lady Maud's Walk.

Beverstone castle has far more to offer the visitor. It is an imposing ruin, probably originally quadrangular, with drum towers at the four corners, and a short stretch of the deep moat is concealed in a wood behind the buildings. In 1330 the reigning Lord Berkeley bought the manor and modernized the castle. The western range and the gatehouse which he added survive, and include the chapel and Lord Berkeley's chamber with its own tiny oratory. The present house, occupying the site of the south range, was probably built early in the seventeenth century and contains a contemporary staircase, but its mullioned and transomed windows and its hipped roof of Cotswold slate seem to date from about 1690.

The earliest buildings on the present site at Sudeley date from the fifteenth century, when the castle came into the hands of the Botelers, who lost it again to the Crown during the Wars of the Roses. A fine bay window belongs to a suite, probably added by Richard of Gloucester, afterwards Richard III. In 1547 it was given to Admiral Lord Seymour, then husband of Henry VIII's last queen, Katherine Parr, who died here and is buried in Sudeley church. The present house was built by Lord Chandos about 1572 in Boteler's outer court, and on the eve of the Civil War Sudeley was described by a contemporary as 'of subjects' castles the handsomest habitation, and of subjects' habitations the handsomest castle'. After the Civil War the castle, which had been held for the king, was 'slighted', or rendered untenable and probably uninhabitable; its restoration began only in the middle of the nineteenth century and was completed about 1936. The elevations to the court retain much of their original form but the interior has been remodelled. Some contemporary chimney-pieces and Flemish

13. *Beverstone Castle.*

glass have been introduced, but most of the stained glass and fittings are in gothic style by nineteenth-century craftsmen.

Broughton Castle near Banbury, on the other hand, is virtually the same house in which Lord Saye and Sele plotted the Parliamentary rebellion, and in whose attics he quartered his troops. One of the most attractive, perhaps the most interesting of the great houses of our region, it is not in origin a castle at all, but an early fourteenth-century moated manor house, later fortified by William of Wyckham, the founder of Winchester and New College. It was modernized and greatly enlarged about 1554 by Richard Fiennes, the third Lord Saye and Sele, whose descendants still live there, and there have been only minor alterations since his day. The castle lies low in an undulating park, completely surrounded by a moat, usually green with water-lilies but at the time of writing undergoing dredging. The single narrow bridge is guarded by a small medieval gatehouse. Within this beautiful frame an almost symmetrical Tudor elevation, built of the local warm brown stone, shows only at the eastern end some of the medieval windows and crenellations. The mixed character of the building can be better appreciated from the exquisite little 'ladies' garden' at the rear. The fourteenth-century great hall is still in use, lit by a fine bay window added by Richard Fiennes, and visitors are also shown the groined passage and vaulted undercroft of the principal chamber of the medieval house, now a bedroom with a magnificent chimney-piece; from it a window looks down into the original chapel, which retains its floor-tiles and heraldic glass. Most of the superb ceilings and woodwork installed by Richard Fiennes are still in place.

The picturesque ruins of a smaller unfortified manor house, built in the fourteenth century, remain on the bank of the Windrush at Minster Lovel. This was the ancestral home of Francis Lovel, Richard III's minister:

(The Cat, the Rat, and Lovel that Dog
Rule all England under the Hog)

Lovel supported the cause of Lambert Simnel, who was a local boy. The Pretender's army was defeated at Stamford Bridge, and Lovel was last seen struggling to climb the bank after swimming his horse across the Trent. In 1708, workmen repairing a chimney at Minster Lovel Manor broke into a secret room and found the body of a man sitting at a table with a dog at his feet. Both crumbled to dust as they looked. On this frail evidence a story grew up that Lovel came home and was fed by one faithful servant, whose sudden death left his master to starve locked in his hiding place.

The Norman Conquest brought peace and growing prosperity to England, making trade with the continent easier and safer than ever before. In Flanders, the cloth manufacture had already begun to expand in the eleventh century, and English wool was regarded as the best in Europe, commanding the highest prices both in Italy and the Netherlands. When the Conqueror gave the manor of Minchinhampton to the nuns of the Holy Trinity at Caen, he was not offering them a mixed upland farm too remote from the abbey to be economically managed, but a valuable share in the resources of his new kingdom. Later the nuns are found running 1,700 sheep on Minchinhampton Common.

Domesday records the existence of only two markets in the south Cotswolds, at Bradford-on-Avon and Cirencester, and none at all in the northern half of the region, but the famous survey is notoriously incomplete in several particulars. At least as many as in Roman Britain would have been required by the rural community in 1086. The boroughs of Winchcombe and Malmesbury were certainly market centres, and since the royal manor of Cirencester had a market, others such as Bloxham and Deddington surely had markets too. Close to the one-time royal manor of Chedworth stands a farm called Newport. Anglo-Saxon *port* means market, and this five-way junction is probably the place where, according to Domesday, tolls were charged on salt coming into the manor. The manor of Burford appears in Domesday as a small and purely rural community, yet within a year its owner, Robert Fitz Hamo, was granting his tenants there the right to form a merchant guild, which was normally given only to an established mercantile community. In 1107 Henry I made a grant to the abbot of Evesham licensing him to hold a market at Edwardsstowe (Stow-on-the-Wold), but the presence of a market at this important cross-roads may well have been the reason for chosing it as the site for a monastery more than fifty years before. Banbury did not obtain a market charter until 1152, but the market was already there, and at such an important river-crossing, the centre of a huge episcopal estate, it had probably been a place of trade since time immemorial.

By the thirteenth century the whole economic and political structure of the kingdom was beginning to revolve round the export of wool. Any extraordinary expense or shortfall was met by an increased tax or levy on the trade, an example being Richard I's ransom, raised by an extra tax on wool, and the whole crop for the season 1193–4 was taken from the Praemonstratentian and Cistercian abbeys besides. We may imagine in what terms this event was discussed on the manors belonging to Kingswood, Bruerne and Monkton Farleigh.

The wool of Cotswold ranked second only to the 'Lemster Ore' of Hereford and Shropshire, and was much more plentiful. The sheep were noted for their large size, long necks, and the depth and whiteness of the fleece. In the thirteenth century the city of Gloucester owed 30,000 bales of Cotswold wool to the Crown. The abbot of Gloucester was shearing 10,000 sheep, and it was probably to store the wool-clip as well as corn that about 1300 he built the great barn still standing at Frocester. Another splendid medieval barn at Stanway, now used as a village hall, was built by the abbot of Tewkesbury. Stanway with Taddington, a hamlet high in the hills, gave him his share in the harvest of the wolds. All the neighbouring abbeys, and some distant ones, had their sheep-walks, Evesham in the parishes round Stow-on-the-Wold, Pershore at Buckland, Cowley and Hawkesbury, Westminster at Bourton-on-the-Hill, St Frideswide's, Oxford, at Tackley, the bishop of Worcester at Blockley and Bishops Cleeve. It was in order to increase his flocks that Lord Berkeley bought Beverstone.

Until the reign of Edward I, English and foreign dealers had equal access to the sources of supply. Italian firms such as the Bardi, Peruzzi and Frescobaldi of Florence specialized in large dealings with monastic houses, frequently in forward transactions in which the annual clip would be sold on the sheep's back, or even several years ahead. Some of the wool sold came from their tenants. Every parish within the wolds had downs similar to Minchinhampton Common on which the peasants had the right to run their sheep. A proportion of their produce would be absorbed by dues to their landlords and tithes to the Church (often in the Cotswolds the same ecclesiastical body), but the poorer wool would remain to be disposed of in the local market, and provide the peasants with money to spend there.

Before the twelfth century was out, markets had been set up at Campden, Dursley and Wotton-under-Edge, these last depending partly on the produce of the Vale. A market was proving a very good way of raising the value of an estate, to be followed, if the venture showed signs of prospering, by a charter granting the enviable status of burgesses and a measure of self-government to the inhabitants. A new market-place would be laid out, designed to attract the settlers who would be needed to turn the new borough into a profitable speculation. With his castle as a natural focus for traders, William de Braose had only to set up his market-place at Tetbury on the main road which passed by; similarly at Chipping Norton and Campden it was only necessary to choose a fairly level stretch of the important thoroughfare passing through an existing settlement, but the matter was not always so simple. When the abbot of Gloucester decided to set up a market in the central Cotswolds, he had to place it at the extremity of his vast estate extending from Ampney St Peter, and Eastleach up the Coln to Coln Roger and across the Leech to Aldsworth, in order to find an ideal site where an ancient thoroughfare up which merchants would come intersected with the Fosse Way. The market grant for Northleach is dated 1227. The town never equalled Burford and Campden, but it became quite an important centre, the home of some outstanding woolmen, some of whose doings have come down to us in the Cely papers.

Map 6 *The Cotswolds from 700 to 1535.*

In the same year William le Gros established a market at Old Sodbury. Fifty years later William de Waylaund obtained another market for Sodbury, and his son yet a third ten years after that. Probably it was the Waylaunds who realized that the steep village street would not do, and laid out a new market-place, which became Chipping Sodbury, on level ground at the foot of the hill, close enough to the main road to encourage the traveller to turn aside and come through.

Between 1200 and 1400, Marshfield, Hawkesbury, Kings Stanley, Minchinhampton, Painswick, Brimpsfield, Lechlade, Fairford, Guiting Power, Cheltenham, Prestbury, Moreton-in-Marsh, Blockley, Witney, Woodstock, Charlbury and Deddington were given markets, by far the majority before 1300. In the Cotswolds a good position on a main road almost guaranteed success. Hawkesbury, Brimpsfield, Guiting and Blockley had no chance on this account and Prestbury was too near to Cheltenham, but of the rest all except Charlbury and Deddington, achieved the status of a borough. The foundation charters of such boroughs rarely survive. We first hear of burgesses at Sherston in 1404, though this attractive hill-top village, which had already been ancient when Edmund Ironside fought Canute there in 1016, had gained a market licence in 1252.

The grant of a fair normally accompanied the market charter, and would be fixed to coincide with the parish dedication feast or one of the great Christian festivals. It was intended to attract traders from far and near, and to become the great event of the neighbourhood, celebrated with pageants, sports, feasting and all kinds of revelry. When the bishop of Lincoln started a new Whitsun fair at Banbury in 1154 the abbot of Eynsham was willing to assist a fellow churchman, and glad to contribute to the economic opportunities of his north Oxfordshire estates, so he ordered that the Pentecostal procession of three rural deaneries which normally came to Eynsham, should in that year go to Banbury. At the Midsummer Fair at Burford a great golden dragon used to parade through the streets in memory of a battle fought there in 752 between Cuthred of Wessex and Ethelbald of Mercia. According to tradition, Aethelhun the standard-bearer brought down his opposite number by running him through the body with the pole bearing the dragon banner of Wessex, and thus hastened the rout of the Mercian army. This pageant was unhappily discontinued some time in the eighteenth century; the Whitsun procession lingered on at Campden into the present century.

If a town prospered, further market days and fairs would be added. By the eighteenth century there were five at Banbury, of which the most important was the five-day horse-fair in January; on the first day the best horses were sold, and so on to the last, 'Gipsy Day', which was devoted to the nags and donkeys. At one of these fairs, usually in the autumn, the workers of the district would seek a year's contract of employment, standing in the market-place with the tools of their trade. Was it a kind of compliment, or just because women were in the majority on these occasions, that the hiring fair became known as the Mop? The October fairs at Cirencester, Chipping Norton and Banbury are still so-called.

14. *Aerial view of Stow-on-the-Wold. The burgage strips of the medieval town can be seen ringing the market-place.*

From fifty to a hundred burgages, freehold tenements with special privileges attached, clustered round or along the market-place. These consisted of houses occupying a narrow frontage with a long strip for yard, warehouse or stables, and garden behind. In several towns, notably in Chipping Campden where it is known as Back Ends, a lane still runs along the end of these burgage strips. Perhaps as many more cottages, a few farmsteads, and one or more mills would lie within the borough boundaries.

The houses at first would all be of wood and thatched. In 1221, after a disastrous fire, the prior of Winchcombe built two houses of stone, roofed with Cotswold slates, which were probably the first of their kind in the borough. By the end of the fourteenth century some inns and houses of the principal inhabitants were being built of stone. Six stone-built houses built before 1400 survive in Burford, though with much alteration from the fifteenth century. The Chur in Bisley Street, Painswick, has a late fourteenth-century stone doorway, but the original building may have been of timber. It was probably an inn. Campden in this period was catching up on Cirencester in importance, and William Grevel, 'the flower of the wool merchants of all England', who died in 1401, built himself a stone house whose arched doorway and long low roof still adorn the High Street; the very fine bay window was added perhaps a hundred and fifty years later. Monmouth House in Thomas Street, Cirencester, is a fourteenth-century house modernized in Tudor times. In all Cotswold towns the occasional fragment of a vault, doorway, or a piece of carved stone indicates the remains of a stone building of this period. Examples of fifteenth- and early sixteenth-century houses and other buildings are far more numerous, though towards the end of the period there seems to have been some sort of fashionable revival of timber framing. The George Hotel at Winchcombe is a pre-Reformation inn presumably built by the abbot to cater for pilgrims, for the carved spandrels of the doorway bear the initials of Richard Kidderminster who resigned in 1525.

There are quite a large number of medieval survivals among the manor houses of the Cotswolds. The most interesting houses from this point of view are Horton Court and Buckland Rectory. The north wing at Horton is dated about 1140, a high bare hall of stone, with open roof and fireplace of later date, entered through a chevron-moulded doorway. The rest of the house was built about 1521 by William Knight, Henry VIII's envoy to the pope in the matter of his divorce, and later bishop of Bath and Wells. Evidently captivated by the Italian way of life, he made an Italianate loggia in his garden which still contains four medallion heads of Roman emperors in stucco. He also added bands of renaissance ornament carved in oolite to the porch of his house, for which he must surely have brought home the drawings, for they are some of the very earliest examples of such design in the country. House and garden lie with the church in a romantically secluded cup beneath the wooded scarp.

Buckland Rectory also lies at the foot of the scarp. The timbered hall has a magnificent roof of two bays, with two tiers of windbraces. The hammerbeam truss is carved with angels holding shields and the north window contains contemporary heraldic glass. The badges of Edward IV and the rector from 1466 date the building within twenty years.

15. *Courtyard at Elm Tree House, Chipping Campden, 1916 (woodcut by F. L. Griggs). A typical Cotswold town rear view showing the wooden partitions customarily used inside the stone*

Great Chalfield Manor, two and a half miles north-east of Bradford-on-Avon, is built of Cotswold stone, one of the most perfect surviving moated manor houses in the country, dated about 1480. There are medieval halls at South

Wraxall, Down Ampney House, Icomb Place, Little Sodbury Manor and Daneway in Sapperton, incorporated in later building with various alterations. The east wing of Owlpen Manor, one of the most attractive on the wolds, is the medieval house, but the Great Chamber was added about 1540 and the whole house was completely remodelled in 1720. At Shipton-under-Wychwood Prebendal House contains fifteenth-century work, and the tithe barn belongs to this period. The splendid Shaven Crown Inn is said to have been built for visitors to Bruerne Abbey. Many villages can show stone cottages dating from the early sixteenth century which were originally occupied by small farmers rather than labourers.

Sheep-farming was by no means the exclusive preoccupation of Cotswold farmers, even at the height of its importance. On the ironstone corn and cattle were the principal themes, along the Cornbrash grain was the more important crop, and the quarries offered good opportunities for successful enterprise. Even on the high wolds landlord and peasant aimed to grow their own bread, drink and seed-corn, as well as a great deal of winter fodder, reared their own plough-beasts and drove their swine to the dwindling woods. In the south Cotswolds and along the Edge the forest was still being pushed back to make room for the plough. The villages of Cranham, Stockwell and many other hamlets, were wrested from the woodland in the thirteenth century. Ecclesiastical bodies were not indulgent landlords; labour-services on the Cotswolds were abnormally high, and the tenants could be sure that every half day, or its money equivalent, would be exacted. By the early fourteenth century, landlords had begun to prefer the money, and the Black Death, a fearful epidemic of bubonic plague which carried off nearly a third of the population in 1348–9, accelerated the change. At this period the ploughlands were still cropped on the two-field principle, half the arable remaining fallow each year. In many parts of England a three-field rotation was being introduced, reducing the fallow to one-third, but on the wolds the greater area of fallow was probably needed for sheep and cattle.

It seems that great proprietors such as the abbots of Gloucester and Winchcomb and Lord Berkeley generally managed their sheep-flocks outside the self-contained life of the village communities on their manors. When Lord Berkeley bought Beverstone in 1330, he bought out the freeholders and eliminated the arable, stocking it with 1,500 wethers. Such flocks were under the care of a master shepherd (a salaried official) and his deputies, and probably moved about from place to place. In May each year the abbot of Winchcombe moved his household over to Sherborne for a month. Here he had a large mixed farm whose production was geared to supplying the abbey and victualling this annual event, and there were broad meadows to accommodate his flocks from the upland manors of Snowshill, Charlton Abbots, Hawling and Roel when they were driven down to be washed before shearing in the limpid waters of the Sherborne Brook. In 1355 most of the peasant households of Sherborne owed service to the abbot, washing, shearing, and sewing up the wool in packs of over two hundred fleeces apiece, for which they received an allowance of food while at work. Hired labour was also required, drawing in, probably, every able-bodied man, woman and child in and about the village. At the end came the shearing feast. Four miles downstream at Barrington, the prior of Lantony, a cell of the Welsh abbey near Gloucester, carried out the same operation with his flocks from Colesbourne, Turkdean, Cherington and South Cerney, if not from Painswick and Haresfield as well. The abbot of Gloucester presumably held a similar shearing on the Coln or the Leach.

To the shearing also came the dealers. An Italian known as Bernard Lumbard was at Sherborne in 1436, and was probably a regular visitor. By this date, however, the home market absorbed more wool than the export trade. In some counties many villages are known to have been obliterated to make room for sheep, and this may have been the fate of the abbot's village of Roel, whose turf-covered ruins are clearly visible in the field next to Roel farm, and of Upton in Blockley when the bishop had increased his flocks about a hundred years before. During the hundred years of the three Edwards, however, the wool tax passed on by the merchants to the growers with a bonus for themselves, had so depressed prices that many great sheep-farmers began to lease their acres and their flocks to the peasants. Only two thousand sheep came to the abbot's shearing in 1436, but we may suppose that on upland manors a rustic festival was in progress which would continue long after the abbey had been forgotten – that scene which Shakespeare immortalized in *The Winter's Tale* where the saltiers perform a horn dance, Autolycus steals from men and teases the girls, and the buxom mistress of the feast

> . . . was both pantler, butler, cook,
> Both dame and servant; welcomed all, served all,
> Would sing her song and dance her turn; now here
> At the upper end of the table, now in the middle,
> On his shoulder, and his; her face afire
> With labour and the thing she took to quench it,
> She would to each one sip.

To assist in levying the wool tax and disposing of levied wool, various measures had been taken at different times to concentrate the export trade in the hands of an English monopoly. Thus emerged the Company of the Staple, and the Staple, that is, a fixed market through which all wool for export had theoretically to pass, was located finally at Calais in 1335. Although the Italians managed to secure exemption, the importance of middlemen, up-country wool-brokers, was increased, and by the end of the fourteenth century a class of merchant princes was beginning to emerge, with the merchants of the Staple at its apex. Such was William Grevel of Campden, whose house we have already noticed, whose descendants are the Earls of Warwick. Such, a generation later, were the Gibbes of Campden, the Midwinters, Forteys and Taylours of Northleach, the Pynnocks of Burford, the Thames of Fairford, whose great fortunes were involved as much with the home market as with the export of raw wool.

Already in 1086 many Cotswold villages had a water mill: the Trinity mill at Bagendon, the old mill at Stonehouse, and no doubt others stand on a Domesday site. Within a hundred years a momentous discovery had been made. The first recorded fulling mill in England (1185) was at Barton in Temple Guiting on the infant Windrush. It was probably alongside, or even within the same building, as a corn mill. A fine seventeenth-century house, perhaps formerly inhabited by generations of millers, still stands at this historic spot, but only a choked mill-pond remains of any mill. Another fulling mill is on record at Bourton-on-the Water in 1206. A few years later Abbot John of Winchcomb was making a cut to improve the flow of water to his fulling mill at Sherborne. Roger the Fuller appears in a Customal of Minchinhampton in 1272 and other fulling mills in the neighbourhood of Kingswood and Wotton-under-Edge appear in the records about the same time. After this the references are plentiful. In 1409 Sir John Fastolfe, a soldier in the retinue of the Duke of Clarence and an astute man of business, acquired the manor of Castle Combe by marriage, and for the next thirty years he was constantly recruiting men for the French wars and clothing them in the red and white cloths bought from his tenants at Castle Combe. By 1454 the village was almost entirely occupied by seventy clothworkers with their apprentices and servants, and their scarlet cloths were widely known as Castle-combes. Other colours on record are 'plover subtil' and 'frost green', names for dun and dull green as picturesque as those now used to sell brown stockings. Cloth from Cirencester and other centres was being sent to the village for dyeing. About fifty new houses had been built in the village in Sir John's time, and the manor court had imposed closing times (8 p.m. in winter and 9 p.m. in summer) on the local taverns.

Fulling is the process by which the open mesh created by the weaver is shrunk and thickened into cloth. Until the advent of the mill, the makers of fine cloth, apart from domestic weaving for home consumption or purely local trade, were concentrated in the cities, where the fullers, walkers or tuckers, as they were variously called, carried out the laborious finishing process by treading the cloth hour after hour in an alkaline solution. By the fourteenth century the stringent regulations of the Weavers' Guild at Bristol, designed to safeguard quality, included one forbidding clothiers to send their pieces into the country to be finished (i.e. to the fulling mills in the south Cotswolds). At the time the object of this provision was to prevent an expanding industry from migrating altogether to the valleys, as ultimately it did. Owing to the heavy export duty, English clothiers were buying their wool at a fraction of the price foreigners had to pay, and in consequence could offer their cloth more cheaply; merchants found that the export of cloth, on which the duty was small, was far more profitable than that of wool on which a crushing duty had to be paid. Thus by 1500 English cloth had overtaken the Flemish on the European market. The main demand, however, was for white broadcloth to be worked by the highly skilled dyers and finishers of Antwerp, and the trade was dominated by a new monopoly, the Merchant Adventurers Company, with headquarters in London. Probably many merchants of the Staple, however, had a finger in both pies.

To these woolmen the self-destroying baronial struggle known in history as the Wars of the Roses (1455–85) was a nuisance rather than a disaster. It is doubtful if Cotswold folk ever saw the march of contending armies, unless when the battle of Tewkesbury was fought fifteen miles from the foot of the scarp. Their role, as usual, was to supply the 'sinews of war', mainly, one must suppose, to the Yorkist cause, since the 'king-maker' Warwick held the Staple town of Calais, and Edward IV had business dealings as a merchant (Burford itself belonged at that time to Warwick). The Yorkist sympathies of the wool merchants are plentifully displayed in their great churches.

Perhaps it was partly because, with so much of the wolds in ecclesiastical hands, they found difficulty in investing in land, that the merchants spent so lavishly on their parish churches. There they lie, with their wives beside them, under monumental brasses as grand as any nobleman's, clothed in ample fur-trimmed robes instead of knightly armour, with a large purse instead of a sword at the waist, and their feet resting, not on some heraldic beast, but upon the humble sheep. There is a unique collection of these brasses in Northleach church.

6

'As sure as God's in Gloucestershire'

Considering the great opportunities available to sheep-farmers, it is not surprising that there is hardly a church on the Cotswolds that does not show traces of Norman work. In the remoter upland villages many retain the simple character of a Norman 'field-church' (a chapel which was the property of the man who built it where there had never been a church before), consisting of a little hall with the tiniest chancel beyond a low narrow arch, sometimes even lacking an east window and lit by mere slits. One or two windows, a bell-turret or a tower and a slightly improved chancel are their only later additions. The churches of Brimpsfield and Ozleworth are the most interesting of this group.

St Michael's, Brimpsfield, is a very early Norman structure. The chancel was slightly extended, and a bell-turret added a little later, and then in the fifteenth century a tower was ruthlessly thrust into the centre of the church. The effect is quaint, and shows by contrast how sophisticated and sympathetic were the masons responsible for most medieval rebuilding. St Nicholas's Ozleworth, has a central hexagonal tower, extremely rare in Norman times; it was probably built by Roger de Berkeley who died in 1131.

The churches of Avening, Hampnett and Elkstone have Norman stone-vaulted chancels. St Mary's Kempsford, has a Norman nave (*c.* 1120) with its four windows, and exterior carved door-frame, pilaster buttresses and zig-zag string-course intact; at Coln St Denis, South Cerney, Great Rissington, Stowell and Withington the Norman central tower has survived. Bishop's Cleeve has a splendid church with many Norman features, notably the long dragons and dragons' heads carved on stops and corbels. However, the elaborately carved doorway is undoubtedly the most arresting feature of Norman village churches. The door-frame is chiefly made up of geometric ornament, especially the chevron pattern, occasionally of stylized beaked heads, of which particularly fine examples are to be seen at Windrush, Burford, Great Rollright and Barford St Michael. At Condicote, Farmington, Southrop, Winstone and Bloxham the tympanum within the carved frame is relieved by a diaper of star, fish-scale, honeycomb or lozenge, but many tympana display somewhat crudely executed figures and symbols: Christ in Majesty and the Harrowing of Hell are the commonest subjects, both favourite Old English themes, but there is great variety. On the south door at Quenington, the Coronation of the Virgin is surrounded with a particularly rich frame; at Church Handborough, St Peter is seated between a winged lion and an Agnus Dei with a cock at his feet; at Harnhill, St Michael tramples the Dragon; Salford has a centaur or Sagittarius; Ampney St Mary has a primitive design said to represent the Lion of Righteousness; at Brize Norton, a notable Norman church, the tympanum carries the Tree of Life; at Stratton, the same symbol with dog and serpent on either side; Lower Swell has the dove plucking the olive branch; Dowdeswell's tympanum is said to represent the seven-branched candlestick of Zachariah.

St John's, Elkstone, built about 1160–70, is undoubtedly the best-preserved and most interesting Norman village church in the Cotswolds. Originally there was a central tower, and the low round arches which pierced its walls to give access to the chancel are framed with a chevron pattern within a pelleted hood-mould. Stops and responds are carved with long dragon-heads. The Norman chancel is intact with its tiny east window and the ribs of the stone vault meet in a flat boss formed of four grotesque masks. Outside, the corbel-table beneath the eaves shows animals, birds and signs of the zodiac. Within the south porch a surround of beaked heads varied with an elephant, a horse and several demons encloses a rich doorway, the subject of the tympanum being Christ seated in Majesty with emblems of the evangelists, a seraph, and the hand of God. The central tower perhaps collapsed in the thirteenth century, and the lower chamber was replaced by a dovecot, a very unusual feature. The existing tower was added about 1370. Postlip's simple chapel has received even less alteration.

Three remarkable Norman fonts remain to be mentioned. That of Rendcomb shows formalized reliefs of the apostles within an arcade below a patterned frieze; at Hook Norton a rather similar design gives us Adam with spear and rake, Eve with the tree of life, a centaur, and other grotesques; the finest is at Southrop, which shows Moses with the tables of the Law, Ecclesia in a symbolic scene, and Virtues trampling Vices, all carved with a good deal more freedom and realism than the other examples.

Everything in the village churches, however, pales into insignificance compared with the south porch at Malmesbury. Of this great abbey church, which had a spire taller than Salisbury's, only six bays of the nave remain Norman up to and including the triforium, with a decorated clerestory and a tall decorated window next to the sadly mutilated Norman tower at the west end of the south

16. *Romanesque sculpture in the north porch of the abbey church at Malmesbury.*

aisle. The porch must have compelled the respect even of sixteenth-century vandals. The outer door is surrounded with eight bands of ornament, narrow bands of leaf design alternating with wider bands bearing panels sculptured in relief, displaying the bible story. The innermost band of eleven panels shows the creation to the death of Abel; the next carries the story as far as David in twelve panels, three devoted to the ark, three to Samson and three to David. It is evident that the sculptor found some characters more inspiring than others, for the number devoted to Samson could hardly have been justified in the context of Christian symbolism. The next group follows the New Testament from the Annunciation to Pentecost in thirteen panels. Reading horizontally, the link between some of the scenes, for example Moses striking the rock and the Last Supper, is a good deal more obvious than others. Finally there are eight panels depicting Virtues trampling Vices, a subject perhaps inspired by a poem of Prudentius called '*Psychomachia*', or 'The Combat of the Soul', for the abbey had a copy which is now in the library of Corpus Christi College at Cambridge. These panels have suffered greatly from the weather and are only partly decipherable, but were evidently designed and carved by sophisticated craftsmen. Within the porch a second less elaborate but no less finely executed doorway has a tympanum displaying Christ in Majesty, and across the east and west walls of the porch are two friezes of six apostles with an angel extended in flight over them in each; the stylized drapery is characteristic of Romanesque sculpture, and reminiscent of the Burgundian style of about 1130. There is hardly anything equal to these on this side of the English Channel, and they are happily in a good state of preservation.

The windows of Norman village churches were in general very small because there was no glass for them. The east window at Elkstone retains the rebate for a folding wooden shutter. In the thirteenth century better windows began to be installed for the priest to read by, often in an enlarged chancel. The east end of St Laurence's, Wyck Rissington, is very unusual: four lancets grouped in pairs, each pair surmounted by a lozenge-shaped light, the whole framed by an elaborate string-course, hint at the traceried windows to come. A feature special to the Cotswolds began to be added in this period, namely the small saddle-backed towers found at Syde and Eastleach Turville and (a later example) at Duntisbourne Rous.

The Decorated style of the late-thirteenth to mid-fourteenth centuries coincided with bad times for sheep-farmers, and therefore left little mark on the wolds. At Minchinhampton, however, there is a most exquisite window in the south transept. The church of Eastleach St Martin was virtually rebuilt at this time; and the churches round Banbury, where corn was more important than wool, have some fine decorated features.

The church of St John the Baptist at Burford, best seen from across the Windrush beyond the town, seems to have been in an almost continual state of alteration. The Norman west door and central tower indicate that the twelfth-century church must have been a large one, but in the thirteenth century transepts were added, and the merchant guild built a detached chapel of Our Lady on a different alignment. Individual merchants then began to add chantry chapels, and in the fifteenth century a fine south porch linked the enlarged and modernized Lady Chapel with St Thomas à Becket's chapel to form a second south aisle, a clerestory was added to the nave, and a new sanctuary, and all the windows were enlarged in the Perpendicular style.

In the fifteenth century work usually began with the tower, and at Burford a spire was added. Spires were first introduced in the late-thirteenth century and remained in fashion for about a hundred years. We may imagine that travelled merchants and experienced masons in the local quarries, then supplying stone for the buildings of Oxford and even London, would still have wanted for their own church the features they had admired on their journeys or supplied to their customers for some years after new ideas had been introduced by the avant-garde of the building trade – the porch at Northleach is another example of such conservativism.

The people of Burford may have wished to rival Witney, only ten miles away, where a splendid tower and spire had been built early in the fourteenth century. This is a large, handsome church, a Norman shell greatly enlarged and enriched in the thirteenth and fourteenth centuries, but cruelly restored by G. E. Street in 1865–9.

There are not many spires in the Cotswolds, but the region has one at Bloxham to compare with the finest examples in the East Midlands. This majestic church is built almost entirely of the local rich brown ironstone. The main fabric belongs to the Early English period, but in the fourteenth century the beautiful windows were added, using on their inner arches decorative mouldings from the original Norman church. The tracery of the west window in the north aisle incorporates a cross with the head of Christ in the centre and emblems of the Evangelists on the arms. Pillars with richly sculptured bases and capitals divide the aisles from the shallow transepts, and there is a fine wooden roof contemporary with the Perpendicular clerestory and chancel windows. The west doorway is framed by an unusual representation of the Last Judgement, and above it the superb tower and spire soar up 189 feet.

A local rhyme comparing three spires of the Banbury region praises

> Bloxham for length,
> Adderbury for strength,
> King's Sutton for beauty.

but many people would give Bloxham the palm for all three, and praise Adderbury for its sculpture and the beauty of its setting. The main fabric here is of the

17. *St Mary's, Bloxham.*

local purplish marlstone with its characteristic pearly lichen, but the freestone used for the splendid Perpendicular windows and decorative detail is the gold-peppered grey oolite from Taynton. A string-course below the roof of the nave portrays jugglers, strange beasts and musicians. The gargoyles are very large and vigorous. Within, two slender pillars with capitals and bases carved with heads of men and beasts similar to those at Bloxham divide the transepts, but here corbels supporting the roof and the window stops are equally lively.

With the recovery of sheep-farming, which accelerated in the fifteenth century, come the great 'wool' churches which are the pride of Cotswold towns.

Of the most outstanding, Northleach has a very beautiful south porch which retains most of its medieval statuary, and a noble nave, but the church is chiefly famous for the woolmen's brasses, among them that of John Fortey (d. 1459) who gave the great clerestory. The roof of the nave and the north chancel chapel are contemporary. St Mary's Fairford, was thoroughly rebuilt in 1490–1500 by John Thame, wool merchant, and his son. The designer evidently felt that some splendidly grotesque figures from the old church were too good to lose, and placed them on the tower, together with heraldic carving, Thame's trademark and occupational emblems sharing the honours with Yorkist devices. On the west side a figure of Christ is placed below Thame's armorial wyvern and lion in combat, flanked by a salt-trader's shell and woolman's shears and gloves. The string-courses bear a number of large and very lively figures. As in all the churches of this period the windows are very large, but unlike the others the medieval glass is here preserved intact. (During the last war it was all removed and stored in safety.) From the north aisle round to a dramatic Last Judgement in the great west window the story of Salvation from Eve to the Fathers of the Church is set out in brilliant contemporary colour. They are thought on stylistic grounds to be the work of Barnard Flower, a Fleming who as Henry VII's master glass-painter worked on Westminster Abbey and King's College Chapel at Cambridge. The designs are derived from a book of woodcuts popular in the early sixteenth century, known as the *Biblia Pauperum*, or *The Poor Man's Bible*. The church at Campden has a certain coldness for all its fine symmetry and truly splendid tower. The nave arcades display in their coved octagonal piers a feature shared with Northleach alone, and probably designed by the same master-mason, who may have been the Henry Winchcombe who scratched his name on one of the bases in the latter church. Campden church makes its chief impact as an important element in what is perhaps the most perfect street-scene in England.

Cirencester, as befits 'the capital of the Cotswolds', has the finest church of all, and here we know in some detail the story of rebuilding. In 1400 the people of Cirencester held up the westward march of the Earls of Salisbury and Kent, Richard II's half-brothers and supporters, at a critical moment for the usurping Henry IV; the earls were captured and beheaded in the market-place. Both abbot and townsfolk reaped a lavish reward, and the people immediately put the new tower in hand which ever since, as they no doubt intended, has dominated the approach from the west, and rises up before the traveller on Ermine Street as if the Roman road itself had been aligned upon it. They meant to add a spire, but even before the tower itself was finished it showed signs of movement, and the two buttresses which give it an appearance at once of daring and strength were added and incorporated into the west walls of the aisles. This was about 1430, and already the Garstangs, a family of a northern woolman who had settled in the town, had begun to rebuild the south aisle, with a chapel at its eastern end. They made a pair of fine new windows, and an oak screen bearing their arms and trademark. Almost at the same time, Richard Dixton and William Prelatte, household officers of the Duke of York and members of the weavers' guild, had begun on the northern aisle with a guild chapel of the Holy Trinity. Yorkist emblems, not trade symbols, adorn the Weavers' chapel.

The next additions were the arcades of the Lady Chapel and St Catherine's chapel, followed by a new chantry of St Catherine and St Nicholas added to the latter by John Chedworth, bishop of Lincoln, whose name suggests that he was paying a debt of affection to his native country. In 1508, Abbot Hakebourne added the fan-vault to this chapel.

The parishioners made the crowning effort soon afterwards. The nave was completely rebuilt by 1521 and the church flooded with light from a clerestory supported on tall slender piers above which, borne by angels, appear the shields and trademarks of numerous subscribers. A distinctive feature of the great 'wool' churches included here is a large window over the chancel arch. This glorious work was finished off by exquisite pierced battlements equal to those of Westminster and Windsor.

Meanwhile, about 1490 the abbot, who required an office for the transaction of secular business outside the precinct, had added a great south porch, three stories high, elaborately decorated with blind arcading, canted oriel windows, buttresses and niches. This soon came to be known as the town hall, and was used for the town's business long after the abbey and its dealings had sunk into oblivion.

Many a dim little village church was provided during these years of prosperity with fine large windows, or a clerestory, enriched with an additional aisle, a vaulted south porch, or a taller tower. The beautiful tower at Kempsford, the north aisle at Chedworth, fine carving in the north aisle at Aldworth, a surprising richness in the interior at Bledington, an arcade in the nave reminiscent of Northleach and Campden, a stone pulpit and a beautiful wooden rood screen at Church Handborough are some of the more outstanding memorials to this happy epoch. Not surprisingly, stone pulpits are quite common in the Cotswolds, notably in the south, for example at Cirencester, Chipping Sodbury and Cold Ashton, wooden screens extremely rare. St Peter's, Rendcomb one of the finest village churches in the region, was completely rebuilt about 1517 by Sir Edmund Thame, John Thame of Fairford's son, and bears a marked resemblance to his father's church. About the same time the rector is reputed to have paid for the rebuilding of the church at Cold Ashton. St Mary, Marshfield, close by, had been rebuilt in 1470.

At the very beginning of this period the monks of Eynsham built a fine new church at Combe to replace one in the original settlement on the banks of the Evenlode. This is specially notable for its wall-paintings. The finest frescoes in

18. *St Peter's, Rendcomb – a sixteenth-century woolman's church.*

the region are to be found, however, at St Peter-ad-Vincula, South Newington. Fragments of a Last Judgement over the chancel arch, and a beautiful series in the north aisle, are of the fourteenth century, and much cruder paintings of the late-fifteenth century remain in the nave. Hornton, Horley and Swalcliffe in the same district also have some good frescoes. In Gloucestershire there is nothing to equal these except perhaps at Hayles, although Ampney St Mary has one with an unusual subject – Christ wounded by manual work on Sunday.

Four great Benedictine abbeys – Malmesbury, Gloucester, Winchcombe and Eynsham – with the bishop of Worcester, already dominated the Cotswold scene when Hastings was fought, but the Normans were not content merely to enlarge and beautify existing churches and Saxon foundations; they added as many more abbeys of their own, as well as a number of insignificant priories, and two preceptories of the Knights Templars, at Temple Guiting and Quenington.

By the twelfth century the Benedictine Rule was no longer in fashion, so when about 1107 Henry I refounded the monastery at Cirencester he gave it to the Order of Augustinian Canons, and another important Augustinian house which came to own a good deal of land in the south Cotswolds was founded at Bristol in 1142. In 1229 Ela, the dowager countess of Salisbury, founded a house of Augustinian Canonesses at Lacock. This is beyond the south-eastern fringe of the Cotswolds, but built of stone from the Hazelbury quarry.

The Saxon church recently excavated on the abbey site at Cirencester had been staffed by a college of secular canons, who served both the town and the country round about. According to a thirteenth-century tradition, St Aldwyn (Coln St Aldwyn) had been a member of this community in the time of King Egbert (802–39). Now the members of the old community were obliged to join the new enclosed community or accept the humble position of a parish priest on one of its dependant estates in the surrounding villages. With the great sheep-runs all round, with splendid communications and with a thriving market at the gates (which Henry I in his foundatign charter referred to as a borough), the abbey of Cirencester became immensely rich, but relations between town and cowl were never very happy. They might cooperate in a moment of political crisis to overthrow the two earls, the abbot undoubtedly contributed lavishly to the building of the parish church, and probably to the upkeep of a grammar school, but successive holders of the office did all they could to deprive the towns-people of the beginnings of self-government which they had enjoyed until in 1342 the reigning abbot, after an unedifying struggle, succeeded in buying from the Crown the suppression of their borough court. When Henry IV rewarded the townsfolk for their assistance against his enemies with a merchant guild and its privileges, the abbot succeeded in getting the royal charter annulled. This humiliation must have been hard to bear, and there can have been little love lost between the parties. Perhaps that is why so few bits of sculpted stone taken from the abbey, or even a commemorative inn sign, are to be seen in the town. Apart from remains of the Norman gatehouse in Grove Lane, it is as if the great abbey had never been.

In the second quarter of the twelfth century the Cistercians arrived in England, bringing with them enormous religious prestige. Numerous houses were founded, of which the most successful were those established in the remotest places, 'far from the habitations of men' as the rule demanded. The economy of the great houses of the north was necessarily based on sheep-ranching, and it must have seemed likely that a Cistercian house would thrive in the Cotswolds, the only difficulty being that much of the best country was already in ecclesiastical hands. It was not until 1139 that the Cistercians arrived at Kingswood on the Little Avon, two miles from Wotton-under-Edge, endowed with several Cotswold manors. One of these was Hazleton, and to this place the monks retired during the anarchy of King Stephen's reign. Anyone who has visited this remote upland village will readily understand that the supply of water there was quite insufficient for the relatively sophisticated standards of plumbing of a monastic community. They returned to Kingswood in 1147, after a brief attempt to establish themselves at Tetbury. In the same year twelve monks from the first English Cistercian house at Waverley came at the invitation of a certain Nicholas Basset to found the new community of St-Mary-in-the-Heath or Bruerne on the banks of the Evenlode, in his manor of Tretone or Drayton, a name which in consequence disappeared from the map. Most of the new abbey's land lay in the neighbouring parishes of Sarsden, Kingham, Churchill, Westcott Barton and Fifield, but they had also many scattered properties in the wolds, and Holwell in Swalcliffe away towards Banbury. Nevertheless, the community was never very numerous, and apparently seldom very prosperous. At the Dissolution their income appears to have been no more than £124 per annum, and there were again only twelve monks besides the abbot. The income of Kingswood was nearly twice as large, their numbers about the same. Perhaps the Bruerne estate was too scattered to be administered economically. Early in their history we find them obtaining from the Crown a grant exempting their flocks from distraint so long as they had anything else to be distrained upon! Like most religious houses they suffered at least one disastrously spendthrift and profligate abbot, and probably many who were not born administrators. The lean times of the early fourteenth century found them mortgaging their wool-crop in the vain hope of remaining solvent, but on the eve of the Dissolution thee were three thousand sheep on their pastures, and even Cromwell's commissioners reported that the house was in good order and the abbot a learned and virtuous man.

The last major foundation in the Cotswolds became one of the greatest. It was the fulfilment of a vow made some time before 1246 by Richard, Earl of Cornwall, King of the Romans, and later Emperor, when he was in danger of shipwreck crossing to England. He had acquired the manor of Hayles from his brother, Henry III, perhaps for this very purpose. Between 1246 and 1251 he expended 10,000 marks on the building of church, cloister, dormitory and refectory, which were immediately occupied by twenty Cistercian monks and ten lay brothers from Beaulieu in Hampshire, and the abbey was consecrated with the utmost pomp in the presence of the king, queen, and thirteen bishops, most of the barons, and three hundred knights, for whom the earl provided a magnificent entertainment. The same day he gave to the new community 1,000 marks to purchase land and houses for their support, remarking, 'I wish it had pleased God that all my great expenses in my castle of Wallingford had been so wisely and soberly employed'. When he died he was buried with his wife Sanchia of Provence in the abbey church.

The domestic quarters of the abbey had probably been built largely of wood, for within twenty years of that great inauguration they were almost completely destroyed by fire, and even the church was gutted. Their founder had just died, but his son Edmund came to the community's aid in this crisis with a timely gift, the famous relic of the Holy Blood which Edmund had bought on the continent. By 1275 the new church, containing a shrine fit for this sacred and valuable object, was ready for consecration. As had doubtless been intended, the relic spread the fame of Hayles far and wide and brought a flock of pilgrims.

After this chequered start, the community settled down to the austere life of the Cistercian rule, and the exploitation of their estates. About half of these were on the wolds, a great block on the hills immediately behind the abbey, Stanton, and Coscombe above Stanway, property in Swell, Longborough, Charingworth and North Leigh in Oxfordshire; these were stocked with sheep. The great woods clothing the steepest parts of the scarp, of which a considerable area remains to this day, yielded a valuable crop of timber, and the swine flock seems to have been an important element in the abbey's economy. A smaller number of manors in the Vale no doubt supplied their corn and other crops. At the time of the Dissolution there were twenty-two monks, and the abbey's property was valued at £357 a year. This places their income in relation to the size of the community between those of Bruerne and Kingswood. The abbot received the customary pension, a prebend at York, and the manor of Coscombe, and retired to this sheltered spot about half-way up the scarp within the lea of Stanway Wood.

The abbots so adorned and embellished the church they found at Hayles that little Norman work remains there. Its most notable feature is the thirteenth-century wall-painting. Frescoes in the chancel display the heraldic devices of the King of the Romans and Eleanor of Castille; over the rere-arches of the windows are fantastic monsters, and in the splay of the Norman windows rather later frescoes of St Catherine and St Margaret, each with a monk at her feet. There are also some nice seventeenth-century fittings.

Hayles is the only abbey site worth visiting within the Cotswolds, and is carefully preserved by the Department of the Environment. The positions of the pillars in the nave is marked out by yews planted early in this century when excavation was begun. The great church had an apse in the French style, with five radiating chapels. A substantial part of the east range of the cloister has recently been excavated, including the chapter house, where the bases of handsome blue lias pillars dividing its three aisles have been revealed. There are some very beautiful bosses in the museum, and a number of tiles and other fragments in the church. A gated road still connects Hayles with its manors on the wolds above, a quiet bird-haunted ascent past sloping woods and bumpy turf, which leads to the tiny church of Farmcote, standing lonely in a field with a splendid prospect of the Vale, with Bredon and the Malvern Hills in the distance, and the abbey site, neat but desolate, below.

At Lacock Abbey the cloisters are nearly intact, and the chapter house, sacristy and warming-room may be visited. Above it the fine fourteenth-century roof of the dormitory and the refectory roof in the western range are exposed within the house. The shady character (Sir William Sharington) who bought up the abbey in 1540 moved into the abbess's lodging in the southern range, and this still contains the principal rooms. He embellished it in Renaissance style. The buildings were subsequently much altered by the architect Sanderson Miller for his descendants, mainly in the Gothick style, so that the four cloister ranges became a mansion. In the nineteenth century it was the home of W. H. Fox Talbot, an outstanding pioneer of photography, and a museum of his work occupies a barn at the abbey gate.

The village of Lacock, a delightful mixture of stone and timber, contains the nunnery's tithe barn, and the Angel inn, which has a sixteenth-century doorway and is probably in origin a pre-Reformation hostelry. The whole is most admirably preserved by the National Trust.

Between 1535 and 1539 all these monastic houses were surrendered to the Crown. The sheriffs in charge of the dismantling process were supposed to see that valuables were preserved for the Crown, but they turned a blind eye to an immense amount of pillage and destruction. At Hayles a maid-servant who had the courage to protest was answered by the sheriff himself: 'Hold thy peace for it is there now. Catch as may catch.' No doubt there were plenty of people in the wolds who felt as she did, but at least as many had a rod in pickle for exacting monastic landlords, or were simply out for what they could get. The would-be burgesses of Cirencester perhaps welcomed a chance of revenge; land-hungry gentry anticipated a rich harvest. An old saying, 'as sure as God's in Gloucestershire', is thought by some people to have been a pious reference to the Precious Blood of Hayles, by others to the number of abbeys in the county, but with three-fifths or more of the wolds in the hands of the Church the saying could well by 1535 have carried ironic overtones.

The large estates of the bishop of Worcester would remain virtually intact, and the new bishoprics of Gloucester and Bristol, with the abbey churches of St Peter and St Augustine saved to be their cathedrals, were endowed out of monastic lands, but the vast estates of the great Cotswold abbeys, and the properties of the smaller houses and more distant abbeys – Evesham, Tewkesbury, Pershore, Lantony, St Friedwide's at Oxford, and even Westminster – were now to be scrambled for, and in many cases to remain subject to the vicissitudes of family fortunes instead of the relatively immutable tenure of an ecclesiastical corporation. These accounted, probably, for nearly half the acres of the wolds. In the face of such temptations, ordinary men will leave the religious implications to look after themselves. Few regions of England can have experienced a more drastic change, and yet while the west of England, Lincolnshire and Yorkshire mobilized their doomed resistance, the people of the Cotswolds in general accepted the religious upheaval calmly. In 1544, however, the parish priests of Bloxham, Chipping Norton, Deddington and Duns Tew were sentenced to be hanged from their church towers for resistance to the new Prayer Book.

No doubt there were genuine converts to the new religion, especially in the towns; a blanket-weaver of Witney was fined in 1521 for possessing a copy of the Scriptures in English. William Tyndale was born at Slimbridge in the Vale and already had his translation of the Bible in contemplation when as a young man Sir John Walsh of Little Sodbury Manor appointed him tutor to his sons. There is a most interesting early Baptist chapel and a contemporary meeting house in Chipping Sodbury. However there seem to have been relatively few iconoclasts. The glass at Fairford was untouched, that of Cirencester left to fall out during centuries of neglect. The ancient statue of St Aldhelm at Sherston became Rattlebone, a mythical local figure, said to have died fighting under Edmund Ironside against Canute in a battle fought at Sherston in 1016.

7

Clothiers and Gentlemen in the Sixteenth and Seventeenth Centuries

The dissolution of the monasteries came just in time for the wool merchants and clothiers who had been growing rich during the previous hundred years on the trade in undyed broadcloth. They had been able to dress in silk, lend money to kings and nobles, build great churches, found schools and almshouses, represent their town in parliament. At last they could consolidate their success by entering the ranks of the landed gentry, building themselves fine houses on their new manors, often with stone quarried from monastic ruins. It may be said that the release of monastic land, coinciding with a climax of prosperity in the cloth trade, led directly to the first flowering of the Cotswold style of domestic building, and the story of the cloth trade is in effect an account of the making of the south Cotswold landscape. It begins at the southern extremity, in the new county of Avon, and the borders of Wiltshire.

In general the Crown sold monastic property to speculators who disposed of it subsequently in convenient parcels. At Malmesbury the abbey buildings were placed in the custody of Sir Edward Baynton, who had been the abbey steward, and his deputy William Stumpe, a remarkable (but representative) figure in the scramble for monastic spoils in the Cotswolds. Stumpe's father was a Gloucestershire weaver who had risen to be a small clothier at Nibley. (Clothier is the word historically used to describe a capitalist employing a workforce for the production of cloth either domestically or on his premises, and trading in the finished product.) Stumpe and his contemporaries were entrepreneurs, not craftsmen, though they seem often to have been weavers, fullers or millers in origin. The first step was indubitably the acquisition of a fulling mill, usually on lease. Stumpe himself, until the Dissolution, was merely a tenant of the abbey, but when he became Sir Edward Baynton's deputy he was already one of the four richest men in Malmesbury and had represented the town in parliament for ten years. His association with Baynton enabled him to secure the abbey site for himself, and he died possessed of a good deal of land scattered through the neighbouring shires, having been a justice of the peace for fifteen years in both Wiltshire and Gloucestershire, besides holding several lucrative public offices, and at last the high office of sheriff. He had successfully penetrated the social stronghold of the landed gentry and seen his eldest son James knighted and married to Sir Edward Baynton's daughter; to him he left his landed possessions. His business interests he left to his younger sons. James was survived by an only daughter and this heiress's four daughters all married into the nobility. One of the younger children's sons, the Reverend William Stumpe, is recorded as having used the priceless manuscripts from the abbey library to stop the bungs of his wine barrels in his rectory of Yatton Keynell.

Stumpe's treatment of the abbey site was characteristic. To recover the purchase money he pulled down the chancel and transepts and sold the lead and stone apart from what he needed to build himself a house in the precinct consonant with his ambitions. The house still stands, an early example of the style that was to become a beautiful commonplace in the Cotswolds. The large halls of the abbey, such as frater, dorter, chapter-house and misericorde, he filled with broadcloth looms, and turned the remainder into tenements for his weavers and spinners. (He planned to set up a similar establishment at Osney Abbey near Oxford, but failed to find in that locality the two thousand skilled hands he needed for the venture.) The six remaining bays of the abbey church at Malmesbury he gave or sold to the town for a parish church, which was licensed by Cranmer in 1543. According to legend, when Henry VIII was huntng in Braydon Forest he descended upon the clothier, who managed to provide for the king and his followers by giving his men porridge for the day.

Stumpe or one of his rivals also filled with looms the old church alongside the abbey (of which only the tower remains today). Abbey buildings at Cirencester were also being used as loom-shops at this time. This development has been seen as a premature attempt to adopt a factory system of production, but perhaps it had more to do with housing shortage as more and more workers were drawn in from the countryside to the vicinity of the fulling mills, and with the unsuitability of countrymen's hovels to accommodate a broadcloth loom. The need for cottages large enough to take the broadloom and light enough to work it widened the scope of an evolving building tradition which is displayed in the farmhouses, cottages and barns built within the next hundred years as well as in mansions and manor houses all over the Cotswolds.

One or two drives along the southern flank of the region between Cricklade and Bradford-on-Avon will provide ample illustration. Cricklade lies beyond the edge of the wolds but most of its buildings are of Cotswold stone. The church has a tower in the characteristic Wiltshire style, with very large pinnacles at the four corners. It is dedicated to a Celtic saint, St Samson, whose bones are said to rest beneath a small earthwork on Cairn Hill south-west of Malmesbury. Though a few Roman objects have been found, the town owes its existence to Alfred's *burh*; Ermine Street crossed the river to the east and many Roman objects have been dug up in the parish of Latton, famous for the wild fritillaries which grow in the meadows hereabouts. Our route follows the Roman road northwards for two miles and then turns west to South Cerney, a true Cotswold village where the sequence of noble domestic and farm buildings begins. The church is notable for its Norman features, especially the north doorway, dated 1134–54. We take the lane leading westward and follow signs for Ashton Keynes, a lovely village with the headwaters of the Thames flowing through it in several pretty brooks; it has many good stone houses and cottages.

From here to Oaksey we are in the watery pastures very early reclaimed at the edge of the now almost vanished Blaydon Forest. Somerford Keynes is chiefly notable for a basically Saxon church, with some features which may date from the late seventh century when the manor came to St Aldhelm. Oaksey church has two early frescoes, St Christopher, a very common subject, and a much rarer one, Christ of the workers with symbols of various occupations. We reach A429 at Crudwell, where the church is the centre of a fine group composed of the Old Rectory, Crudwell Court with its fifteenth-century barn, and a schoolhouse (1670).

We follow A429 to Malmesbury, standing high on a spur of the oolite between the Bristol Avon and one of its feeders. This is a busy little town, its main street a good deal disfigured by modern shop-fronts, but it still contains houses and cottages dating from Stumpe's day. Stumpe's own house, however, is not visible from the streets. The centre of the town is a pretty stone-canopied butter-cross, dominated by the great church. King's Walk commemorates one of Stumpe's rivals, Matthew King, who made the path along the town wall to reach his mill on the Avon, now incorporated in a modern factory. Malmesbury boasts three worthies: St Aldhelm, the medieval historian William, and Thomas Hobbes, the seventeenth-century philosopher, who was born here in 1588 and educated at the grammar school before going to Oxford at the age of fourteen. His father was the drunken and scandalous vicar of Westport, a medieval suburb. The philosopher's birthplace was on the site of the Congregational chapel. He has been called the Father of Political Science, and his works have had a continuing influence on the continent, especially on Rousseau, Spinoza and Leibnitz. As far as is known, none of his active life was spent at Malmesbury.

From Malmesbury we follow B4040 to Sherston, pausing perhaps at the crossing of the Fosse Way (or Akeman Street), here a muddy track, to visit the site of White Walls in the pastures half a mile down on the left. Shipton Moyne, the most southerly of the Cotswold Shiptons, is one and a half miles across the fields to the north.

Sherston is a charming decayed market town standing on a low cliff above the Avon on the southern fringe of the Jurassic belt, here only about seven miles wide. It has a large rectangular market-place (obviously planned), round which stone and colour wash are pleasantly mixed. Behind the eastern range of houses rises an interesting church, mainly Early English but with a Norman arcade and later features of various dates including an ornate tall tower, a remarkably successful gothic reconstruction, designed in 1730 by a local architect, William Sumpsion of Colerne. The Anglo-Saxon origin of the name, *Sceorstane* (= a steep place + stone), is thought to describe natural features, but the town is said to be built within a prehistoric earthwork, and local legend has it that this is the real White Walls referred to by the bard Lywach Hen as a scene of British struggle against the Saxons. Sherston's first certain appearance in history is the battle in 1016.

By taking a minor road leading southwards out of Sherston it is possible to join the Fosse Way, now a lane, and follow it (with a brief detour through Grittleton) to the intersection with B4039, which leads down towards Castle Combe. Sir John Fastolfe's industrial enterprise laid the foundation for its famous beauties, church, manor house, clothiers' houses and weavers' cottages forming a wholly harmonious group in the shelter of hanging beechwood. Returning to B4039, but forking right along a lane through Biddestone, we come next to Corsham. Biddestone is prettily grouped round a green and the church contains late-eighteenth-century box-pews and gallery.

At Corsham we are in the heart of the great clothing district centred on Chippenham. Corsham does not seem to have been a medieval borough, but it grew into a small town exceptionally full of good building, and has besides the Jacobean mansion, Corsham Court, the core of which is a grand Elizabethan house built by a London merchant in 1582. The Methuens have owned it since 1728, and it contains their famous collection of pictures. Corsham undoubtedly owed part of its growth to the quarries; the hamlet of Westwell, where they were mainly situated, became a large suburb and is still expanding, with commuter houses added to those of workers in H.M.S. *Royal Arthur*, the naval depot which now occupies the quarries.

From Corsham we follow the relatively modern turnpike road down to Box. After running down the side of the dramatic By Brook valley it offers a view first of Brunel's monumental tunnel-entrance, and then of pretty houses and cottages beneath the causeway on which the road is carried, before climbing gently along the handsome high street. The church lies below this on the right in an attractive cul-de-sac. It seems to have been built in the fourteenth century and is dedicated to Thomas à Becket, and was destined to supersede, quite early, the old parish church at Hazelbury on the hill above, of which nothing now remains. Beside the church stands an eighteenth-century school now divided into flats (Springfield House). At the traffic lights we turn left on to A365, but turn again left to skirt the village and climb Quarry Hill. Within the woods on the right, amid beech, thorn, and sycamore saplings, carpeted with ivy and tufted with Harts Tongue fern, lie tumbled rocks and great blocks of stone, some still showing the marks of the quarrymen's tools. Towards the top the beech takes over and it is easier to move among the workings. Hazelbury itself is effectively screened from all the roads. Turning right we reach B3109. Beyond it lie the tile pits from which the houses of the district got most of their roofs. We turn right again to reach the travellers' hospice at Chapel Plaister. (The tiny chapel is usually open.) The lane signposted to Wadsworth is the old London road. Continuing along B3109 another two and a half miles brings us to the turn for South Wraxall manor house, the home since the fifteenth century of the Longs, one of the most notable clothing families.

Robert Long, a contemporary of Sir John Fastolfe, built the Gate House and the Great Hall which has a glorious timber roof. Another Robert (probably he who paid for the north aisle in the greatest of the Wiltshire clothiers' churches at Steeple Ashton) added a wing and other improvements. Finally, about 1598 (the date on the huge fireplace in the Great Drawing-Room) Sir Walter Long made the house suitable for his new dignity by adding this and another grand room, with large windows and lavish decoration in the currently fashionable Renaissance style. He probably left the trade to become a gentleman, but other members of his family continued to be working clothiers for at least two hundred years. The house is barely visible from the road, and is, unhappily, seldom open to the public. According to legend it was here that Sir Walter Raleigh received a drenching from a servant who saw him smoking a pipe and thought he was on fire. Sir Walter certainly visited the house.

Returning to B3109, at the next cross-roads a lane on the right leads to Great Chalfield Manor (National Trust). We now come to Bradford-on-Avon, a Cotswold clothing town second only to Stroud in size and infinitely more attractive. It is so full of good building that the perambulation occupies eleven pages

19. *South Wraxall manor, a successful clothier's mansion.*

in Pevsner's *Wiltshire* volume, to which the reader specially interested in architecture must be referred. Just beyond the town lies the abbess of Shaftesbury's manor farm. The farmhouse contains a number of fifteenth-century features, and the great thirteenth-century tithe barn is one of the largest in England.

We reach our southernmost point at Westwood. Westwood Manor is described by Pevsner as 'a perfect Wiltshire manor house', but it is pure Cotswold in style. Although certain features are earlier, including traces of an open hall, the house as it stands is chiefly the work of Thomas Horton, who made his fortune as a clothier in Bradford, where a memorial brass records his death in 1530, and of John Farwell, who married a Horton girl. Farwell modernized the house between 1616 and 1632, enriching it with plasterwork, panelling and decorative fireplaces. The church at Westwood is notable for a fifteenth-century east window depicting a crucifixion against a background of lilies. The fine tower was the gift of Thomas Horton.

The return journey might be made through Monkton Farleigh and Colerne. At Monkton Farleigh there was a Cluniac priory founded in 1125. The manor house is basically of the twelfth or early fourteenth century. Colerne is a well-built hilltop village with a fine church which contains a fragment of an Anglo-Saxon cross-shaft admirably carved; the splendid tower was clearly Sumpsion's inspiration in the Sherston design. This itinerary might be extended via the delightful town of Marshfield (p. 145) and Cold Ashton, where the stone pulpit inserted into the rood-loft stair built only a few years earlier shows the Reformation in action, to Old Sodbury Manor house where Tyndale lived and preached for two years and Chipping Sodbury, a true Cotswold town at the foot of the scarp; continuing via Horton Court where Tyndale discussed the future with William Knight (p. 186), Hawkesbury, and the 'clothing' villages of Alderley and Hillsley, the deep valleys of Kilcot and Ozleworth (see below) at the head of the little Avon with their splendid woods including the Midger nature reserve, returning across the wolds via Westonbirt (p. 153) to Sherston.

Several houses farther north belong to the same period as Westwood and Wraxall. Chavanage House near Tetbury is not known to be specially connected with the cloth trade, but we may be sure that wool was the crop which made the builder's fortune. Only the west front remains of another, Newark Park, built by Sir Nicholas Poyntz, previously steward of Kingswood Abbey, with stone quarried from the abbey buildings supplemented, according to local tradition, with material obtained by pulling down all the village crosses in the neighbourhood. Chastleton House was built in 1603 by a Witney wool merchant, ancestor of the present owner; it contains much contemporary furniture, and interesting royalist relics, with a topiary garden dating from about 1700. Stanway house is another, a grand extension of the abbot of Tewkesbury's manor, built well before 1630, the date ascribed to the remarkable gatehouse. Rousham Court on the Cherwell is another Jacobean house full of historical interest with famous gardens by Kent. These great mansions undoubtedly supplied inspiration, but the fine flower of the distinctive Cotswold style is better seen in lesser houses, for example in Upper Slaughter Old Manor House, Bibury Court, Ablington Manor, Shipton

Court (Shipton-under-Wychwood), Hidcote House, Hidcote Manor (which has famous gardens), Througham Slad (in origin a medieval house) and Iles Green among many noble farmsteads with barns as handsomely finished as the houses and often larger than the parish church. The Great Rebuilding which took place all over England in the seventeenth century began at least a hundred years earlier in the Cotswolds, and, thanks to wool and the superb quality of the building material, was more extensive and produced a larger number of houses capable of serving the needs of generation after generation.

The clothier's mill had less ornament but it was as substantially built. To it the raw wool was brought, to be doled out after washing to his spinners and weavers who worked either in their own cottage or sometimes in barns or workshops. The woven cloth returned to the mill for fulling and finishing, and from the mill most of it went to Blackwell Hall in London, the market of the Merchant Adventurers' Company which held the monopoly of the export trade in undyed broadcloth to Germany and the Netherlands.

The Wiltshire clothiers put all their eggs in one basket, but Gloucestershire men, while they took advantage of the boom in white cloth, never abandoned their traditional product, a coarse material dyed dun, olive or blue, and they were already famous for their scarlets, which they now began to make on the broadloom. William Halliday of Fromehall Mill must have been a wealthy man when he died in 1519, and was commemorated by a fine brass bearing his mark in Minchinhampton church. Thomas Gardner, a mercer of Painswick, who built the beautiful Court House just below the church about 1604, was a member of a well-established clothing family. When in 1557 the government had passed a law containing an abortive clause forbidding the manufacture of cloth outside cities and market towns, they made exception for 'any towns and villages near the river Stroud . . . where cloths have been made for twenty years past'.

The jealousy of city manufacturers, and especially London cloth-workers, which had had something to do with this futile piece of legislation, eventually sparked off disaster. In 1613 a certain Alderman Cockayne managed to induce James I to transfer the Merchant Adventurers' monopoly to a new company which was to undertake the dyeing and finishing of cloth before export, and discovered too late that he could neither get enough work efficiently done in London, nor sell dyed cloth to German and Flemish customers who were in the market only for material for their own expert dyers and finishers. The Thirty Years' War, which closed many of the traditional outlets, came hard upon the collapse of this ill-timed experiment, from which the 'white' industry never really recovered. From this time the cloth manufacture of Cirencester and

Map 7 *The south Cotswold clothing district.*

Malmesbury dwindled away, and the clothiers of the Windrush Valley turned their attention to blankets.

For the clothier who had made a fortune during the boom years of the sixteenth century, now was the time to retire into the ranks of the gentry, acquire a patent of Arms, and build an appropriate house. The Hall at Bradford, built by the clothier John Hall in 1610, is the somewhat pretentious mansion of a successful businessman who got out just in time. It was used as a model for 'the English House' for one of the great Exhibitions at Paris in the last century.

The great depression in the 'white' industry produced a period of dire misery among unemployed weavers, and shrill recrimination among the clothiers and the Merchant Adventurers. The latter blamed the clothiers for including too much bad cloth in their packs, and succeeded, under Charles I, in getting a new Commission sent out authorized to overhaul the whole system of inspection and bring delinquent clothiers to book with the assistance of the Justices. The new inspector, Anthony Wither, had actually been associated with Cockayne's venture, and his interference was very ill-received by the clothiers and their friends and relations the Justices. While inspecting some cloth in Bradford he was tipped into the river: '. . . the place was twenty feet deep and nine cloths then in the water, under any of which if I had risen I had inevitably drowned. . . .' The standard broadcloth was over 60 inches wide and 24 yards long so he was not exaggerating his danger. He encountered less crudely-expressed but not less effective opposition from Sir Edward Baynton. Eventually he made Wiltshire too hot for him, but he was still His Majesty's Commissioner for Clothing in 1634 when he fell foul at Blackwell Hall of a Painswick clothier over the position of his cloth-mark.

This was Thomas Webb, with a name which suggests an ancestry of weavers; he had relations all over the clothing district who claimed descent from Flemish craftsmen. He was even then building himself Hill House in the neighbourhood of Painswick, where the date may still be seen on the porch. He called down the curses of the poor on Wither, and swore that his mark was in the right place, and there it should stay as long as he lived. The slump in the white trade was bad enough for poor weavers; if the government, egged on by Wither, suppressed the gig mill, Webb and his friends declared, even more people would be thrown out of work. The gig mill, a recent invention, was properly used in Gloucestershire in finishing coloured cloth; in Wiltshire it had been used by dishonest clothiers to overstretch their pieces.

The Wiltshire clothiers laid the blame for their defective cloths on wool and yarn merchants; but the more enterprising among them were turning to new lines of merchandise, of which the most promising was the revival of the coloured cloth trade. The Gloucestershire men were beginning to apply their skill in dyeing to a finer broadcloth, and to extend their range of colours. The clothiers also began to import dyed Spanish wool to make a material known as Spanish cloth or Medleys. Benedict Webb of Kingswood and John Ash of Freshford were among the pioneers of these, while along the Somerset Frome they were experimenting with a cloth of similar quality made from English wool dyed after weaving and before fulling. Others turned to worsted and even serge, but the latter never took root in the south Cotswolds. The Spanish cloth and the very similar English cloth dyed 'in the saye' proved very successful. The latter was the line developed by Paul Methuen, who arrived from his father's vicarage at Frome to join his father-in-law in business in Bradford, and became one of its leading clothiers; indeed John Aubrey calls him 'the greatest clothier of all time'. His grandson was able to buy Corsham Court, which has remained to this day in the family. The negotiator of the Methuen treaty with Portugal, and founder of Corsham's famous collection of paintings was a cousin.

Paul Methuen brought over skilled workers from Amsterdam in 1659, probably to introduce the making of finer warps, and settled them in Bradford in the place near the parish church known ever since as Dutch Barton; another group were settled at Westwood, where some of the buildings are thought to show Flemish influence. These were not the first Flemish immigrants in the Cotswolds. According to tradition, clothiers from the Netherlands had been established at Seend in the reign of Henry VII, from whom, indeed, the Methuens may possibly have been descended. The great family of Clutterbuck had arrived in Gloucestershire in the sixteenth century. The Pauls of Woodchester came from the continent in the seventeenth century. This family always claimed to have been exiles on religious grounds, but there is no doubt that the Cotswolds must have seemed to offer settled conditions and a demand for new technical knowledge very appealing to enterprising clothiers in war-torn Europe at this period.

The success of the new materials created much jealousy; it upset the wool market, and produced a new and much-abused middleman, the yarn-brogger or market-spinner. During the reign of Charles I, the clothing districts were in a turmoil which was exacerbated by ill-conceived government interference.

The Restoration ushered in a period of relative stability in the Cotswolds. Within the next thirty or forty years, the towns and villages acquired their characteristic appearance. The traditional mode of building was modified by the prevailing classical ideas. The houses, retaining of necessity their unfashionable steep gables, became more symmetrical, sometimes almost square with two gables on each front. Four-light mullioned and transomed windows became more or less standardized; chimneys were gathered on interior walls, their stacks of coved and moulded ashlar providing an elegant finish to the whole; gable-ends, labels and porches were adorned with ball finials, shells and other restrained classical ornament. Among dozens, Egypt Mill House, built by a clothier, and Cassey Compton in Withington, built by the Howe family, are arbitrarily chosen examples. These beautiful houses continued to be built well into the next century alongside others displaying more fashionable features such as hipped roofs, parapets and balustrades, tall sash windows and elaborate door-cases on absolutely regular elevations. Most of the older manor houses, too, were enlarged and beautified with fine staircases, panelling and plasterwork. Hundreds of less impressive buildings – town houses, farms, cottages and splendid barns – have survived.

During the Commonwealth even the 'white' trade had made some recovery, and coloured cloth and the 'new draperies' forged ahead. In Uley church a tablet records the death in 1731 of the nonagenarian John Eyles, 'the first that ever made Spanish cloth in this parish'. Eyles's mill at Wresden within the same parish must be one of the oldest cloth mills in the region; there are two circular openings in the north wall through which perhaps the weavers handed in their woven pieces and received new 'chains' in old John's day. (The 'chain' was the quantity of raw material, partially prepared, required for a length of cloth.) Groups of primitive mills like this were replaced by a single larger establishment as machinery improved, but in the Painswick, Pitchcombe and Slad valleys the cloth industry was dying out when the factory mills were beginning, and many old buildings survive.

Sheepscombe is a true eighteenth-century clothing village at the head of the Painswick valley; mills and weavers cottages cling to the side of a deep and intensely green valley fringed with beechwood. The principal mill was still working in 1820, when the people of this remote hamlet were looked on as a very rough and lawless lot. Tocknell's Court, a mile or two further down the valley, was a clothier's domain, and a little farther on we come to Damsell's Mill, probably a seventeenth-century building, which has been skilfully converted but retains some of its machinery. On the edge of Painswick, mills, mill-houses and silted-up mill-ponds occur every few yards. Lovedays Mill at the foot of Vicarage Lane, the seventeenth-century house with early-nineteenth-century mill attached, forms a striking group. Probably one of the oldest surviving mills stands in the yard of Cap Mill House, one which can never have held more than two pairs of fulling stocks and may have been in use as early as the sixteenth century for the manufacture of felt caps. The porch of this handsome house bears the initials and cloth-mark of the clothier who built it, with the date 1678. In 1729 the mill was in the hands of the Packer family. Only a little way downstream we come to another beautiful mill house, until recently the Painswick Nurseries, but the mill buildings attached to the house have vanished. The last of the series,

20. *Lovedays Mill, Painswick.*

below the town, is King's Mill, a large house built in the traditional style, having an especially attractive situation. It incorporates an extensive range of workshops used in the ninteenth century as a pin factory. A footpath leads past the mill by way of the fine seventeenth-century Sheephouse to Stroud. On the other side of the narrow spur on which Painswick stands, the road to Edge plunges immediately into the Washbrook valley, and Washbrook Mill, Upper and Lower Doreys Mills, all now dwelling-houses, may be glimpsed on either side. Another relic of the industry is the roundhouse in Kemps Lane, used for drying and storing wool.

The Bradford neighbourhood also offers unspoilt clothing villages at Freshford, Avoncliff and Stowford on the Frome. A little further upstream from the latter at Tellisford, the narrow bridge with the ruined mill beside it across which the packhorse train used to start out on the journey to Blackwell Hall in London has never been widened or adopted by the Somerset County Council. The clothier's house above shows the original owner's fashionable taste, having a hipped roof, four-light windows and a handsome doorcase.

Even in the more heavily industrialized Stroud and Nailsworth valleys one encounters a few early mills, and many handsome Jacobean and Georgian houses among nineteenth-century buildings. The picturesquely named millers, 'Kings of Egypt', occupy a range of buildings (very run down) at Egypt Mill where in 1675 Edward Webb worked two fulling-mills, a gig-mill and a dye-house. There was a 'tenement' also on the site, which may refer to the beautiful four-square Cotswold house which is part of the group lying alongside A46 where it enters Nailsworth from Stroud. This house is described in 1814 as having a wool-store in the attic – perhaps most of these high Jacobean clothiers' houses included one. St Mary's mill-house at Chalford, probably almost contemporary with Egypt Mill, shows the new fashion coming in, having a classical front with balustraded parapet, hipped, roof, and shell-hood doorcase, while the mill itself is an early-nineteenth-century building.

After fulling-stocks, the gig-mill was the first extension of the use of water-powered machinery in the manufacture of cloth. It was presumably similar to the modern machine – a drum packed with teazel-heads (wire is now used except for some very fine cloth), over which the material was passed to raise the nap after fulling. It was becoming widespread in the sixteenth century until it was outlawed in 1552, mainly on account of its improper use by the 'white' trade. Gloucestershire clothiers took little notice of this, except to change the name of the machine, which appears in seventeenth-century deeds as a mosing-mill. Further improvements which were introduced during the eighteenth century drew more and more of the manufacturing processes into the mill complex, and burling shops, scribbling shops, teazel-houses and dye-houses were added to the original buildings, many of which have been converted into dwelling-houses.

Chalford village well illustrates this later period, beginning in the valley bottom. Chalford Place, the manor house, is within a few yards of St Mary's Mill. This fifteenth-century house became the Company Inn in the seventeenth century, where the East India Company's buyers came to do business, but it is no longer an inn. Gradually the village climbed the hillside, which was terraced to accommodate drying racks and tenters; weavers' cottages and substantial clothiers' houses cling to the steep slopes. At the top, Chalford Hill is an industrial hamlet, its centre the Duke of York inn, a predominantly early-eighteenth-century building likely to be in origin a farmhouse, for it contains such antique features as a spiral stone staircase. At Grey Cot Huguenot weavers were at work in the seventeenth century. The narrow high street (signposted Chalford Vale) follows the old road to Cirencester, and is full of fine clothiers'

21. *Chalford: The Company's Arms Inn (formerly the manor house and now again a private dwelling. Canal Lengthman's cottage now a museum.)*

houses and contemporary cottages, inns and converted mill-buildings lying alongside the derelict canal. One or two side valleys have buildings to show how tiny some of the enterprises of those days could be, and how small the force of water needed to drive their machinery. A mile beyond the village, Twizzell's or Baker's Mill's beautiful house, with its mill-dam now a stretch of ornamental water, marks the end of the series. By the close of the eighteenth century the owners had been born up on a tide of improvement to Frampton Place, leaving this delightful dwelling to their manager. The mill itself is no more, but the house has been recently restored.

8

The Civil War and its Aftermath

The good fortune which in previous centuries had preserved the Cotswolds relatively immune from struggles raging elsewhere did not hold in the seventeenth century.

When in 1642 civil war broke out in England, it might have been expected that, as a result of the Cockayne incident, the clothing interest would not be very friendly to the Crown, still less after, very early in the war, the king ordered all the cloth in the Gloucestershire centres to be commandeered to clothe his soldiers. Samuel Webb of Ham Mill in the Golden Valley (now a carpet factory) and others who could find the money, paid heavily, and more than once, for immunity from confiscation, but they were still vexed by contradictory royal mandates, on the one hand forbidding them to trade with rebellious London, on the other forbidding them to stand off any of their work-people; nor could they escape the demands for quartering, provisions and contribution from both sides. A horse-train of cloth on its way to Coventry (whither some Cotswold cloth was regularly sent for dyeing), though escorted by a Gloucestershire troop, was set upon by the Earl of Northampton on behalf of the king, and the cloth taken. Toll had to be paid to garrisons along the road, and, as the broadweavers of Chippenham put it: 'It is feared that in these times they will measure with the spear and not by the yard.' Support for the Royalist cause could only be had at the sword's point from the clothiers, an integrated community alike through business interest and family connections, and one of them, Edward Ash of Freshford, threw himself into raising arms for Parliament.

One of the first battles of the Civil War was fought at the northern extremity of our region, below Edgehill, five miles north-west of Banbury. The royalist forces were drawn up between the Rising Sun Inn on A433 and Bullet Hill east of B4086, from which Prince Rupert made his successful charge. Edgehill Tower, part of the Castle Inn, is a sham castle on the spot where the king raised his standard, built about a hundred years after the battle by Squire Sanderson Miller of Radway (which lies between the foot of the scarp and the battlefield proper), an amateur pioneer of romantic architecture. Today the splendid panorama of the midland plain with the battlefield in the foreground is sadly obscured by trees. In a cottage close to Radway House, King Charles breakfasted before the battle, dressed, we are told, in a suit of silver armour with a surcoat of velvet and the garter jewel on his breast. It was a brave show for a man who could seldom pay his army, and a brave day, for the king had the best of the bloody battle which followed, securing possession of Banbury and establishing himself at Oxford. Many of the victims are recorded in the parish registers of Warmington, a charming stone-built village to the east of the line at the foot of the scarp.

With Charles's headquarters at Oxford, the Cotswolds became a vital area. Beyond the hills lay reinforcements in the south-west and across the Severn, and the Severn valley itself was a rich potential source of revenue and provisions. The key cities, Bristol and Gloucester, however, were held for Parliament, as were Bath, Cirencester and Malmesbury, all walled towns. The king's ultimate failure to secure Gloucester was fatal to his cause, and the manoeuvres of 1642–4 were largely concerned with the capture of Bristol (a rich prize in itself), and the command of the Severn. A necessary preliminary was to secure Cirencester and Malmesbury.

Cirencester was altogether the more important of the two, and the harder nut to crack, for it contained a worthwhile arsenal. When in the autumn of 1642 Lord Chandos came from Sudeley to execute the king's Commission of Array, or Call to Arms, he was set on by a mob who tore his carriage to pieces while he himself barely escaped. The first assault in January 1643 by Prince Rupert was successfully repulsed, but in February, after the best of their arms and men had been drawn off to assist in the capture of Sudeley for Parliament, the town fell after a fierce resistance lasting seven hours. One of the clothiers who fell on the barricades has a memorial tablet in the church. Prince Rupert locked his prisoners in the church for the night, without food and water, and according to tradition their friends began the destruction of the stained glass windows in order to relieve them. The next day the prisoners were roped together and marched to Oxford with their governor, Colonel Fettiplace of Swinbrook, and they promised not to take up arms again in return for pardon. This Colonel Fettiplace is one of those heroes reclining on his elbow in Swinbrook church. No doubt among the rank and file were some of the many disgruntled and unemployed weavers who supplied cannon-fodder to both sides in the war. They had a reputation for religious zeal and bad discipline.

In February, Malmesbury fell easily to Rupert, and the king was lavishly entertained by the corporation. Less than a month later Sir Edmund Waller secured the surrender to Parliament by a trick, after a stiffish resistance during which a gap was made by an explosion in Abbey Row which has never been filled except by a fine magnolia tree. The royalist garrison's cavalry was quartered at Sherston at the time, after a skirmish there, but it too was routed in a night attack. In April and May the town changed hands twice more without bloodshed.

In the summer the royalist army from Cornwall crossed the Avon at Bradford, and swinging round through Bathford, met Waller on Lansdown Hill in a fierce battle in which they lost more than half their cavalry, but, falling back on Marshfield, held the road to London. Waller hastened after them but was soundly beaten at Roundway Down near Chippenham. Some of the prisoners were executed against the west wall of the abbey church at Malmesbury, where the bullet-marks may still be seen. After this, the royalist armies joined forces to seize Bristol. This was their high-water mark.

On his way to settle the quarrels within his victorious armies, the king spent one more night at Malmesbury. By this time Cotswold people had had a year of plunder and exaction in the name of contribution and provisions, to say nothing of assaults and executions, and he had a cool reception. 'The Mayor and Corporation have deserved so ill of me that I will neither be reasoned by them nor admit them to my presence until this business be settled,' wrote Charles. He hoped that Gloucester would not hold out. The attitude of the governor, Colonel Massey, was doubtful. He was a highly efficient professional soldier with plenty of battle experience on the continent, and had only offered his services to Parliament because the king would not give him the command he thought his due; might he not surrender? However, the siege lasted through August, and by the beginning of September Parliament had managed to raise an army which was sent under the Earl of Essex to the relief of the city. The lack of food they suffered on the two-day march from Adderbury testifies to the dire effect of royalist foraging on the Cotswold flocks. Near Stow-on-the-Wold, around the ruined windmill seen on the south side of A436, Prince Rupert tried without success to check them, and the king then withdrew to Painswick, hoping to give battle on the open wolds where his cavalry could operate to advantage when Essex set out on the return march.

Local legend says that in this retreat from Gloucester one of his sons asked him when they should go home, and he replied that he had now no home to go to; but can he have realized so soon that the tide had indeed turned? Another story associates the hamlet Paradise (A46) with Charles II, who is said to have called it so after a night spent on Painswick Hill. If indeed he gave it its name, it was probably on this occasion and not, as the story says, on his flight from Worcester when he was never near Painswick. At all events, the inn has long been called the Adam and Eve.

Essex managed to draw the royalist army eastward, and then turned swiftly south, surprising Cirencester at 3 a.m. and easily capturing it on his way back to London. The king followed a parallel line through Stow, and the south Cotswolds saw him no more.

The royalist garrisons in both Gloucestershire and Oxfordshire now came in for the full attention of the redoubtable Massey, who is said to have overwhelmed eight of them in eighteen days. The following May he set out to take Malmesbury once more, in preparation for the assault on Bristol. Tetbury offered no resistance, but Beverstone Castle was stoutly defended by its amateurish garrison until the commander, Colonel Ogilthorpe, slipped out by night, escorted only by six troopers, to keep an assignation with a girl in Chavenage House, falling straight into the hands of the watchful Massey's men. Malmesbury was stormed the following day, and Bristol fell to Cromwell's New Model Army in the course of the summer.

The Oxfordshire Cotswolds continued in the thick of the war to the end. Banbury was twice besieged and finally fell to Parliament, who ordered the destruction of the castle in 1646. The bells of Deddington, out of action because the church tower was in a ruinous condition, were commandeered by the king for cannon. The final battle was fought in the spring of 1646, when the last royalist army, despairing and demoralized, was defeated at Stow-on-the-Wold; the battle is said to have raged through the market-place.

There remained the aftermath. In 1649 Cromwell defeated a rebellion of the Levellers within his own army at Burford. The delinquent soldiers were locked in the church for the night and the next morning were marched to the roof of the Sylvester aisle to see three of their ringleaders shot in the churchyard. In 1651, after the battle of Worcester, Charles II, disguised as a servant to Miss Jane Lane who rode with him, passed uneventfully down the Fosse Way and spent a night in Cirencester and another at Boxwell Court, where the jewel he gave his hostess is faithfully preserved.

We possess an eloquent picture of what the war had meant to country people in a statement made by John Chamberlayne, the squire of Maugersbury, close to Stow-on-the-Wold, who was obliged, like other royalists, to redeem his sequestrated estates with a heavy fine. 'A Note of the quartering, Contribucion, and Provisions sent to the armyes . . . since the war began' records fifty-eight items.* There were large contributions to various royalist regiments; contributions to royalist garrisons (two months provision to Beverstone Castle); contributions to the Parliamentary garrison at Gloucester and the Parliamentary siege of Oxford; crops to the value of £40 were spoiled when Essex clashed with Rupert on the way to relieve Gloucester, and Chamberlayne had to provide some quartering and provisions to both sides as well as to my Lord Wilmot at Moreton-in-Marsh, who had harassed the approach of Essex's army; when 'Sir Edmund Waller chased the king's army to Worcester', and again when the king came back, when the Parliamentary army 'returned from Newbury Fight', quartering and provisions again; seven men and horses of Major Cromwell's one night; 'after Stow fight' (the last battle) quarter and provisions again, and so on; besides which he lost seventeen plough horses and at least a hundred sheep 'by souldiers'. It is not difficult to imagine what farmers and small-holders, who would have been treated with even less respect, suffered 'by souldiers'.

It cost Chamberlayne the huge sum of £1,246 to redeem his estates, but Edward Yerbury, a rich clothier of Bradford, the only one of any substance who supported the king, got off with a mere £150. As the king's Commissioner he had treated his parliamentarian friends with so much consideration that they got up a petition for him, and even helped him to pay his fine.

Others managed to make friends in high places. John Dutton, the son of a woolman who had acquired the abbot of Winchcombe's manor of Sherborne, and had held high office in the county under the king, was able to persuade Cromwell that he had followed his master under duress. He was building at Sherborne during the Commonwealth and later became Lord Sherborne. Lord Herbert, grandson of the Marquess of Worcester who had lent enormous sums to the king and in addition suffered a disastrous siege of his castle of Raglan, played his cards even better. He dissociated himself from his grandfather's politics, abandoned the Catholic faith to which his family had clung, called himself Mr Somerset, and gained the friendship of Cromwell. During the Commonwealth he regained part of his inheritance, and Badminton itself came to him from a cousin. Here he began to build a new seat after the Restoration, and lived in quasi-royal state for the rest of his life, becoming the first Duke of Beaufort in

* H. P. R. Finberg (ed.), *Gloucestershire Studies* (Leicester University Press, 1957), pp. 184–9.

1678. The descendants of so staunch a cavalier as the old Marquess of Worcester naturally possess a number of royalist relics.

Nor was it quite plain sailing for the winning side. The war divided many families. Anthony Kingscote of Kingscote, the representative of a far older family but a man of similar substance to Chamberlayne of Maugersbury, had no fines to pay, but that did not mitigate his bitterness against his eldest son who sided with the Crown. When the old puritan died during the Commonwealth, his will not

22. *Broughton Castle.*

only disinherited his heir, but grossly insinuated that his daughter-in-law was not legally the luckless cavalier's wife. The couple had perhaps been married according to the prescribed Anglican rite, for their children were always recognized as legitimate. The execution of the king was too much for many parliamentary supporters. According to tradition, Cromwell came himself with Ireton to persuade the owner of Chavanage House, who was a member of the Long Parliament, to show himself in the House and sign the death warrant; the rooms they occupied are shown. Lord Saye and Sele, who had done so much for the parliamentary cause, made a strategic withdrawal to Lundy Island, which he owned. This prudent course secured his pardon at the Restoration, and indeed he obtained the office of Lord Privy Seal. He was known among his contemporaries as Old Subtlety, and no doubt they appreciated the Latin inscription he had carved on the rich screen he erected round his dining-room door: 'There is little pleasure in the memory of things past.'

After the 'revolution' of 1688, remote areas like the Cotswolds harboured many a discontented gentleman. We catch an unexpected glimpse of middle-class life in our region in the diaries of John Wesley. As fellow and later tutor at Oxford from 1725 to 1735, the ardent young don found his greatest pleasure in riding over the wolds to stay in the sheltered villages at the foot of the northern scarp. Probably he was introduced into this cultivated and relaxed society by a fellow undergraduate, John Griffiths, whose father was vicar of Broadway, and whose sister Nancy was immediately attracted to him. In the same parish lived the Winningtons, small gentry with whom he went hunting, and the more aristocratic Granvilles, descendants of the cavalier Sir Bevil Grenville who perished at Lansdowne in 1643, and now, as Jacobites, living in temporary eclipse in this retired spot. There were two daughters, Mary, two years older than Wesley and as beautiful as she was intelligent, and Anne. It was a wonderful October when he first visited them, with the *aurora borealis* flashing night after night over the wide flat Vale of Evesham to the north, lighting them home from supper at Buckland rectory. The rector there was Trethewy Tooker, another Jacobite, an eccentric, witty divine who wore rough country clothes, and 'never appeared to so little advantage as in the pulpit' according to the sharp-tongued Mary Granville. His household included another Jacobite refugee and a merry, good-humoured daughter Fanny, who could listen to poetry but was better at a Christmas frolic than a deep religious discussion. Two miles further along the scarp at Stanton, the rector, the Reverend Lionel Kirkham, was a jovial, hospitable gentleman with several sons and three daughters. Stanton boasted at that time a private Academy kept by the Reverend John Chapone, who was engaged to marry the eldest daughter Sally. He had been persuaded by her to employ as assistant her friend and protege Elizabeth Elstob, who was deep in the study of Anglo-Saxon texts. The two girls had become acquainted through their dressmaker, George Ballard. This remarkable young man lived and worked at his trade in Campden, and studied Anglo-Saxon in his spare time until in the closing years of his short life Lord Chedworth of Stowell Park and some of his friends provided him with an annuity to enable him to devote himself to scholarship. Elizabeth Elstob had by 1726 already published a grammar, and was working on translations of the Saxon poets after the school day was done. There were other Oxford friends in Mickleton, Guiting and Notgrove, and a host of acquaintances around this charmed circle.

Wesley was very recently ordained, and had preached his first sermon while staying at Witney the previous year. He preached in the ensuing years in Buckland, Broadway and Stanton, and the young ladies listened to him eagerly; they seem all to have been more or less in love with his romantic looks, earnest eloquence and tender interest in their spiritual lives. He, in his turn, learned with

23. *The Jacobean pulpit from which Wesley preached at Stanton.*

them easier social manners, to bandy compliments and the currently fashionable nicknames. He was Cyrus to his Cotswold friends, and his two favourites among the girls were Varanese and Aspasia, Sally Kirkham and Mary Glanville. There were Christmas revels and long summer days spent with the Kirkhams, sometimes with tea among the haycocks, and often with dancing and cards after supper which might last into the small hours. He would wander into the kitchen to help Mrs Kirkham whip up a syllabub, or join a fatigue party shelling peas in the arbour. Best of all were the afternoons sitting in the garden reading poetry, plays and sermons with the girls, or climbing the scarp to sit beneath a fringe of ash trees looking out over the fruitful vale, receiving their confidences and giving advice about their souls. Sally Kirkham was a serious, well-read and intelligent young woman, three years older than Wesley, and well able to meet him in conversation. A tender friendship sprang up between them at once, which continued to thrive unchecked by her devotion to husband and children, and ended only when Wesley left for America in 1735.

Only a little less ardent was his feeling for Mary Granville, also soon married and a widow by 1730. Mary Pendarves, as she had become, soon returned to the great world and became at last tired of his unfashionable enthusiasm. She became something of a figure in Georgian society and was a friend and correspondent of Dean Swift. After her second marriage, as Mrs Delaney, she features as a charming and gracious woman in the diaries of the novelist Fanny Burney, whom she introduced at court. It was through her that Sally Chapone eventually obtained from Queen Charlotte a pension for Elizabeth Elstob to enable her to give up teaching.

When Wesley returned from America, the rest of his life was given over to missionary labours, during which he preached from time to time in the Cotswolds, but never again at Stanton, the delectable mountains of his earthly pilgrimage. His influence in the Cotswolds was markedly less than that of George Whitefield, founder of the Primitive branch of Methodism, who was born in Gloucester, and spent many years in Bristol. The sparse hamlets on the edge of wood and common which became populous villages in the clothing districts offered a challenge to missionary zeal which was taken up by nonconformist preachers sooner than by the clergy of the established church.

Wesley's 'dear delightful Stanton' is still a beautiful and extremely well-preserved village. It was one of the first, indeed, to be protected from inharmonious intrusions. There are many seventeenth-century houses and cottages, and even some council houses built of traditional materials, and there is no through traffic to mar its character, for the main street ends in a track up the face of Wesley's beloved Horrel Hill. (Another track leads ultimately to the Iron-Age fort on Shenberrow Hill.) The pulpit in which he preached, bearing the date 1684, and a memorial tablet to some of the Kirkhams, are to be found in the church, which is chiefly interesting, however, for the glass and furnishings (including reredos and organ loft) designed by Ninian Comper early in this century.

In 1657, a year before the Lord Protector died, there had been formed a royalist club, the Gloucestershire Society. This club continued to flourish long after the king was safely back on the throne, and was still flourishing in the nineteenth century. Meanwhile, an apparently independant offshoot had been formed, the Gloucestershire Society of London, which had the charitable object of raising money to apprentice poor children, and had 299 members of the nobility and gentry of the county on its subscription list. In the course of the years, one drinking-song gained pre-eminence over all others with the two societies. *George Ridler's Oven* is one of those rambling folk ditties eleven verses long, with perhaps a touch of salacious innuendo, and a rousing chorus to roar out as bottle and keg went round.

The stones, the stones, the stones . . . [9 times]
The stones that built George Ridler's oven
And they came from the Bleakeney's quar,
George he was a jolly old man,
And his head grew above his hair.

The stones, the stones, *etc.*

There's Dick the treble and John the mean,
(Let every man sing in his own place)
And George he was the elder brother
And therefore would he sing the base.

The stones, the stones, *etc.*

Mine hostess maid, and her name were Nell,
A pretty wench and I loved her well.
I loved her well – good reason why
Because she loved my dog and I.

The stones, *etc.*

My dog has gotten such a trick,
To visit maids when they be sick.
When they be sick and like to die,
Oh thither go my dog and I.

The stones, *etc.*

My dog is good to catch a hen
A duck and goose is food for men
And where good company I spy
Oh thither goes my dog and I.

The stones, *etc.*

When I go dead as it may hap
My grave shall be under the good ale tap.
In folded arms there will us lie,
Cheek by jowl my dog and I.

By 1800 the London Society had a well-sculpted model of George Ridler reclining on a barrel, pipe in mouth and grog in hand, accompanied by his dog with a dead fowl in its jaws. The song, led by a trio of voices, was the climax of the annual dinner, held at the height of the London Season on the second Wednesday in May. Meanwhile, an edifice of symbolism was being woven about this raffish folk image. George himself had become King Charles I (the crown was the head which grew above his hair). Who were the stones, his dog and the maids this creature visited, had become a subject for endless discussion at club meetings and in the local press. In 1867 a letter in the *Wilts and Gloucestershire Standard* revealed that Bleakeney's Quar was Black Nest quarry in Bisley parish, yielding stone considered specially suitable for ovens, and the Ridlers a numerous farming clan in the neighbourhood. The elucidation of these local and personal allusions did not diminish the attractions of the political game. J. Arthur Gibbs, in his *A Cotswold Village*, published in 1898, devotes five or six pages to the ballad without mentioning them. He describes the artistry and enthusiasm with which it was rendered in pubs and smoking concerts and at every parish entertainment, and in an appendix offers what he deemed to be the most likely among many political interpretations. Whether they were genuine or not, the ballad had become a sort of regional anthem.

9

Roads, Canals and Railways

The road system of the Cotswolds, though it has remained surprisingly unchanged through the ages, has naturally been subject to changes of emphasis. The Roman system centring on Cirencester, the provincial capital, consisting of new trunk roads supplemented by prehistoric tracks, in many cases improved by Roman engineers, has already been described.

Akeman Street never recovered its position as a trunk road. In the Middle Ages the importance of Bath had greatly diminished, and travellers proceeding thence to Cirencester followed the ancient trackway (keeping to higher, less marshy ground than that crossed by the Fosse Way between the two towns), and passing through the new borough of Tetbury, which was already a growing wool market by the thirteenth century. At this period the most important road on the Cotswolds was the link with Salisbury and Southampton along which came wine and other luxuries to be exchanged for Cotswold fleeces, and on which the wool-trains started out on their long journey to Flanders and the Mediterranean. This is now A361, which enters our region at an immemorial ford crossing the Thames at Lechlade. The name means 'the crossing on the Leach (estate)'.

Evidently there was a Saxon settlement, but Lechlade first appears as a market and borough in the thirteenth century, when no doubt its situation on the Southampton road offered promising opportunities for commercial enterprise. The new borough barely succeeded in establishing itself, and it is now hardly more than a busy village, though with several good inns on the market-place, and a number of substantial houses demonstrating the importance of its position at the head of the navigable Thames in the eighteenth and nineteenth centuries; a typical Cotswold 'wool' church stands a little back in a spacious churchyard.

Two lines from Shelley's 'Ode written in Lechlade Churchyard' are carved on a stone at the gate.

From Lechlade, traders bound for Cirencester turned westwards (along the High Street), but those with business in the central Cotswolds, Campden or the Midlands continued northward (A361) to the Windrush, where a flourishing settlement had grown up on the south bank. Burford obtained its charter as early as 1087, and it was along the Southampton Road, on a gentle slope, that the burgage tenements were laid out, the road forming the market-place. The parish church alongside the river clearly indicates the site of the pre-Conquest village thus elevated by its first Norman owner, and indeed the medieval guildhall appears to have been in this corner of the town. To the new market-place came Italian merchants during the next three hundred years to buy wool in the fairs. Here beyond question Bernard Lumbard halted on his way to the abbot of Winchcombe's manor at Sherborne, and others bound for the abbot of Gloucester's shearing at Eastington and the market at Northleach stopped to shoe their horses if not to dine and sleep. Here quarry-owners and masons discussed contracts for dressed stone destined for Oxford, Windsor and London. The George and the Bear are the oldest recorded inns, but Reaveley's shop in 1485 was the Novum Hospitium Angulare (the new inn on the corner). Already in the thirteenth century the built-up area was climbing the steep hill beyond the intersection of the road to Witney (Witney Street) and that to Cirencester and Northleach, along which a new market-place was designated for sheep rather later. The oldest houses here (Sheep Street) date from the fifteenth century.

By the fifteenth century the burgesses had established a grammar school – as the Chantry Commissioners reported in 1547: 'The guild of our Lady in the said parish church founded to give to the poor people of the town, and to the mending of highways and bridges . . . and did build a chapel annexed to the minster there to teach children freely.' This obviously refers to the Lady Chapel west of the porch, originally a detached guild chapel enlarged and linked with the church in the fifteenth century, very likely in order to accommodate the school, which was an addition to the original objects of the chantry probably made at that time. The little west doorway would have been preserved for the use of the children. Perhaps significantly, St Anne, who is often depicted teaching her daughter, was joined with our Lady when the rebuilt chapel was dedicated. Twenty years after the Chantry Commissioners' report, the burgesses managed to refound their school (1570), and in time to give it a building of its own. Several of the Sylvesters, a rich family of clothiers, were buried in fine tombs in the guild chapel, and it became known as the Sylvester aisle.

In the sixteenth century, cloth-making throve in Burford; Edmund Sylvester built one of the finest houses in the town, now known as Falkland Hall. However, the Sylvesters and several other clothiers seem to have migrated to Witney, where the blanket manufacture was flourishing when the 'white' trade collapsed. Whatever the vicissitudes of the cloth trade, the town was in no danger of stagnating; it was the centre for the great quarries of the Windrush valley, there was an active tanning industry, and a thriving manufacture of horse clothing. A local saddler was claimed to be the best in Europe in Charles II's reign, and two of the famous Burford saddles made an acceptable pledge of loyalty to William of Orange when he visited the Cotswolds in 1695.

Probably the route from London to Gloucester became well known when the king was at Oxford during the Civil War. The most direct road between Oxford and Witney then ran from Botley across the marshy Thames valley to Eynsham, and was often altogether impassable in winter, always too miry for wheeled traffic, which made a long detour (A34 and A4095) through Long Hanborough. Previous ages had therefore preferred to reach Gloucester via the Bath road (A4) and Ermine Street, in wet weather avoiding the marshy miles between Stratton St Margaret and South Cerney by passing through Lechlade, Fairford, Barnsley and Perrots Brook. This route (now largely unclassified) later gained the name of the Welsh Way because generations of Welsh drovers used it to bring their cattle destined for the London market to be shipped downstream from Lechlade.

In 1726 a good causeway was put across the Thames marshes and the Toll Bridge at Swinford built, opening the direct route to Witney to wheeled traffic. In 1735 we find Wesley riding out from Oxford to meet Mary Pendarves on her journey to London from Gloucester. In 1761 a certain Thomas Castell of Burford started a coach service to London, one of the pioneers of the route which was soon to be the established coach-road to Gloucester and South Wales. At this time the road entered the town along Witney Street and left along Sheep Street, and two of the most important inns were the Bull on the corner of Witney Street, rebuilt in classical style in 1620, and the Lamb in Sheep Street.

The Burford Roads Trust had recently been formed, and this road had been turnpiked in 1751, with a branch to Cheltenham in 1756 to improve the prospects of the budding spa, in which Lord Sherborne had an interest. The Burford–Cirencester road (A433) was dealt with in 1753, and the ancient Southampton road from Lechlade to Stow through Burford (A361 and A424) in 1755. The other roads converging on Stow were turnpiked in the same few years. This meant that an attempt was made to give roads and bridges a standard width, and a foundation of stone, surfaced if possible with gravel, and accurate signposts and milestones were provided. The material for Cotswold roads still came from diggings alongside the highway, of which the made-up-road seldom occupied more than half, and these diggings have left humps and hollows on many verges to this day. There was no gravel on the wolds, and the brashy oolite used for surfacing

Map 8 *Stroudwater clothing district.*

all too easily dissolved under heavy traffic into dust and mud – Cotswold turnpikes had a bad reputation.

The cost of these operations and of maintenance was met out of the parish rate, heavily subsidized by the tolls collected at gates set up by the trusts along the route. Turnpike trusts were private enterprises set up by local people. The tolls were mortgaged in advance, their collection at each gate being auctioned separately, so that administrators knew what income they had at their disposal to inaugurate and supervise necessary work, but there was also a profit to be made by the purchasers of the tolls from each gate; thus abuses crept in. Turnpike roads were sometimes little better than those which remained in the care of the parish. Nevertheless the improvements effected by the trusts made regular coach services possible, and their schedules were constantly improved.

Burford's ancient reputation as a halting place revived and grew with the expanding coach traffic. Between 1800 and 1840 the coach trade was the most important element in the life of several Cotswold towns, and an ample incentive to the turnpike trusts. Soon after 1800, thirty coaches passed each way along A40 every day, and the fame of Burford's inns, with their sideboards loaded with venison (much of it illegally obtained in Wychwood Forest) and noble sirloins from the Windrush water-meadows, had made 'Burford Bait' a colloquial expression for a good blow-out anywhere south of the Trent. In 1812 the Burford Road Trust made the relatively straight and level length of A40 which by-passes the town and the fierce hills in and out of it on the old road. The Bird-in-Hand and the Ramping Cat were built at the new cross-roads above the town to cater for through traffic, but the inns in the High Street continued to flourish for another generation on local trade and on the wagons and fly-vans which carried heavy goods and light packages repectively, and the travelling poor. The town was not growing, but it was holding its own. Hardly any new houses had been built since the close of the seventeenth century, but the existing stock was constantly enlarged, modernized and divided.

The high spots of Burford's year were the Midsummer feast and Bibury Race Week, when every inn was crammed to the roof. George IV might be the guest of Lord Sherborne and all the gentry round about entertained large parties; tradesmen in the surrounding villages slept on their counters in order to let their rooms to visitors. This annual event is said to have been first held in 1621, when a visitation of the plague at Newmarket prevented a regular meeting from being held there, and Charles II made it popular. The course, of which nothing now remains, was on the downs above Aldsworth (now under arable crops) to the south of A433 midway between Burford and Bibury. An engraving exists showing a grandstand of some pretension, with an ornamental cast-iron balcony, but the races were discontinued in the last century.

Tetbury also had its coach trade, though less than Burford's; on the other hand its wool market retained its importance well into the nineteenth century. The town also had its race week, another gay event with balls every night and venison suppers. The little town has finer houses and grander inns than Burford's, with a pleasant market house on stone columns in the centre. The races survive, and some new light industry and a small housing estate, together with the revived traffic on the road, keep it alive. No two towns in the Cotswolds, however, were more blighted by the coming of steam than Burford and Tetbury.

Northleach had only a moderate share of the coach traffic on A40. The Flyers avoided the steep descent into the town and the marshy transit of the Leach valley by using the ancient ridgeway to the east of it through Hampnett, now a green road, which had been superseded centuries before when the abbot of Gloucester had founded the borough; probably they changed horses at Frog Mill on A436, and later, after the new descent into Cheltenham had been made, at a new inn at Andoversford. There was enough slower traffic to keep one good inn going in Northleach but the town had no other resource, and in spite of its glorious church it is easily the smallest and least impressive of the Cotswold wool markets. Even the revival of the road has done little for it; the heavy traffic grinding through its single street deters visitors to the church from lingering. It cries out for a by-pass but is probably unlikely to get one in the near future.

The main road from London to Worcester has always passed through the north Cotswolds; Ogilby's chart marks it *The Great Road*. At that time, however, travellers from London came via Wheatley and Islip to Glympton (B4027), and thence by the lane through Cleveley to Enstone, crossing the modern road there to Chalford Green, and thence to Chipping Norton on an alignment which is still a parish boundary. In 1718 the road from Oxford to Woodstock was turnpiked, and in 1736 an entirely new turnpike road was built between Woodstock and Chipping Norton. The method used here was probably employed wherever new roads were to be built. It is recorded that a team of eight oxen ploughed the whole length in sixteen-mile furrows. From that time the route through Oxford and Woodstock (A34) superseded the old road. Another great improvement made about the same time to this 'Great Road' was the Five Mile Drive over Bourton Downs between Bourton-on-the-Hill and Broadway (A44). The Great Road over the Cotswolds was as lonely as A40, passing through few villages or even wayside hamlets. About 1806, travellers on both are known to have been terrorized by an outbreak of highway robbery. The culprit was presently found to be a certain Mr Freeman, who was living in style in the manor house at Minster Lovel and lavishly entertaining his unsuspecting neighbours, after having made the Home Counties too hot for him. He was eventually caught and hanged.

Meanwhile the Bath road was being steadily improved until by 1800 it was the best in the country. In 1727 the first Trust was formed to take the road through Chippenham, avoiding the marshy length around Lacock, and a new length (A3509) was made from Corsham to rejoin the old road at Chapel Plaister, where the chapel is a travellers hospice. The old road ran thence along Kingsdown and is now unclassified. In the same year improvements to the road between Chippenham and Bristol via Marshfield and Tog Hill were put in hand. The Corsham–Batheaston section of A4 was not made until 1756.

Considering the industrial activity in the Stroudwater valleys, progress with the roads was surprisingly slow. Cloth for Asia and the New World went away by water, but the bulk of the trade passed through London. Gradients in the Stroudwater Hills were almost impracticable for wheeled traffic, and no amount of contemporary surfacing could have withstood the fierce rivulets which inevitably coursed down them in the torrential rains of the district. It took a whole day for a wheeled vehicle to go from Stroud to Chalford, following lanes high up along the valley side and up and down the steep re-entrants. The road over to Nailsworth via Minchinhampton was equally bad. The road from Stroud to Cirencester also went up by Rodborough to Minchinhampton (a terrible hill for horses), then along the ridge to Sapperton (unclassified now most of the way) and at Park Corner joined the ancient Cirencester–Bisley road, which between here and Oakridge negotiated the atrocious gradients of the Frome valley, a route now deservedly abandoned. Thus Cirencester was entered north of the Park. Travellers from Chalford followed the attractive and precipitous lane up the valley through Frampton Mansell to Sapperton. These roads were too bad for the kind of engineering that was undertaken in mid-century to effect more than marginal improvement. However, in 1746 the road between Gloucester and Stroud via Painswick (A46) was turnpiked, and the Bath road beyond Nailsworth (A46) about the same time. After an appalling climb out of Nailsworth, this road soon joined the line of the immemorial Cotswold Ridgeway. In 1758 a now unclassified road from Bisley through Brimpsfield to the Ermine Street was improved and extended down the Toadsmoor valley into the busy industrial village at Brimscombe on the Frome.

In 1780 the Nailsworth Valley Trust was formed to build the much-needed new road (A46) between Nailsworth and Stroud, and the lovely Nailsworth–Tetbury road through Avening. The next thirty years saw most of the worst gradients on the older turnpikes eliminated by new lengths laid out in wide loops: Fish Hill, Edge Hill, Stanway Hill, Frocester Hill and the Nailsworth horseshoes are the most spectacular of these. There was a new gentle descent to

Cheltenham from Andoversford, cutting out the cruel gradient through Dowdeswell village, and a by-pass for another severe climb out of Naunton.

A new road between Stroud and Cirencester was of less importance to through coach traffic than these, but much needed by local people. A419, serving the whole Frome valley and the heart of the clothing district, and avoiding the great detour round Cirencester Park, was made in 1814. The Frome valley is said to have been called the Golden Valley by Queen Victoria; before this road was built she could hardly have seen it.

As early as 1697, schemes began to be discussed for making the Frome navigable between Stroud and the Severn. The navigation of many English rivers was improved about this time, including the Thames and the Kennet, by means of new cuts and flash locks. The latter consisted of a narrow channel with a single pair of gates, which when opened released a sufficient tide of water to carry flat-bottomed craft safely to a lower level. There is an old sloping stone weir at Little Barrington supposed to have been made about this time to assist the transit of barges laden with stone from the quarries of Windrush, Sherborne and Barrington, but it may be older, since those quarries were sending stone to Oxford by water as far as Eynsham in the Middle Ages. Plans for improving the Stroudwater Frome all foundered on the conflicting demand of the mills for water power. A canal was another matter, and between 1776 and 1779 the Stroudwater Navigation was built terminating at Wallbridge, even then a suburb of Stroud. It proved a godsend to the people of the district, though more for the import of coal and other heavy goods than for the despatch of their merchandise. Most clothiers continued to send their goods by road. The canal continued in use until 1941. Lately conservation groups have been at work on it and much of it is now navigable for pleasure craft. Most of the stylish lengthmen's cottages with doric features survive.

When this canal was opened, the Severn was the chief outlet for Birmingham and the Black Country, and the proposal to link the Stroudwater Navigation with the Thames, providing a through inland waterway to London, met with massive support. Four years later (1783), work began on the Thames and Severn Canal, 28¾ miles from Wallbridge to Lechlade. This formidable under taking was completed within six years, with a branch to Cirencester. Forty-four locks were required between Wallbridge and Daneway, where the canal entered the 2⅜-mile-long Sapperton tunnel, the longest that had so far been built. It was a great day when the first boat went through (November 1789), but within a matter of months the Oxford canal up the Cherwell valley to Rugby had provided Birmingham with a shorter and more reliable route (it was found to be extremely difficult to keep up the level of the water in the long summit between Sapperton and Siddington on account of the porous nature of the oolite bed). The Thames and Severn was thus an unprofitable venture almost from the start, and as early as 1860 the company already had a scheme, which came to nothing, for turning it into a single track railway. The section between Stroud and Chalford continued to be well-used for local deliveries throughout the nineteenth century. After various vicissitudes, the canal came into the hands of the Gloucestershire County Council, who tried to revive it, but the last commercial craft passed the summit in 1911, and in 1933 the whole was abandoned.

24. *Tunnel portal on the Thames and Severn Canal at Coates.*

The most imposing relic of this great enterprise is the monumental portal in Coates parish, easily seen from Tunnel House, once a lonely bargees' port-of-call, and now a popular inn. The western end is less ornate and much overgrown. From the Daneway Inn, whose car park is built over the last of the 44 locks, down to Chalford the towpath is a public footpath leading down from ruined lock to ruined lock through a beautiful valley fringed with woodland, along whose shoulder the Western Region expresses break the silence from time to time as they thunder down towards Gloucester. At Chalford one of the unique round lengthmen's houses is used as a canal museum; others survive near Lechlade, Marston Meysey, Cerney Wick and Coates. Close to each of the shafts that were made to build the tunnel the spoil was collected in neat mounds and planted with beech saplings. These symmetrical knolls crowned with mature trees mark out the course of the tunnel through Sapperton parish.

The Kennet and Avon canal skirts the southern extremity of the Cotswolds, where it follows the course of the Avon from Bath to Bradford. Like the Stroud Navigation it was long under consideration; at one period a ship canal was even contemplated to permit ocean-going vessels to pass from Bristol to London, and the canal is substantially wider than was customary at the time. Digging was begun at Newbury and Bradford-on-Avon in 1794, in the latter about half a mile west of the town, where a pretty little suburb (it might almost be called a port) subsequently grew up; canal wharves are still to be seen. Later the Somersetshire Coal Canal branched off here. John Rennie was the Kennet and Avon's engineer, and he was the designer of the handsome aquaduct at Avoncliff which carries the canal across the river. About four miles downstream, the canal crosses the river again on an aquaduct 150 yards long with doric ornament, designed by Charles Dundas, another of the canal's engineers. William Smith, the pioneer of British geology, died in a cottage near this spot. At Claverton there is a pumping station dated 1813 containing some contemporary machinery in process of restoration. Here traces of the railroad made to bring stone down from the Bath quarries on Monkton Down may still be seen. This western end of the canal was opened in 1796, but the remainder was not operational until 1810 when the Wilts and Berks canal was also opened, linking the Thames through Abingdon with the Kennet and Avon canal at Semington, a few miles upstream from Bradford, with branches to Chippenham and Calne. From that date Bath stone, chiefly from Box and Corsham, was used extensively in Oxford. In 1830 the Wilts and Berks carried 70,000 tons of freight.

In 1852 the Great Western Railway bought up the Kennet and Avon, the Wilts and Berks being left to die of natural causes. Both lingered on till the end of the century; only the dry bed of the Wilts and Berks remains, but part of the Kennet and Avon is still navigable and conservation groups are at work.

The Oxford canal has never ceased to function, although Nuffield College now stands on the site of the principal wharf. Coal still came to the brewery by canal as late as 1961, and by then the pleasure boats had already begun to cruise on it. It is now one of the most popular of English canals. It winds through the

Arcadian Cherwell valley, for the most part on the Buckinghamshire side. James Brindley treated the river with small respect, several times impounding it to form a length of his canal. One of the longest of these lengths begins half a mile below Shipton-on-Cherwell, whose church, a pretty piece of Gothic revival by the painter William Turner of Oxford, juts out, shaded by lime trees, above its placid waters. The wharf here has vanished, but at Thrupp, the next hamlet downstream, the wharves and pleasant inn are always thronged with cruisers.

The first railroads, primitive tracks with horse-drawn trucks, appeared in the region in connection with the stone quarries. As early as 1731, Richard Allen had a pioneer tramroad made between his new quarries on Monkton Down and Bath for his great project there. In 1798, at the order of Charles Brandon Trye, newly come to his inheritance in the manor of Leckhampton, and with an interest in Cheltenham, a gravity inclined-plane was constructed, enabling trucks of stone from the ancient quarry beneath the edge of the scarp to reach the turnpike (B4070) a mile outside the growing town. The success of this enterprise probably encouraged Lord Sherborne to make a tramroad, opened in 1811, to bring coal from Gloucester Docks to the spa; on the return journey trucks carried stone from the Leckhampton quarry brought down by two further inclined-planes. The tramroad was closed in 1859, but the inclined-planes continued to serve the quarry until 1924, and the track is now a much-frequented path onto Charlton Kings Common, beloved for its bracing air and splendid view. Coal and stone were the only items for which such enterprises were worthwhile in the Cotswolds. Coal would then cost twice as much in upland towns and villages as it did in those served by the new canals. In 1826 a tramroad between the navigable Avon at Stratford and Moreton-in-Marsh was opened, with a branch to Shipston-on-Stour ten years later; a proposed branch to the quarry at Bourton-on-the-Hill was never made. The track between Moreton and Shipston was taken over by the railway in 1889; the old tramway between Moreton and Stratford was not superseded and seems to have fallen out of use as late as 1904. The track may be seen beside the Fosse Way north of the town.

As early as 1824 Bristol magnates were thinking about a line to London, and the famous John Loudon Macadam, who was road engineer to the Bristol trust, surveyed part of the route, but it was not until 1833 that the company to be known as the Great Western Railway was launched, and 1841 before Brunel's broad-gauge track was complete. The line declines gently from Chippenham, plunging just beyond Corsham into a 'monstrous and extraordinary, dangerous and impracticable' tunnel, the longest railway tunnel that had so far been made, but by no means so long as some canal tunnels. It emerges into the valley of the

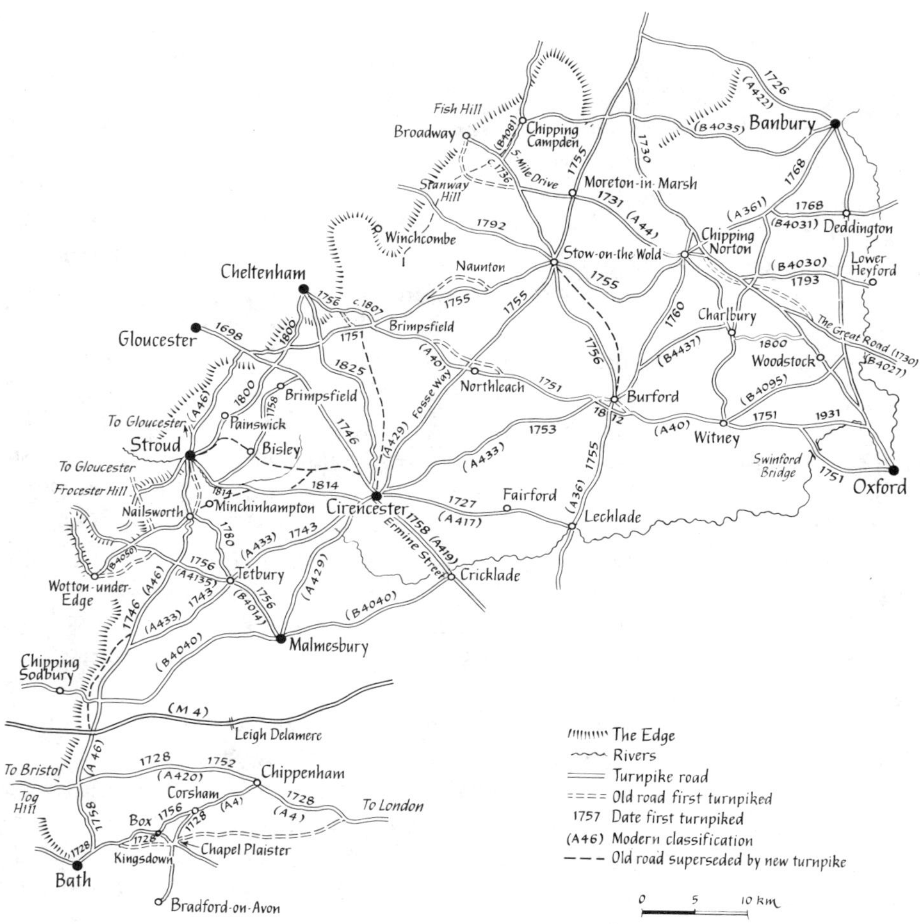

Map 9 *Turnpike roads.*

By Brook just outside Box village, and Brunel's stately portal can be seen from A4. An even handsomer entrance to a smaller tunnel is less accessible in fields a quarter of a mile north of the church. A branch from Swindon to Cirencester was also opened in 1841, but the station at Kemble, now the only one of importance on the south-eastern flank of the Cotswolds, was delayed until 1883 by the implacable opposition of the local squire, a Scot who, not content with blocking the proposed station and obtaining £7,000 compensation, insisted on an unnecessary tunnel 500 yards long to hide the obnoxious intruder from his offended gaze.

Almost at the same time (1839–44) Brunel was laying, for the Bristol and Gloucester Company, the line which skirts the foot of the southern scarp, soon to be absorbed by the Midland, which reached southward with a narrow-gauge line to Gloucester and Cheltenham in 1840. The Cheltenham and Great Western Union Railway Company was also at work under his direction on another formidable tunnel through the scarp to extend their Cirencester branch from Kemble down to Gloucester and Cheltenham via Stroud. This line was opened in 1847. It passes close to the monumental entrance to the Thames and Severn canal tunnel at a higher level, and crosses the course of the canal underground.

The next important addition to the Cotswold network was completed in 1853, again by Brunel, for the Oxford, Worcester and Wolverhampton Railway. The making of this line up the Evenlode valley produced one striking incident which features in all railway histories, the battle of Mickleton tunnel between a gang of 2,000 navvies raised by Brunel and the gang of a defaulting firm of contractors who were occupying the workings. Lord Redesdale of Batsford Park made a stipulation that every passenger train should stop at Moreton-in-Marsh. They still do, to the great advantage of well-to-do commuters from London and the Black Country, and indeed of every dweller in the north Cotswolds, who without his lordship's intervention might well have found themselves without any fast trains at all. The company was absorbed by the Great Western in 1861. The line up the Cherwell valley to Banbury was opened in 1852 as part of the Great Western's route from London to Birmingham, Shrewsbury and Birkenhead.

One more line was added to this basic network after the Severn tunnel had been opened in 1886; it was completed in 1900, offering a slightly shorter route to Bristol and South Wales from London. This line crosses the south Cotswolds mainly underground between Acton Turville and Old Sodbury. The Duke of Beaufort demanded that every train should stop at Badminton, and they continued to do so on request until shortly before Badminton and Chipping Sodbury stations were closed. A private Act of Parliament was required to bring this about.

This network survives to this day, providing an indifferent railway service to the region. Subsequent additions, however useful to local people, never really paid their way, and fell beneath the Beeching axe between 1961 and 1964.

Within ten years of its completion, Chipping Norton and Bourton-on-the-Water had been provided with links with the Oxford–Worcester line from Chipping Norton Junction (now Kingham); Dursley, a busy clothing town, got its branch from the Midland in 1856; Nailsworth, just as busy, had to wait, disastrously, another seven years. In 1872 a branch reached Malmesbury from Dauntsey. The Cotswolds had proved a surprisingly formidable obstacle in the creation of a rational system south of the Trent. Most additions within the region in the 'seventies and 'eighties were made with the object of improving links with the West Midland cities rather than to supply the needs of the little upland markets which incidentally benefited. A line intended to run from Oxford to Cirencester through Witney and Bampton reached Fairford in 1873 and got no farther. A long-projected line between Banbury and Cheltenham was completed in 1889, incorporating the Chipping Norton and Bourton-on-the-Water branches. This offered a shorter route from London to Cheltenham, but the switchback twenty-four miles between Kingham and Cheltenham took an hour to travel. The line was chiefly useful for conveying ore from the Banbury iron-field to South Wales. Two years later came a still more ambitious and uneconomic line between Cheltenham and Swindon via Cricklade, Cirencester, Chedworth and Withington; the hamlet of Andoversford became a junction and achieved the dignity of a cattle market. The train took twenty minutes to cover the 7½ miles between Chedworth and Cirencester, and though a carrier's cart would have taken at least three times as long, not surprisingly the company was already in the hands of a receiver when the line opened. Tetbury, which had entered upon a decline with the virtual disappearance of the great wool market, temporarily postponed by the growth of coach traffic, was in a bad way when a branch line reached it from Kemble in 1889.

The last line serving the region was built after the turn of the century. In 1900 the Great Western laid a track between Leamington Spa, Stratford-on-Avon and Cheltenham, via Broadway and Winchcombe, which served all the villages at the foot of the northern scarp as far as the Stour. The station at Toddington, on this recently reprieved line, is now used as a store for the movable fittings from abandoned lines beloved by railway enthusiasts.

Three Cotswold towns, Burford, Northleach, and Marshfield, were left high and dry by the railway system. J. Arthur Gibbs in his *A Cotswold Village* (1898) describes an expedition from Bibury to Burford in a horse bus, along an empty dusty highway to arrive in an almost ghostly high street. Alone of the three, such a calm now broods over Marshfield, once a busy stop where horses were changed for the last time on the road to Bristol. Like the others, it came to life again with the revival of the road, but has been deserted since the M4, the London–Bristol–South Wales motorway, was opened.

The borough of Marshfield is first mentioned in 1397. At that date there was a little Norman church with a central tower; a hundred years later the existing noble structure had been built round it. Several of the cloth-making tribe of Webb are buried in the church, and it is natural to link the town's growth in the fifteenth century with the expanding cloth trade. The largest accessible deposits of fuller's earth are found in this vicinity, and indeed the name probably refers to its characteristically sticky cloggy soil. The Tolzey Hall is dated 1695, and there are a number of good houses and inns of the eighteenth and nineteenth centuries. The long main street is less spectacularly picturesque than those of Burford and Campden, and has therefore not caught the imagination of tourists, but it displays an almost stately charm, and the wondrous harmony of Cotswold stone as much as any.

M4 makes a minimal impact on the Cotswold landscape. It enters the region about Leigh Delamere service station, and leaves it after ten featureless miles at Dodington. It is the only motorway at present crossing the Cotswolds, and fortunately no other is in contemplation.

10

Mansions and Churches since 1660

The Cotswold style developed in the mansions of the gentry and the houses of the merchant princes in the sixteenth and seventeenth centuries had been a variant of the building fashions of Tudor and Jacobean England, and this 'vernacular' continued long in use for cottages, farmsteads and small public buildings after the rich had followed the fashion into the classical proportions and decorative devices introduced from Italy by Inigo Jones and his contemporaries. These made their first appearance in the Cotswolds at Badminton.

Badminton House was begun by the first duke of Beaufort within a few years of the Restoration. The first stage, whose architect is unknown, is best represented (in spite of many additions) by the north front, and by the hall and adjoining rooms by which the public enters. The dimensions of this hall are those of the Badminton court, for the game was first played here. To this stage also belongs the three-mile vista, one of twelve spectacular radiating avenues laid out at the same time. Another of the avenues, not now visible from the house, but extending five miles into the next parish, is still popular with riders, but most of the avenues were destroyed by William Kent about 1746, just as they were approaching maturity, when the third duke employed Kent to enlarge and embellish his mansion, and give a more fashionable aspect to the park. Kent built the monumental gateway at the end of the three-mile vista, the main entrance on the Bath road (A433). This is Worcester Lodge, probably the most magnificent summer-house in England, with a Palladian dining-room above the gateway containing a beautiful plaster ceiling representing the Seasons; the whole is crowned with a saucer-dome, and flanked by smaller ornamental gates with a gazebo beyond each.

The descendants of the cautious and politic first duke remained Jacobites at heart, but did not meddle in such dangerous politics. They made Badminton their chief interest, adorning and enlarging the house, and hunting their chief occupation. Perhaps hunting was in the blood, for the dukes of Beaufort are descended from John of Gaunt, and the medieval kings of England were nearly all passionate hunters.

About six thousand people sat at the first duke's table in an average year, of whom in 1705, 1,451 were the duke's guests, and the vast quantity of game they consumed nearly all came from his estates. There was venison from June to January, duck, quails, partridges, hares, rabbits in the autumn and winter, larks in October and thrushes for three weeks in November. The third duke was a friend of Beau Nash, whom he tried (unsuccessfully) to infect with his own passion for hunting. Stag-hunting, coursing and hawking were his favourites, and those of most Cotswold men. The fifth duke is said to have introduced fox-hunting to the county, having enjoyed a magnificent run in Oxfordshire when the stag-hounds were set to draw for a fox at the end of an unsuccessful day. In 1770 he took over this Oxfordshire country, then known as the Old Berkeley, which embraces virtually the whole of the Oxfordshire Cotswolds, and hired the earl of Shrewsbury's magnificent house at Heythrop, whither he moved his household and his hounds each year for part of the season. This hunt is now called the Heythrop.

The builder of Cirencester Park, Allen, first Earl Bathurst, was a man of a very different origin from the second duke, whose contemporary he was. His father was Sir Benjamin Bathurst, of a family of Kentish woolmen. He was the only one of seven brothers to survive the Civil War. Having made his fortune in the East India Company, and served as Treasurer to the Princess Anne, in 1695 he bought a large estate, the centre of which was Oakley Grove near Cirencester. The son, another staunch Tory, began to build a new mansion in 1714, and is thought to have designed it himself. The most distinctive feature of his design is the great yew hedge encircling a grassy court in front of the house, an idea ultimately derived from Bernini's Piazza, transformed by the conventions of an English garden. He was a man of literary tastes, and was interested in garden design; he possessed also a wide knowledge of trees and a keen business sense. Unable to play a political part during the Whig ascendancy, he made his estates the business of his life, and instead of calling in a professional designer, laid out the park himself, with some help from his literary friends, notably Alexander Pope. His park was to be not the usual grassland sprinkled with isolated trees, avenues and patches of woodland but a forest, intersected with formal radiating avenues, a grand vista, glades and bowers. The woodland screened by these formal or semi-formal effects was destined to produce profitable crops of timber. Pope himself seems to have invested £1,500 in the enterprise, and the earl, writing in 1730 to urge his return, promises him 'three or four million plants out of my nursery to amuse yourself with'. Around the Horse Guards, the centre of radiating avenues each with a stone sentry box, yew, cherry and box mingle with forest trees in beautiful profusion; there are many splendid beeches, and avenues of elm and horse chestnut. Among the other buildings they devised, Alfred's Hall is the first castellated folly in England (now sadly dilapidated), Pope's seat a more conventional little rusticated pavilion. This glorious park extends seven miles to the edge of Sapperton village, and the whole has long been open to pedestrians. The second earl introduced the kennels into the park. He hunted with his own pack, as well as his own country, that country pertaining to the Vale of the White Horse, and part of the Cotswold country as well.

We shall find a member of the Whig ascendancy in the extreme south of the Cotswolds. William Blathwayt was a civil servant who helped to pave the way for William of Orange, and was his Secretary of State. He married the heiress of Dyrham, an Elizabethan manor house lying in a wooded cup below the scarp not far from Bath. In 1692 he began to refashion this house, employing a Frenchman, Samuel Hauderoy, who rebuilt the old hall and added a delightful two-storey, slightly foreign-looking western range, with a fine view into the Severn Vale across the canals and cascades of a Dutch garden. After 1698 the building was in the hands of William Talman, an adjutant of Wren's, who added the imposing eastern range facing the wooded slopes of the deer park. The house is built of Box Ground stone by masons from Corsham. Dyrham and its contents was bought from Blathwayt's descendants in 1957 by the National Trust and it is regularly open.

Barnsley Park in the central Cotswolds is a more beautiful house than any of the three already mentioned, but unhappily is not open to the public. It is built in the baroque style introduced by Vanbrugh and Archer, by a little-known architect, using stone from the estate's own quarry. Archer himself was the designer of Heythrop House, begun in 1706; indeed the splendid central block is one of his most important works. His flanking wings unhappily have been several times rebuilt, and his interior gutted by fire. The region can boast of having also, at Blenheim Palace, the most famous example of Vanbrugh's genius, conceived as a national monument and built at the nation's expense for the first duke of Marlborough, and still inhabited by his descendants. The building was in the hands of Nicholas Hawksmoor from Wren's Office of Works, and a notable architect in his own right. The stone came from Taynton and Barrington quarries and has weathered superbly.

Blenheim Palace is one of three notable houses on the eastern skirts of Wychwood Forest. It replaced, though not on the same site, Henry I's hunting lodge of Woodstock. Wychwood was one of the English kings' favourite hunting grounds until the seventeenth century, and every king down to Charles I spent some time at Cornbury Hall, a second lodge built originally by Henry I nearer the heart of the Forest. Here Elizabeth I's favourite, Robert Dudley, Earl of Leicester, died in 1588. According to a manuscript quoted in *Athenae Oxoniensis*, 'the erle, after his gluttonous manner surfeiting himself with much eating and drinking fell so ill that he was forced to stay there. Then the deadly cordial was propounded to him by the Countess.' In the next two reigns it became something of an intellectual centre, visited by Lord Herbert of Cherbury and probably others of the metaphysical poets. After the Restoration Charles II bestowed it on the Earl of Clarendon, who largely rebuilt it, though the south wing of an older rebuilding survives. The building of Cornbury was carried out by succeeding generations of the Strong family, master-masons and owners of Barrington quarry, though some local stone was used by Clarendon's architect, Hugh May. Later the house was a centre of Jacobite intrigue, and it is even believed that Prince Charles Edward visited it incognito in 1750. The park preserves the last remnant of the great Forest, some of it probably virgin woodland, but it is seldom open to the public.

Ditchley House, the third of this distinguished trio, is a masterpiece of James Gibbs. He was commissioned in 1720 by the second earl of Litchfield to replace the old house in which his ancestor, Sir Henry Lee, had often entertained Queen Elizabeth I. The first earl, Edward Lee, was ennobled on his marriage with Charles II's daughter. They were said to be the handsomest couple at court. These noblemen, and a number of their distinguished descendants, have a notable series of monuments in Spelsbury church, itself largely rebuilt in the eighteenth century by the Lees, and altered to make a suitable frame for their monuments.

After the excitements of Vanburgh and Archer's Baroque, Ditchley House is a restrained and beautifully composed pile, with flanking service wings linked by a quadrant arcade. The interior decoration is mainly the work of William Kent and Henry Flitcroft, the stuccoists were Italians, Artari and Serena, brought over by Gibbs himself. Their magnificent saloon has mounted between the pilasters antlers from deer caught in the Forest in hunts got up for the amusement of

James I and his son Henry. The building accounts of Ditchley are preserved in the county archives. The Italians charged £100 for their work and the whole house cost no more than £9,000. It is perhaps the most beautiful in the Cotswolds, apart from those built in the traditional vernacular. It has been well looked after, sensitively restored in the 'thirties, and now cared for by the Ditchley Trust, founded by the last private owner for the promotion of Anglo-American cooperation. Conferences are held there throughout the year, but it is

25. *Ditchley Park.*

open to the public daily during the first fortnight in August. Churchill came frequently during the Second World War, and held a meeting with President Truman there.

One other mansion in the classical tradition must be mentioned. Dodington Park was begun in 1795 for Christopher Bethel Codrington, a nabob from the plantations of the West Indies. The interior is very fine. The architect, James Wyatt, died before the building was completed, in a carriage accident while returning from London with his client. The house lies somewhat low, in a fine park clothing the slopes of the scarp, which was laid out by Capability Brown about 1764 for a previous owner of the estate. It is open throughout the spring and summer, and there are a number of fairground attractions in the park.

Romantic ideas took early hold among the Cotswold gentry. Adlestrop Park is the work of Sanderson Miller of Radway a (highly successful amateur architect and the builder of Edgehill Tower) in his own pioneer version of the Gothick, carried out between 1750 and 1762. The north-west front survives from the previous house, a monastic barn converted between 1690 and 1700. The village has some charming eighteenth-century cottages, a Regency *cottage-orné*, a 'Tudor' school-room and a handsome rectory seen against a background of splendid cedars. It has two literary associations. Jane Austen stayed with her uncle Leigh at the rectory, now Adlestrop House, and Edward Thomas's most famous poem was inspired by an unscheduled stop at the station:

Yes. I remember Adlestrop –
The name because one afternoon
Of heat the express-train drew up there
Unwontedly. It was late June.

The steam hissed. Someone cleared his throat.
No one left and no one came
On the bare platform. What I saw
Was Adlestrop – only the name.

And willows, willow-herb, and grass,
And meadowsweet, and haycocks dry,
No whit less still and lonely fair

Than the high cloudlets in the sky.
And for that minute a blackbird sang
Close by, and round him, mistier,
Farther and farther, all the birds
Of Oxfordshire and Gloucestershire.

Less than two miles away, Daylesford House was designed by Samuel Pepys Cockerell for Warren Hastings in 1787. Cockerell was architect to the East India Company, and he added to a conventional design with a doric portico, a dome which must have been intended to remind them both of Indian Muslim architecture. The house also contains a sculptured marble fireplace depicting a Hindu sacrifice. This mixture of classical and eastern inspiration did not deter the architect and his client from adding a Gothick conservatory. Perhaps it was to reproduce as nearly as possible Indian colouring that the brown Hornton stone was chosen. Samuel Cockerell's brother Charles, who had made a fortune in the service of the Company, settled a few miles off at Sezincote. For him Samuel designed a far more exotic and picturesque composition of Indian–Muslim inspiration, though with a classical interior. The stone is said to have been artificially coloured. Thomas Daniell, the topographical artist, designed the garden and various ornamental buildings in the park. This house preceded the Pavilion at Brighton and is a happier example of the English genius for assimilating and domesticating alien ideas. Unhappily none of these three houses is normally open to the public.

Victorian styles executed in Cotswold stone blend marvellously with more traditional buildings, but the Victorian age added few notable houses to the Cotswold scene. In 1863 R. S. Holford commissioned Lewis Vulliamy to build him a mansion at Westonbirt. The chosen model was Wollaton Hall, a palatial Elizabethan mansion on the outskirts of Nottingham. Vulliamy's design produced an admirable pile, as grand as Wollaton, but blending more harmoniously with its surroundings. It is built of Box Ground stone with dressings of yellow Ham stone (the Somersetshire oolite). Holford was passionately interested in gardens and arboriculture; there are the most beautiful Italian gardens attached to the house, and lawns and groves planted with a great variety of splendid trees. The house is now an expensive girls' school, and only open two or three times a year, the gardens once a week in summer. To most visitors, however, Westonbirt will mean Wolford's Arboretum on the other side of A433, owned and much enlarged by the Forestry Commission. It covers 160 acres, and contains almost every tree which can be made to grow in the somewhat chilly climate of the Cotswolds, over 5,000 species, some of them very rare. Most of these, planted in or soon after Holford's time, have reached a splendid maturity, and the Forestry Commission is continually replanting and adding to the interest of the more recently added woodland. The Arboretum is open all the year round and is at its best in spring and autumn.

The classical style was little used for Cotswold churches. Jacobean pulpits and sanctuary rails are not uncommon, but for repairs and restorations to the fabric an attempt was generally made to preserve the ancient character of the building. Painswick's attractive spire, for example, which perfectly harmonizes with the rest, was built as late as 1632; the tower of Deddington was rebuilt, equally harmoniously between 1634 and 1689, that of Bishop's Cleeve in 1707–9. When fire destroyed the medieval church at Tetbury, the tower was still sound enough to preserve, and to this the architect, Francis Hiorn of Warwick, added (c. 1780) a fine light gothic church (as the style was then understood) with very tall, slender, clustered columns of wood about an iron shaft to support the roof, tall windows and galleries and pews with gothic panelling, lit on winter evenings by two magnificent brass candelabra. Even those who are not confirmed church-crawlers will find this one worth a visit. At Bourton-on-the-Water a beautiful fourteenth-century chancel was preserved in

1784 when a nave and domed tower in the masterly and sympathetic style initiated by Wren replaced a Norman church on Saxon foundations. The nave of this church was torn down about 1870 in a burst of high Gothic–Revival enthusiasm, and rebuilt by Sir Thomas Jackson.

26. *St Kenelm's, Sapperton.*

St Kenelm's at Sapperton offers a mixture of styles. It is an attractive church in a wonderful setting, largely rebuilt in the time of Queen Anne within the medieval shell. It contains many classical features and a remarkable monument to Sir Robert Atkyns, author of *The Ancient and Present State of Gloucestershire,* the earliest history of the county. In the churchyard is one of the best collections of brass inscription-plates from 1697 onwards, including excellent modern examples (Ernest Gimson, 1919, and the Barnsley brothers, 1926). These brass plates are a distinctive feature of Cotswold graveyards, for the oolitic freestone was found to lend itself marvellously to decorative sculptured headstones and table-tombs but to be too soft for deeply incised and enduring lettering. Delightfully sculpted headstones are common all over the Wolds, but the table-tombs and monuments in Painswick churchyard are altogether outstanding, the work of local masons in the many nearby quarries. Another notable group is to be found

27. *Tombstones in Painswick churchyard.*

in the quarry district around Burford. This neighbourhood has a highly individual style known as the bolster type and it is touching to find one as far afield as Fairford inscribed to the memory of Valentine Strong, the great master-mason of Taynton.

Some churches were so badly neglected in the eighteenth century that restoration became a very costly matter. The people of Banbury allowed their splendid medieval church, said to have been equal in beauty with those of Adderbury and Bloxham, to become so ruinous that it was cheaper to pull it down and rebuild, which they shamelessly did. The new church was given a very fine classical exterior of glowing Hornton stone by S. P. Cockerell but the interior is bare and characterless. Two churches in the region were rebuilt to suit the taste and convenience of the local grandee. The exterior is uninspiring in both cases, but at Dodington an admirable coffered dome is supported internally on fluted Doric pillars and the sanctuary pavement is of Sienna marble. At Badminton the fifth duke pulled down the old church and built another linked with and harmonizing with the house. Within is a shrine of ducal magnificence. The font, chancel rails and pavement are of beautiful and varied Italian marbles, some of those brought back from his Grand Tour by the third duke, which had lain unused for the previous fifty years. There are outstanding monuments to the first duke by Grinling Gibbons, and to the second, third and fourth dukes by Ruysbrack. It is treated almost as a private chapel by the Beaufort family; humbler parishioners' memorials are banished to the porch, and the church is normally open, apart from Sunday services, only with the house, once a week in summer.

The cottages of Badminton village are admirable examples of the paternal regard very commonly felt for their humbler tenants by rural landlords in the nineteenth century. The squire would give the site and be the largest single contributor to the building of a village school, and head the subscription list opened for the restoration of the medieval church, or the building of a new one in some hamlet whose people had hitherto had only a non-conformist place of worship. The nonconformists had always been very active in the clothing districts, and there are fine eighteenth-century congregational chapels in Stroud and Rodborough, and many less distinguished examples in the hamlets round about. The south Cotswolds, therefore, can show a large number of new Victorian churches; those of Whiteshill, Selsley, Woodmancote near Dursley and Slad may be mentioned. Holy Trinity at Stroud (1838) is one of those financed by the Government's million-pound church-building fund opened in 1820. St Martin's, Horsley, is an interesting example of T. Rickman's work.

The principal architects of the Gothic Revival are all represented in the Cotswolds: William Butterfield at Poulton; Sir George Gilbert Scott notably at Leafield in Oxfordshire, and at Cirencester (Watermoor), as well as in restorations of several important churches; Clutton and Burges at Hatherop; G. E. Street at Whelford and Milton-under-Wychwood; J. L. Pearson at Stinchcombe Freeland and Daylesford; C. F. Bodley at Bussage and Selsley, where there are also some fine windows from William Morris's workshops, and at Filkins; S. S. Teulon at Woodchester, Nympsfield and Uley. Hillsley, Lower Cam and the restorations of Bisley, Ozleworth and Miserden have a certain interest as the work of three clerical amateurs.

Pugin is represented by the Dominican Priory at Woodchester, though his designs for the church were carried out, against his wishes and with modifications, by Charles Hansom. (The priory is now closed, but the church is still in use as a parish church.) One other ecclesiastical building, like Woodchester the product of the Roman Catholic 'second spring', must be mentioned: this is the new Benedictine abbey at Prinknash. The community was established soon after 1928, when the Benedictines of Caldey were given this ancient manor house sheltering beneath the high scarp between Birdlip and Painswick beacon. This beautiful and interesting house was built as a grange and hunting lodge by the abbots of Gloucester. Later it belonged to the lords Chandos of Sudeley, and Prince Rupert occupied it in 1643. When the monks first arrived, plans were made for a neo-gothic abbey church and cloister on the medieval pattern. The Second World War put an end to this grandiose project, and after long delay a new building, modern both in appearance and methods of construction, was opened in 1972 with a temporary church in the crypt. Faced with yellow Guiting stone, from the estate, it juts out boldly from the scarp, a building fully worthy of its magnificent setting. 'On a glorious but impracticable hill, in the midst of a little forest of beech, and commanding Elysium' are the words used by Horace Walpole to describe the site. The design is by F. G. Broadbent, and the beautiful glass in the crypt church, as well as most of the fittings, were made by the monks, who support themselves chiefly by the produce of the estate, and the output of their highly successful pottery.

11

'A truly noble manufacture'; the South Cotswold Scene

Samuel Rudder wrote in his history of Gloucestershire (published 1712) that the clothing industry was so all important in the county 'that no other deserves a mention'. For over three hundred years the valleys of the south Cotswolds echoed from before dawn long into the night with the clatter of the shuttles. A strike brought a shocking silence. 'The shuttles were laid in the silent grave' and 'the resurrection of the shuttles' were phrases which came to the pen of William Playne, member of an outstanding clothing family, when writing his history of Minchinhampton and Avening. The Stroudwater Hills and the deep valleys indenting the scarp to the south of them present us with the landscape of domestic industry, and the scene of many a triumph and tragedy for ordinary Cotswold folk. No study of the region would be complete without this story.

In the eighteenth century much cloth was still exported to Europe, including Russia, but the enterprise of the West of England was directed more towards the home market, towards the Levant, the East India Company's trade with India and China, and towards the growing colonies of the New World. Country squires all over England would wear a coat of Uley Blue to church on Sundays, and ride to hounds on Monday in Stroudwater Scarlet; their soldier-sons wore the same Scarlet on the battlefields of Europe, India and the New World at the head of troops dressed in the coarser cloths dyed in the same beautiful colours. These much-felted materials were virtually waterproof, and a caped coat of heavy broadcloth dyed in one of the sober duns and olives so long produced in the district gave adequate protection to mail coachmen and carriers on their long exposed journeys. The dun-coloured coats said to have been worn by Parliamentarian soldiers still hanging in the hall at Broughton Castle no doubt came from the same source. The Red Maids of Bristol wore Stroudwater scarlet, and coarse cloth was bought in bulk to clothe charity children in Red Coat, Blue Coat schools up and down the country. The polite world bought superfines (fine broadcloth) and cassimeres (twills); the lightest materials were woven for the Turkey trade. It is estimated that early in the century from two to three million fleeces were woven into cloth on Stroudwater alone. Wool from all over England poured into the markets of Cirencester and Tetbury; the luxury goods were made of Spanish wool bought direct from London dealers.

The clothiers constantly sought to improve their methods and to offer new lines to please the world of fashion. Francis Yerbury of Bradford, grandson of the Royalist clothier, introduced the technique of twill-weaving, which he learnt from the silk weavers of Spitalfields while studying for the Bar in London. Onesiphorus Paul of Southfield Mill, Woodchester, invented the knapping engine and various other technical improvements in dyeing and finishing. In the latter part of the century, carding and scribbling were to some extent mechanized, and the great inventions of the cotton industry began to be introduced in Gloucestershire. It was a Stroudwater clothier, Joseph Lewis of Brimscombe, who began the development of the shearing machine. This was patented by Price of Stroud in 1815. Although so much of their equipment was in the pioneer stage, modern manufacturers testify to the excellence of their cloth, and the beauty of the colours they produced with very limited resources, as shown in the surviving pattern books in the possession of some old-established firms. A length of Stroudwater Scarlet hangs in the vestry of Avening church together with other relics. Much must have been owing to the traditional skill of their work-force.

Defoe records that 'many of the great families who now pass for gentry in those counties have been originally raised from and built up by this truly noble manufacture'. This continued. It was possible for a shrewd and enterprising clothier to make a great fortune. Francis Yerbury could afford in 1734 to call in John Wood, then engaged on the creation of fashionable Bath, to make of Belcombe House a perfect specimen of Georgian architecture on a small scale. Westbury House, another of Bradford's Georgian treasures, was remodelled in the same period for a clothier named Phelps. Edward Shepphard of Uley, the largest maker of the famous Blues, created for himself a gentleman's seat when he built Gatcombe House high in the Nailsworth valley (recently purchased by the Queen for Princess Anne and Mark Philips). Onesiphorus Paul of Southfield Mill rose to the baronetcy in 1766 and ambitiously built himself an Italian villa

Map 10 *Navigable rivers, canals and railways.*

up at Rodborough (unhappily burnt down in 1900). The Fort, a folly built as a 'pleasure-house' by George Hawker, a dyer, in 1761 is still a conspicuous landmark in the same parish; part of the buildings of his dye-works are still in use at Dudbridge Garage. Paul Wathen of Gough and Woodchester Mills employed a fashionable architect to turn a fine fourteenth-century house at Lyppiatt, built by the abbots of Gloucester, into a Gothic mansion enclosed in a park. He was a member of the Prince Regent's spendthrift set and soon lost his fortune. By 1800 the head of the family of Halliday, which still owned and worked Fromehall Mill, was a scarlet-coated gentleman who hunted his own pack of hounds.

The intricate system of remote side valleys in the Stroudwater Hills is full of farmsteads built and ornamented with the care and loving detail usually seen only on gentlemen's houses by lesser clothiers, who in many cases engaged in sheep-rearing as a subsiduary enterprise. (The reader is referred to David Verrey's *Cotswold* volume in *The Buildings of England* (Penguin 1970).)

28. *A south Cotswold manor house, Througham Slad.*

One of Gloucestershire's most illustrious sons sprang from the ranks of the gentlemen clothiers. The new baronet, Sir Onesiphorus Paul, the erstwhile inventor and working clothier, excited the derision of the fashionable world when he appeared in Bath ('Sir Onesiphorus Paul and his lady are the finest couple that ever has been seen here since Bath was built'), but his son George Onesiphorus had the education of a gentleman, made the Grand Tour, and took his place as of right in the upper class. After a gay youth he devoted his life to the most harshly treated members of a harsh society, the criminals and the insane. He was among the forerunners who prepared public opinion for the nineteenth-century and all subsequent reforms. Sir Walter Scott dubbed him a wandering knight, which was perhaps a strange title for this austere and diligent character, given to sententious oratory and the minutiae of prison design and discipline, careful custodian of his parish minute-book; but he himself, as an old man, thought he had had as much pleasure in his social work as any of his contemporaries in the hunting field. Southfield Mill has been replaced by a red brick factory, but the gabled stone house behind it where Paul was born in 1746 remains as a more pleasing memorial to a truly great and enlightened gentleman than Northleach Prison, which he designed as a House of Correction for minor offenders, a grim edifice but a palace compared to what it replaced.

The Pauls, Hawkers, Sheppards and their kind could ride out the inevitable fluctuations of trade, but quite short periods of depression often spelt ruin for smaller clothiers, and the majority of enterprises were very small. In the summer of 1768, for example, Daniel Packer of Cap Mill, Painswick, wrote to a business associate: '. . . last Thursday John Harries . . . shot himself through the head; he was deeply in debt for Wooll, and Mr E and I refused to accept his bills in payment thereof.' Packer himself was in difficulties, 'I should be glad to keep on my neighbours if it could be done to pay but common interest' and a little later he turned his weavers off.

The industry was chronically overmanned. A master might employ nine hundred men one year and in another have no difficulty in finding six or seven hundred more. This suited the clothiers, but in the lean years many weavers would be reduced by hunger to stealing, cheating and riot. Hardly ever could they force the piece-rates up. James Wolfe, the hero of Quebec, on duty during the riots of 1758, writes: 'The weavers are so oppressed, so poor, and so wretched that they would hazard a knock on the pate for bread or clothes, and turn soldiers through sheer necessity.'

At all times the earnings of women and children from carding, spinning and winding were an essential element in the weaving family's meagre budget. Joseph White's father, a weaver of Randwick, used to call the child at four in the morning, often to work till nine or ten at night. The boy was one that got away and had a distinguished academic career, but he was permanently deformed by the labours of his childhood. Very few tried to escape to a life of greater comfort and security. When the price of bred fell, they would take frequent days off and work shorter hours; when prices were high, the weaver and his family between them might keep the loom going throughout the twenty-four hours if only the work was available. The liberty to do this they prized above all else when it was threatened by the introduction of loom-shops and factory discipline, so that Timothy Excell, a retired weaver in 1804, thought he remembered a golden age with 'the aged matron carding wool before the door of the rural cottage, the young children handing the fleecy rolls to their parents; while the cheerful song of the healthy damsels uniting with the whirring spindles complete the rural harmony. . . . It was seldom that a weaver appealed to the parish for relief.' But the records tell a somewhat different story.

A popular ballad circulating in the reign of James I expresses the age-long tension between the Yerburys and the Pauls, and the Whites and the Excells who worked for them.

Of all sorts of callings in England there be,
There is none that liveth as gallant as we,
Our trading maintains us as brave as a knight,
We live at our pleasure and take our delight;
We heapeth up riches and treasure great store,
Which we get by griping and grinding the poor.

Chorus And this is the way to fill up our purse,
Although we do get it with many a curse.

In former ages we us'd to give
So that our workfolk like farmers did live;
But now times are altered and we'll make them to know
All we can for to bring them under our bow.
We will make them work hard for sixpence a day
Though a shilling they deserve if they had their just pay.

And this is the way . . .

The capitalist basis of the West of England cloth industry was already breeding its natural corollary – potentially militant workers' organizations. By 1677 the shearmen of Trowbridge were getting that shilling a day, but prices had risen, and some of them struck for a penny more, parading through the streets 'with a fiddler before them', their leader uttering vague threats. The weavers, meanwhile, strove constantly to resist the demand that they should weave at the old rates new materials which had many more threats to the inch, to resist absolute reductions, and the (already illegal) payment in truck, sending petition after petition to the Crown. At last in 1728 a Committee of the Privy Council was set up to investigate. Parliament, chiefly manned by landowners whose interest was to keep the Poor Rate down, and still nervous of political unrest, passed an Act ordering the Justices to fix new wage-scales, but the Privy Council warned the weavers 'not to try to help themselves by unlawful combinations'.

Each trade within the clothing industry appears to have had its own local club, which in the face of a threat to lower wages would organize resistance with the others in a brief combination, Clubs operated at all levels of society in the seventeenth and eighteenth centuries. The Gloucestershire Society has already been referred to and there was a dissident Tory club founded at the Fleece in Cirencester in the years of Jacobite unrest. The workers' clubs were primarily benefit clubs, others had political, others cultural, others purely social objects. They met in inns and commonly had small weekly subscriptions and fines for non-attendance which went towards the cost of an annual dinner, and members paid into a pool for their liquor.

Trouble flared up in a serious recession in 1755, when the weavers' petition declared they were getting no more than fourpence for sixteen hours' work. As a result, the Woollen Cloth Weavers Act was passed, ordering new scales to be fixed but reiterating the prohibition of combinations, and the Justices put forward a new scale with which the weavers declared themselves satisfied. (Clothiers were forbidden by an amendment of 1604 to take part in the fixing of piece-rates.) Immediately there was a counter-petition, deploying the usual argument that a rise in wages would damage the export trade, and the clothiers meanwhile defied the Act.

This was too much for the Stroudwater weavers, who came out on a strike which after six weeks forced the employers to the table in Stroud, in a building surrounded by a mob. When the clothiers attempted to escape through a window, they were dragged back by the coat-tails by the weavers' team, and were forced to agree to the new rates; but the Justices subsequently went back on their new scale, at the same time tightening up the penalties for disorder. That same year a Bradford weaver was hanged for taking part in a riot.

From this time forward the government was deaf to the weavers' petitions, and their spasmodic efforts in their own defence became more violent in Wiltshire. In 1787, for example, 'some 1500 or more weavers from Bradford and Trowbridge, *having compelled their masters to acquiesce in certain regulations* . . . marched in triumph from Trowbridge to Bradford, but were repelled at the entrance to the latter [on A363] by the principal inhabitants'. They then went round another way. 'At Belcombe Brook [on the unclassified road from Bradford to Turleigh] . . . Mr Yerbury had planted two Patereroes at his windows which swept the lawns. Supported by many armed friends he addressed the rioters in so able a manner as to induce them to retire. The military arrived next day and the combination was at an end.' That same year Joshua Clarke of Banbury wrote to a Bradford clothier, 'I wish I could meet with a situation in your part of the country . . . I could make shags full 20 per cent cheaper there than at Banbury.'

In Gloucestershire, where the numbers involved were greater, they began to organize. The Gloucestershire Unions (for such by the end of the century they might be called) began to put pressure on blacklegs. In 1791 a body of eighty weavers gathered at Horsley to compel a weaver who had accepted work at too low a price to return his chain to the clothier, threatening to take the roof (clearly a thatched one) off his brother's house when he took refuge there. It became a common practise to mount the offending weaver on the beam of his own loom and tip him into the nearest water. There was no standard rate, payments being subject to differing deductions and conditions from mill to mill, but the weavers had learnt that solidarity was their only strength, and knew a scab when they saw one.

In 1791 came the first riots directed against machinery. Five hundred people assembled outside Westbury House in Bradford because the owner, Phelps, had converted a carding engine (which had been accepted) into a scribbling machine which was a new device. When he refused to hand over the apparatus, or to promise not to use it, a volley of stones broke most of his windows. He had been expecting trouble and had gathered supporters who at this opened fire, killing a man, woman and boy among the rioters. After this, however, he surrendered the machine, which was burnt in triumph on Bradford bridge.

It is not clear why resistance to the machinery was so violent in Wiltshire. Mr Jones of Staverton, a few miles up the Avon, thought that his men regarded all machines as their enemies. The splendid mill by the bridge at Malmesbury (now used as a store) was built that same year by another Bradford clothier in the hope that there, where cloth-making had virtually died out, he would be able to introduce the flying shuttle without trouble. In Gloucestershire, on the other hand, even the spread of the jenny in the closing decades of the century, which foreshadowed a rapid end to cottage spinning, was calmly accepted. 'It is pretty generally understood,' wrote a clothier in 1802, 'that we have had the market of the world in our hands since the French Revolution.' In those boom years which preceded the Peace of Amiens, weavers and their masters could agree on the need for a better supply of yarn. The flying shuttle or spring loom began to be installed and without opposition. It meant that the weavers who had always been paid by the piece could produce more, and with only a child assistant, so that the proceeds did not have to be shared with a partner, yet there was plenty of work for the extra weavers thus released on to the labour market. The only hint of trouble came when Nathaniel Watts of Wallbridge Mill (now demolished) planned to add a large loom-shop to his premises. Factory discipline, not the machines, was the issue.

Throughout these years the mills were being steadily enlarged or rebuilt to accommodate the new machines. Examples are the four-storey Fromehall Mill with its elegant bridge over the Frome or Stroudwater, St Mary Mill at Chalford (which now makes walking sticks) and Woodchester Mill, both dated 1803–4. The larger clothiers already had a few looms on the top floor of the mill, which was provided with a continuous line of windows, and they were beginning to set up loom-shops in the villages and towns adjacent to the valleys. These plain three-storey houses with flimsy three-light windows on every floor may easily be identified in Sheepscombe, Painswick, Wotton-under-Edge and along the Golden Valley. A notable example may be seen at Avoncliff on the river below Bradford – a large L-shaped building now occupied as flats. After a mass meeting in Stroud Watts agreed to sell spring-looms to his weavers for use in the home.

Lewis's invention was bound to make many shearmen redundant, even in times of maximum prosperity. They were traditionally a rough and turbulent lot, heavyweights who could wield giant clippers with twenty-four-inch curved blades for twelve to fourteen hours a day. Their demonstrations against the new machine ranged from crude threats to arson. In 1802 Paul Wathen of Wood chester received this letter:

> Wee Hear in Formed that you got Sheer in mee sheens and if you dont pull them down in a Forght Nights time wee will pull them down for you Wee will you Damd infornold Dog. And before Almighty God we will pull down all the Mills that have Heany Shearing me Shens in. We will cut out Hall your Damd Hearts as Doe keep them and will make the rest Heat them. . . .

The same summer in Wiltshire, John Jones managed to fight off an attack on his new mill at Staverton (now occupied by Nestlés), but another new mill at Littleton a few miles off was burnt to the ground after the nightwatchman had been surprised. In spite of their blackened faces, he thought he recognized a certain Thomas Helliker in the gang (by his rabbit-teeth). No one else was caught, and though Helliker protested his innocence to the last, the young man was hanged at Salisbury Jail. Huge numbers of his fellow workers came to see him die, and afterwards carried his body in procession back to Trowbridge (some thirty miles), where it was buried with full funeral rites by the curate to the indignation of the gentry; the vicar, however, contented himself with a mild reprimand.

This was during the period of terrible distress, which followed the Peace of Amiens. There were frequent attempts to pull down clothiers' houses, and troops were stationed in many of the clothing towns. The Rev. Lloyd Baker of Uley had a bell to summon help which could be heard by the dragoons in Dursley.

The calmer spirits endeavoured to defend themselves by calling for the enforcement of obsolete statutes: the Statute of Apprentices (1563), to prevent demobilized and unemployed soldiers returning to the already greatly overmanned trade of weaver; the statute of Philip and Mary forbidding clothiers to have more than two looms on their premises, against the hated discipline of the loom-shop; and in Wiltshire they desired to reactivate the Jacobean law against gig-mills as the only legal weapon they could find against the dreaded new machines. The workers' clubs of Gloucestershire, Wiltshire and Somerset were now combined in the Woollen Cloth Workers Society with a membership of twelve or thirteen thousand and affiliations in Yorkshire. It was estimated that nine out of ten cloth-workers were enrolled, and according to the heated imagination of one observer, 'from one end of the country to another by pre-concerted arrangements they can act as one man'. Members paid an entrance fee of one shilling and sixpence a week. This enabled the Society to employ a solicitor to look after the funds and manage the legal activities, but would not suffice for the prolonged legal struggle forced on them by the clothiers. In 1809 the obsolete statutes were repealed without any alternative legislation in the workers' favour, and from this time their earnings were steadily depressed.

Relations in the industry were now very bitter. A Dursley weaver who had migrated to Witney remarked on the happier atmosphere among the blankets. Going before a master in Gloucestershire, he said, had always been like going before a judge. Another weaver, giving evidence before a parliamentary committee, told how the reigning Edward Sheppard said to one of them, 'Do all you can against me and I will do the same against you'. Sheppard was the chairman of the clothiers' organization covering the three counties, and this harsh remark undoubtedly reflected their attitude.

The clothiers' determination to pay no more for pieces with a greatly increased number of threads led to giant protest meetings on Selsley Hill and Stinchcombe Hill in 1825. A strike followed which was brought to an end after three weeks when Edward Sheppard agreed to a higher rate, and eventually Stroudwater followed suit. That Sheppard should have done this is a testimony to the weavers' strength. The strike at Wotton-under-Edge was accompanied by rioting in which the troops were called in and several of the rioters were killed and injured.

Meanwhile the terms of trade still gave the clothiers ample incentive to modernize. Dunkirk Mill near Nailsworth is a long four-storey building repeatedly enlarged between 1800 and 1820, when it was driven by the powerful leat which lies stagnant and weed-fringed behind it. It is said to be the mill described in *John Halifax, Gentleman*, a Victorian best-seller by Mrs Craik.

Most of these extensions were made by Peter Playne, who operated the mill in conjunction with Egypt Mill and nearby Inchbrook Mill. The latter was not modernized, and now makes a picturesque dwelling-house; Dunkirk Mill is now occupied by five firms. Peter Playne's brother William operated Longford Mill in the same valley up towards Avening. In 1806 he built the dam 150 yards long to obtain sufficient power for the new machinery, for which he built Lake Mill, seen in the foreground to the right of the dam from A434, a four-storey building with apsidal engine house (steam was introduced about 1820). Before it is the long cloth-drying stove with ruined cowls on the roof. A few yards further we come to the clothier's stately house, opposite which a lane plunges down to the mill yard. The mill is now used by Messrs Strachan of Lodgemore, who absorbed Playne's firm, to make cloth for tennis balls. The offices contain a date stone from an earlier mill inscribed 1705, and a smaller stone building bears the date 1856. On the left are loom- and spinning-sheds built over the original mill pool in 1912, and beyond them the mill stream flows out beside a row of cottages, possibly old industrial buildings. William Playne was a vigorous and successful clothier. He was the first, in 1808, to introduce German wool from Saxony, which largely replaced the Spanish for fine cloth.

The finest building of this period is the great mill at Kings Stanley, begun in 1813 and built of red brick with stone quoins. No wood was used in its construction; the floors are supported on an interior iron frame such as had been pioneered in Derbyshire only a few years before. The cast-iron arcades survive, one of the marvels of the industrial revolution. The handsome New Mill on the Little Avon just below Brushford Bridge on B4058, the centre of the storm at Wotton-under-Edge in 1825, was built about 1820, but shows a much more primitive system: a row of tie-irons on the façade at the level of each floor secures the iron beams which support it. Since 1844 this mill, now owned by Messrs Tubbs and Lewis, has manufactured silk braid and elastic.

By 1830 the cloth industry was approaching a critical period. Ten years before, Edward Sheppard had sounded a warning, observing how rivals had established themselves in Europe under the protection of Napoleon's Continental System. Yorkshire had already captured most of the coarse trade in which lay the greatest opportunities for expansion, and there was a new tax on wool to be contended with. As John Lewis of Brimscombe said: 'My father used to get more profit by one piece of cloth than I can get by twenty.' It soon became evident that only those who had capital enough to operate on a large scale and take the fullest advantage of the new machinery, as well as considerable business flair, would survive. One of these was Samuel Stephens Marling, who combined shrewd business sense with a romantic imagination. He owned the great mill at Ebley, largely built in 1818, a huge silvery stone pile with stone-mullioned windows, to which he added a wing about 1862 at split level (to reduce the risk of fire) with a staircase tower. He lived up on the Edge at Selsley, where he built himself a house, and a church for the growing village. For the church he employed a famous gothic-revival architect, C. F. Bodley, from whom he demanded a tower which should recall the mountain church of Marling in Austria. Bodley also designed the staircase turret at the mill, using the style of a sixteenth-century French chateau.

Between 1820 and 1844, seventy-eight mills ceased production. The failure of Sheppards of Uley was a catastrophic event. Over a thousand people were thrown out of work and had no hope of finding new jobs in the Cotswold valleys. Some went to Yorkshire, some to Canada, some to Australia. By 1840 the trade had altogether left the valley of the Ewelme above Dursley. It is full of ruins, and only the old press house converted into cottages and a few sheds remain of the great Sheppard enterprise. By this time the power-loom had been adapted for woollen cloth. The younger hand-loom weavers overcame perforce their hatred of the factory, where they could earn twice as much as at home, the older men sent their wives and children. Sir William Marling, looking back in 1900, describes the last of the handweavers as they brought their pieces to the loft: 'a middle-aged or elderly man, rather sadfaced (at least looking as though he had never been young) and often quaintly dressed – sometimes a blue frock coat with copper buttons once gilt, or a swallow-tailed one . . . his pathetic figure now lives only in the memory of a few old clothiers like me'. It had ever been the custom among them to wear their best clothes for this journey. A great industry was passing with them.

No cloth is now manufactured in Bradford-on-Avon and its surroundings; what remains of the Wiltshire branch of the clothing industry is concentrated in Trowbridge. Looking downstream from Bradford bridge one sees an early nineteenth-century clothing mill dwarfed by a much more handsome structure built about 1870 and occupied by the Avon Rubber Company. The busy little town centre east of the bridge, with its Victorian shop fronts, must have been a good deal mauled when the turnpike road (A363) was built to alleviate the precipitous descent into the town down Whitehorse Hill. Middle Tory and High Tory are perched one above the other on the steep valley-side – these charming unspoilt terraces are well worth climbing for. At the end of High Tory the little medieval hospice with its chapel (once used as a loom-shop but now restored), is open at certain hours. West of the bridge stands Phelps's Westburg House.

29. *Ebley Mill, the staircase tower designed by C. F. Bodley.*

Two firms now manufacture cloth in the valleys west of the Edge. Messrs Strachan, Winterbottom and Playne have their offices in the early eighteenth-century clothier's house at Lodgemore, and works at Lodgemore, Longford and Cam Mill near Dursley. They make a great variety of cloth of high quality as well as the famous broadcloth, scarlet for the Guards, hunting pink, green for billiard tables and a special variety for casinos; the Vatican has been a customer since the middle of the last century, buying white for the pope's cassocks and coloured for liveries. The great mills at Kings Stanley and Ebley belong to Messrs Marling and Evans. Their response to modern challenges has been rather different. They produce a large variety of woollen materials, some of it for Marks and Spencer, and also research and make highly specialized materials in man-made fibres, for example Nomex, a fireproof material developed for racing drivers and firemen, a fine thread used in cardiac surgery, and a silvery nylon double material used as shuttering for laying concrete under water. Between them the two firms produce about two-thirds as much as was being made on Stroudwater by the fifty or more mills operating there in 1841. Within Kings Stanley Mill, itself an industrial monument, a shearing machine is preserved made on the same principle as Price's original patent, and no visitor can fail to realize that here is the inspiration for the standard lawn mower, which was invented by Edwin Budding of Dursley and first patented by Messrs Ferrabee, millwrights, of Stroud in 1831.

There are five clothing towns in this part of the Cotswolds, Wotton-under-Edge, Dursley, Nailsworth, Stroud and Painswick. Minchinhampton, up on the plateau, naturally never had any mills and contains no other industrial buildings connected with the trade. It is a quiet grey town with an attractive market hall on stone pillars (1698), and much undistinguished traditional building. Minchinhampton Common is a vast expanse of bare turf which shows up the Belgic lines of fortification well. It is grazed with horses, cattle and sheep by the commoners, and provides a pleasant recreation ground for the folk of Stroudwater, being separated from Rodborough Common only by a narrow strip of development. The two are fringed with charming clothing hamlets such as Box, Amberley and Pinfarthing, linked by a scatter of nineteenth- and twentieth-century villas and stone houses in traditional style, interspersed with woodland.

Wotton-under-Edge is the prettiest of the clothing towns. It stands perched on the marlstone terrace beneath the scarp, a lively little local centre with many colour-washed houses mingling with the grey. The fine church contains an organ built by Christopher Shreider in 1726 for St Martin-in-the-Fields, where it was played by Handel, and one striking epitatph to the Rev. John Tattershall who died in 1801 aged fifty:

> . . . As a determined Foe to all Acts of Oppression
> He dared by a reluctant Appeal to the Laws of his Country
> To maintain the Cause of the Poor,
> To vindicate the Rights of Himself and his Successors

And every suit having been decided in his favour
He was applauded for his perseverance
By the Archbishop his venerable Diocesan
With this strong Encomium,
'Sir! You have done your Duty.'
Muse, Reader, on this interesting Character.
Admire the just Inflexibility of his Principles. And if
Thou seekest the Rewards of Virtue in a better Life
Commend his Zeal! Go and do likewise.

At the east end of the north aisle a Purbeck marble tomb chest bears two beautiful brasses of Thomas Lord Berkeley, who died in 1417, and his wife Margaret. The town owes its charter to the Berkeleys, and boasts a grammar school founded in 1385 by Thomas's mother Katherine, widow of the Lord Berkeley who was implicated in the murder of Edward II; the school building in Gloucester Street bears the date 1726. A more attractive building of the same period is the Blue Coat School in Culverhay, and in Bear Street is another school with interesting associations. This is the British School, a nonconformist foundation of 1843, in which Isaac Pitman is said to have taught shorthand as a voluntary subject. He evolved his famous system at his home in Orchard Street. Edward Jenner (1749–1823), the discoverer of vaccination, was a native of Wotton. He lived and practised as a doctor in nearby Berkeley.

Dursley is less than five miles from Wotton, but cut off by the promontory of Stinchcombe Hill, which from midday onwards casts its shadow over the town. It is a bustling small industrial centre, thanks chiefly to its great engineering works. Though framed by glorious beech woods, its attractions are marred by unsightly development in the High Street and by an extensive red-brick suburb linking it with the village of Cam. There is a charming market house built in 1738, rough-cast and white-washed, on stone columns, with stone quoins and stone-tiled hipped roof, having a statue of Queen Anne facing the market-place which crowds upon a church less distinguished than most Cotswold town churches. There are one or two good clothiers' houses.

Nailsworth lies deep within the southernmost of the Stroudwater valleys. Here is another rather undistinguished little town which nevertheless has a characteristically romantic situation and a number of attractive buildings, notably the Quakers Meeting House on Chestnut Hill and several clothiers' houses on the steep valley-sides. Two streams unite here, one coming down from Cherington to Avening through a secret valley, and thence by Longford Mill; the other, which rises up at Kingscote, reaches Nailsworth through a gorge along which are many old mill buildings, one of which is used by the South Midland Fish Hatchery, with a series of ponds. Above this the road makes a spectacular climb to the important weaving village of Horsley.

The towns of Stroudwater once figured in a local rhyme as

Mincing Hampton,
Painswick Proud,
Beggarly Bisley,
Strutting Stroud.

There can have been nothing beggarly about Bisley in the thirteenth century, the centre of a district in which Stroud was merely a chapelry. The church attained its present size in the fourteenth century, and unlike most large Cotswold churches received relatively little embellishment in the fifteenth – perhaps the rot had already set in. Built over a well in the churchyard is a little lantern-like structure, a thirteenth-century poor souls light, the only outdoor specimen in England. It is said to commemorate a priest who, hurrying out at night to a dying parishioner, fell into the well and was drowned. The Kebles of Tractarian fame were patrons of the living, and Thomas Keble was succeeded by his son, another Thomas, as rector here.

In spite of its presumed decline, this quiet, charming village has a high street which suggests a certain importance, with several old inns. The Bear Inn is the old Court House, and in George Street there is a pretty lock-up with two cells, dated 1824; at Jayne's Court, south-west of the church, an octagonal dove-cot contains a cock-pit. The Kebles restored the town wells, and five gabled water-shuts deliver a plentiful supply of pure water into two great stone troughs in a corner at the bottom of the village shaded by the magnificent sycamores of the Mansion, an early eighteenth-century manor house. Wesley preached at Bisley and lodged in a house in the steep lane leading to the church.

The rise of Strutting Stroud originated in that older industrial revolution brought about by the introduction of fulling mills. Its growth at the expense of Bisley and Minchinhampton no doubt earned it the disagreeable epithet. Since the seventeenth century it has been the industrial centre of the district, progressively modernized. It has a few good Victorian and twentieth-century churches and other buildings, but little now remains of the grace which it must once have had. Victorian additions to the Tudow town hall have produced an attractive pile, which is still flanked by a Georgian terrace. Opposite is a pretty cast-iron arcade. These with the parish church (rebuilt in 1866–8 apart from the fourteenth-century tower) form an agreeable group. The admirable

30. *Painswick street-scene.*

classical Subscription Rooms (1833) and adjacent Congregational Chapel (1837) aptly symbolize the traditional twin pillars of a rising industrial prosperity – nonconformist ethics and a rich middle class. Some pleasant villas built by the latter scattered about the town have been submerged in a tide of intrusive red brick. A much-needed by-pass is in contemplation.

Painswick is one of the brightest jewels in the Cotswold crown. This lovely town, built of the pale silvery local oolite with an efflorescence of attractive detail rare even in the Cotswolds, is perched upon a spur of the upper lias between two deep valleys. Except in the high tourist season it is a quiet place; its historic reason for existence vanished when the mills ceased production before the nineteenth century was well begun. There is no record of it as a town before the fourteenth century and though there is a small market-place the proximity of Stroud must since the seventeenth century have precluded it from gaining any importance as a rural centre. In the nineteenth century, accordingly, it was preserved by poverty from unsightly intrusions; the inhabitants were used to declare, indeed, that they were too poor to live and too healthy to die! Now it is well looked after by the inhabitants themselves with the cooperation of the county planning committee. As an art-centre Painswick has for long rivalled Chipping Campden, and now with its Guild of Gloucestershire Craftsmen, who put on an annual exhibition, has overtaken the north Cotswold town. Painswick's most famous feature is the large churchyard with its ninety-nine clipped yews and remarkable tomb stones, but every street can show some fine houses and pretty cottages, making up a magical whole. The annual ceremony of 'clipping' the churchyard may well commemorate the cooperative duty of caring for it undertaken by the inhabitants long before the present yews were planted in 1792.

The decline of the clothing industry in the south Cotswolds has been attributed to many causes. Perhaps the most plausible concerns the supply of water. Here Yorkshire had a tremendous advantage. The Cotswold streams are not large, nor even very swift. There was enough water, with the aid of a mill-dam, to provide what was needed for all the scouring and washing, and for driving a few pairs of fulling stocks and a gig-mill every fifty yards or so, as they did in many valleys in the eighteenth century, but not enough to drive the larger and more diverse machinery of the early nineteenth century, even with the aid of steam-driven pumps, the principal use for which the early steam engines could be employed. Dunkirk Mill's big leat was Playne's response to this difficulty. In an atmosphere of *laissez-faire* and cut-throat competition very little in the way of cooperation to conserve water could be achieved. Mills were paralysed for days on end by shortages created as often by a neighbour's wilful or improvident action as by drought or frost. The clothier then faced bankruptcy, and his workers drowned their sorrows in the alehouses, often to be told that it was their intemperance that was bringing the industry to ruin! As at Sheepscombe and Longford, it was the big enterprise at the head of the valley which was likely to survive the longest. By the time they could dispense with water-power, only the big manufacturers of fine cloth were still in business.

12

Country Life, 1600–1900

Although the fortunes which built the finest of the great Cotswold houses were usually made elsewhere, the cost of many smaller mansions rebuilt, altered and enlarged all over the region in the Georgian era came mainly from the land.

Cotswold landowners and farmers have always been an enterprising breed. Sainfoin was introduced here early in the sixteenth century as a fodder crop. The system of irrigation designed to produce an earlier growth of meadow grass, invented in Hampshire early in the seventeenth century, was soon established in the Windrush valley where the operation of these water-meadows may still be seen; around Burford the flat fields bordering the stream are saturated artificially in March. It was in the neighbourhood of Winchcombe, Cheltenham and Tewkesbury that an attempt was made, early in the seventeenth century, to grow tobacco on a commercial scale. No serious difficulty was experienced in raising the crop, but the enterprise met with bitter hostility and was suppressed by the government for the benefit of the colonial plantations. In 1667, after repeated prohibitions had had no effect, a company of dragoons was sent to destroy and burn the crop. Tobacco had meanwhile become popular with cottagers and smallholders, who probably continued to grow it for their own use, for it is recorded that in the early eighteenth century mothers filled their children's little pipes to smoke at school in place of breakfast, and men and women were said to fall asleep at night with their pipes still in their mouths.

When the eighteenth century began, sheep-farming was still the predominant enterprise on the wolds, and fodder crops played an important part on the open arable fields of each village. Some of these fields, moreover, had already been enclosed to provide for an enlarged sheep flock in pastures improved by reseeding and manure. The Commission appointed in 1517 to enquire into agrarian distress had found that in Gloucestershire 3,843 acres, mostly in the Cotswolds, had recently been enclosed. The process continued, in spite of hardship and even depopulation in rural communities. The village of Sezincote was a fairly early casualty, for by 1638 the church was in ruins; at Stowell the church became a mere appendage of a great Jacobean house, later the seat of Lord Chedworth, the village a few mounds in the park. The first Earl Bathurst began the enclosure of land round Cirencester:

> Let rising granaries and temples here,
> There mingled farms and pyramids appear . . .
> Enclose whole downs in walls. . . .

Until the middle of the eighteenth century these drastic changes were generally carried out by agreement between landlords and their principal tenants, probably achieved with much patience, and confirmed by private Act of Parliament; they seem in most cases to have concerned the arable fields only, leaving all or most of the commons intact. A few of these indeed remained open into the twentieth century, notably Lower Swell's Cow Common, which features as one of the most important sites in O. G. S. Crawford's *Long Barrows of the Cotswolds*; it used to be a most numinous place, but is now ploughed up. Several commons on the Edge, too high and exposed or too steep for tillage, remain open to this day. At Bisley a proposed enclosure was successfully resisted in 1733 by the many hand-loom weavers living in hamlets on the fringes of the waste who kept a horse or donkey to carry the heavy 'chain' of yarn or length of finished cloth to and from the mill. (These south Cotswold commons were enclosed about a hundred years later, and when Lord Donington, who had been concerned in the business, stood for parliament, crowds ran beside his carriage shouting, 'Who stole the donkey's dinner!') After about 1760 the pace accelerated, so that by 1800 most parishes had undergone a transformation so considerable that the landscape we see today is largely a creation of those years.

The large post-enclosure holdings were often provided with a new farmhouse as well as more extensive farm buildings in the villages themselves, but as a result of the consolidation of the previously scattered strips in the open fields into compact farms, in some cases at a distance from the centre, new farmsteads were also planted in the remoter parts of the parish. Groups of solid buildings by some convenient spring, with a wind-break of fine beech trees, now make many an agreeable oasis in the austere uplands. In 1800 the wolds were bleaker by far, for enclosure had produced a network of dry-stone walls, and new plantations such as Lord Chedworth's great wall of beech at Stowell, now a landmark for miles around, were in ungainly infancy. Many landowners, in fact, had not yet begun to plant. Stow, which is now approached through a beautiful hanger of beech, was then said to lack both wood and water.

The great wool-markets of Campden, Cirencester and Tetbury, which were the admiration of seventeenth-century travellers, were meanwhile dying. In Ogilby's road-book, published in 1675, Campden is described as a town famous

31. *Izod's Barn, Broad Campden, 1916 (woodcut by F. L. Griggs).*

for stockings, and thirty years later an attempt was made to introduce frame-knitting at Cirencester; already much Cotswold wool was only fitted for worsted stockings, having been coarsened by rich feeding in enclosed pastures. By 1800 the local sheep had been changed, partly by cross-breeding, from the bearer of a golden fleece into the 'Cotswold Lion', a large, coarse-wooled animal grown for the table, but a very profitable beast in the days when one gentleman inviting another to take pot-luck would invite him to 'take his mutton with him'. Before enclosure, sheep and cattle, the latter extensively reared on the Forest marble and the Lias on the south-eastern flank of the wolds southwards of Tetbury, Cirencester and Northleach, required fattening for the meat market by a lowland grazier; on enclosed farms it was possible to carry a larger head of both and finish them, indeed Cotswold sheep came to rank first in Smithfield market.

The Cotswolds were already accounted arable country before the great enclosures, though fodder crops dominated the courses of husbandry; the Wolds were not reckoned to be good wheat land, but Cotswold barley (grown partly for feed) already had a reputation. After enclosure, the acreage of both, especially barley, increased, and breweries appeared in Burford, Cirencester, Stroud, Deddington and Banbury. The red land about Banbury, indeed, was regarded as one of England's main granaries.

The Cherwell valley produced the then famous Banbury cheese, a thin white cheese of creamy texture and pronounced flavour. The renowned Double Gloucester cheese is now associated only with the Severn Vale, where it is still made, but in the eighteenth century the south-eastern flank of the Cotswolds produced a great quantity of cheese for the London market which also went by the names of Double and Single Gloucester according to the thickness of the cheese. There was also a longer-matured Loaf of the dimensions and perhaps the character of Cheddar. At that time, apparently, the cheese of Gloucestershire, Warwickshire, Wiltshire and Somerset was sold under the name of Gloucester, much as the name Cheddar is used generically today.

Gloucesters and Herefords were the popular breeds of cattle, but longhorns were being introduced to improve the milk supply. Apart from domestic consumption of milk and butter, all was devoted to cheese-making, and two pigs for every cow were kept to consume the whey. These were usually Gloucester Old Spot, a breed not esteemed for its meat, which was intended only for consumption on the farm. The diet of the poor consisted of bacon, cheese and cabbage. Plough horses, Longhorns, Gloucesters and Old Spots may be seen at the Cotswold Farm Park. The farmers of Bemborough have created on some unprofitable acres pitted by slate-quarrying a zoo of obsolete farm animals. Sadly, the genuine Cotswold Lion is still absent, but primitive breeds such as the Soay and Herdwick sheep represent the kind of sheep shorn by Iron Age farmers on the wolds. The owners are attempting to produce a 'Neolithic' pig by crossing an Old Spot sow with a wild boar.

Readers may have been surprised to find the squire of Maugersbury complaining of the loss of plough-*horses* in the Civil War. Horses were the traditional plough-beasts on the wolds, sturdy all-purpose animals of moderate size, which may well have been descended from the wild horses of prehistoric times. In 1790, go-ahead farmers were introducing oxen, with much approval from agricultural experts, and by 1809 they were thoroughly established on Cotswold farms. Horses came back into favour only very gradually in the nineteenth century, and indeed oxen were still drawing the plough on some farms early in the twentieth. Lord Bathurst retained a team at Cirencester Park, mainly for exhibition, until 1945.

The Board of Agriculture's investigators, William Marshall and Arthur Young who toured Gloucestershire and Oxfordshire in 1796 and 1809 respectively, waxed lyrical about the state of farming on the enclosed Cotswolds, which they said put men working far richer land to shame. They regarded the social cost as a separate problem. Enclosure bore hard upon small farmers, and still harder on cottage smallholders, who could not afford the very considerable expense of fencing their meagre shares and often got left with the less profitable acres. Many of them gave up almost at once. After enclosure, the population of Aston Subedge declined from 104 to 63 within a few years. The parish of Cowley before enclosure contained one farmer with 103 acres, 10 small farmers, and 14 cottage holdings. By 1828, 1,500 acres were divided between 4 farmers, there were 4 smallholders, and 24 landless cottagers. If at first reduced, the population there had recovered by natural increase, but in status and well-being all but eight families were far worse off. William Marshall says that in 1798, about Northleach, where cattle were an important enterprise in the upper valley of the Sherborne Brook, most of the labourers still had a cow pasturing on the old cowdown, an unprofitable piece of high ground which remained unenclosed, and he assumed that formerly most labourers had had one, but Arthur Young, writing of Oxfordshire twelve years later, found nothing of the kind on the wolds, and has much to say of the misery and desperation to which farm labourers were by then reduced, unable even to supplement their miserable wages by the produce of a garden in many cases. Between 1820 and 1830, the period of Captain Swing, sporadic riot, machine-breaking and arson were less frequent in the Cotswolds than in Wiltshire, East Anglia, Kent, Sussex and Hampshire, but were by no means uncommon.

There were at that time various schemes for giving the poor some land to cultivate for themselves, but very few benefited. For several decades agricultural workers lived on the verge of starvation. In one village in the Stroudwater Hills, the only healthy-looking family belonged to a woman who was enterprising and unprejudiced enough to feed them on boiled snails. Perhaps she had gipsy blood, for a generation later, as Laurie Lee tells us in *Cider With Rosie*, gipsies were looked down on by village folk for eating them.

In the 'Hungry Forties' a scheme, associated with the Chartist movement, led to the establishment of small settlements of smallholders, not necessarily farm-labourers by trade, here and there in England. One such Charterville was set up on the Cotswolds on a piece of enclosed downland between Witney and Burford.

The little stone bungalows, each with a tiny gabled porch, can be seen on and adjacent to A40, south-west of Minster Lovell. They were not a success, for the holdings were too small to provide a living for a family, and the situation made it impossible for the tenants to work them as a part-time or family activity.

Against this background of dire poverty, the prosperity of Cotswold landowners came to a grand climax in the middle decades of the nineteenth century.

32. *Calcot, a hamlet in the Colne valley.*

Between 1800 and 1840, the few remaining open fields and almost all the commons had been enclosed, and the staggering increase in the number of English mouths to be fed offered a golden opportunity to Cotswold farmers, busily sowing the wastes and pastures with wheat and barley. Over in the Stroudwater valleys, millwrights and foundrymen began to turn their attention to agricultural machinery.

Landed proprietors great and small were deeply involved in every aspect of development, reorganizing and improving farms, planting coppices and coverts. They went on in mid-century to provide new cottages in their villages, nearly always using traditional materials quarried on the estate, and worked by their own labourers, who could in those days turn their hand to any local craft; they built often, indeed, in so traditional a style that it is difficult now to distinguish their work from that of their forefathers.

There was plenty of work for masons, carpenters, blacksmiths, wheelwrights, harness-makers and country tradesmen generally who had their share in the good times. The chimney sweep of Chipping Sodbury hardly ever missed a run with the duke of Beaufort's hounds, and was often mounted by His Grace. The duke, at the apex of the social pyramid, led the way in increasing the already lavish mode of life in country houses. In 1840, under the seventh duke, only hunt members sat down to breakfast at the famous lawn meets at Badminton, out of about three hundred horsemen present, while hundreds of spectators came out from Bath and Bristol; twenty years later there were about two thousand horsemen on these occasions, and the eighth duke entertained about a thousand to breakfast, three or four hundred to lunch, and visitors wandered through the house at will. When his eldest son came of age, there was a huge expenditure on private and public entertainment; a roasted ox, a ton of beef, and other good things were provided for his humbler tenants. He seems to have possessed great charm, and this, coupled with great extravagance and liberality, made the 'Old Blue 'Un', as he was affectionately called, greatly beloved.

Many freehold farmers began in those days to 'live the lives of squires . . . hunting, shooting, coursing, and sometimes fishing'. They also enjoyed the unsporting but effective method of shooting partridges and rabbits 'under a kite' – the kite cast a drifting shadow like a bird of prey, and the terrified creatures crouched down until the man with the gun was on top of them. Rooks were regarded both as enemies and delicacies. Sparrows also were rigorously controlled; if they became too numerous a Sparrow Club would be advertised, and a meeting held at which the villagers would be told what prizes would be forthcoming for corpses brought in.

The following quatrain was popular among Cotswold farmers, and may be taken as a summary of their attitude to their work-people:

> 'Tis the same with common natures,
> Use 'em kindly they rebel;
> But be rough as nutmeg graters
> And the rogues obey you well.

Farm-labourers obtained some small improvement in their condition during those golden years. The new cottages invariably had gardens; they could grow vegetables, and they often managed to keep a pig, at best killing twice a year, but butcher's meat or poultry they never saw in their own houses. Increasingly there was a school for their children. A telling picture of their lives is to be found in Flora Thompson's trilogy, *Lark Rise to Candleford*, which describes a childhood at Juniper Hill, a hamlet five miles beyond the Cherwell. In the middle years of the century there was plenty of work for everybody, and the few old people who until very recently could recall that vanished society, had many pleasant memories; of harvest suppers; of the squire's occasional bounty, when they would be invited to take their cutlery to a dinner of roast meat in the park; of visits to the Mop and other fairs, and to the races at Moreton, Stow, Bibury, Banbury, Cirencester, Tetbury or Sherston; of the Whitsun festival which survived in many Cotswold villages in spite of all that had been done to suppress the rougher side of the entertainment, of smoking concerts and penny-readings which offered opportunities for local talent and entertainment, held in the new schoolroom which served also as a parish hall.

During the eighteenth century Cirencester had suffered from the decline of the great Friday wool-market, but it gained a rising reputation for the manufacture of curriers' knives, for which, no doubt, some of the old fulling mills were adapted. The growing prosperity of upland farmers after enclosure, followed by the establishment of two breweries, also contributed to preserve the town from serious decline. Soon after the turn of the century, the Cirencester and Gloucestershire Agricultural Association was founded, and it was at a meeting of the Cirencester and Fairford Farmers' Club in 1842 that a lecture was given on 'The Advantages of a Specific Education for Agricultural Students' which led directly to the founding of the Royal Agricultural College under the chairmanship and then presidency of Earl Bathurst. By 1860 a great corn exchange had gone up in the market-place, and Cirencester was fast superseding all the other little markets of the central Cotswolds.

This was a happy epoch in the town's long life. The races on North Cerney Down meant a week of festivity in summer, with balls and dinners. The old theatre attached to the Volunteer inn, where many famous names had appeared on the boards, would be open for this occasion, and perhaps again in the hunting season. Cirencester was thought of as the 'Melton of the West' in sporting circles. Several hundred hunters were stabled there during the season, and the principal inns were full of hunting men who could go out six days a week with one of the five famous packs within reach. Some, indeed, settled in a town which offered such excellent opportunities for sport, and quite a number of pleasant Victorian villas went up on its fringes. Many buildings in the old streets were replaced, refaced and enlarged, though happily (no doubt for economic rather than aesthetic reasons) the traditional materials were mainly employed. By the end of the century the town had a fine library and two museums, and it was managing to retain its position as the 'capital of the Cotswolds' in spite of a disastrous depression in the surrounding countryside, and indeed throughout England, mainly due to competition from the farms of the New World.

The whole region was in fact embarked on a long and grievous decline. The great corn grounds were seeded down, and remained understocked and neglected pasture, sprouting hawthorn, dog-rose, thistles and docks, and along the path of the railways the Oxford ragwort spread in wide destructive yellow swathes. Gates became crazier and walls more dilapidated with every unprofitable decade. Cottagers drifted away and farms stood untenanted.

By 1890 quite a number of the mansions of the gentry were shut up or let to strangers. Even the Old Blue 'Un was affected, though he managed to preserve the princely way of life for the remainder of his days, devoting his closing years to the Badminton Library, a series of informative books on sporting subjects, in the editing of which he took an active part. The first volume came out in 1885, and the twenty-eighth, *The Poetry of Sport*, two years before he died in 1899. His heir was obliged to sell many of the Beaufort acres, and never attempted a similar standard of living; the Beaufort became a subscription hunt.

We have a graphic description of the wolds at the turn of the century in J. Arthur Gibb's *A Cotswold Village*, the first in a long line of Cotswold rhapsodies.

> 'Tis a wild deserted tract of country that stretches from Cirencester right away to the north of Warwickshire. For fifty miles you might gallop across undulating fields and meet no human being on your way. We have ridden forty miles on end along the Fosse Way and, save in those curious half-forsaken old towns of Moreton-in-Marsh and Stow-on-the-Wold, we scarcely met a soul on the journey.

He tells us that, as might be expected, it was the small enterprises which succumbed, while the larger farmers, cushioned by fortunes made in the years of prosperity, absorbed many of the vacated holdings and held their own. Barley remained highly profitable, and so long as horses were unchallenged on the farm and on the roads there was always a good demand for the black oats which did well on the wolds. Sainfoin continued to be a worthwhile crop, for cattle- and sheep-rearing, if conducted on a sufficiently large scale, yielded a decent profit. Large freehold farmers and well-established tenants found themselves with more time to 'live the lives of squires, more especially where there is no landowner resident', but they were dipping into their capital, as they bitterly complained, to pay the wages of their work-people. Among the labourers, struggling along on about twelve shillings a week, malnutrition, if not actual starvation, was rife, so that even a mouldy pudding destined by a middle-class household for the pigs would be gratefully consumed by a labourer's large family.

Those 'curious half-forsaken towns' were in dire straits. Stow now only came alive for the annual fairs (notably the horse fair). Burford, Campden, Moreton, Fairford, Lechlade, Northleach and Deddington, though retaining a consciousness of urban status, would hardly any longer have been regarded as towns by an unprejudiced observer, for the country trades which had formed their mainstay were in retreat. The cobbler still had work, patching the almost upatchable and keeping worn harness going, but very few new suits would be ordered from the tailors. The roads no longer automatically brought such places any business,

Witney, Woodstock and Chipping Norton, having still some larger industry, fared better. Winchcombe was decaying gently between the scarp and the relatively prosperous market gardens of the Vale of Evesham, but it too had one industry of more than local importance on its outskirts. This was the paper mill at Postlip, owned by Messrs Evans, Adlard, who with their work-force formed a sort of community within a community, directors, managers, and operatives passing on their skill and experience from father to son. The Postlip mills make their first appearance in Domesday Book; as paper mills they were already active in 1752, manufacturing boards and coloured papers. The purity of Cotswold water makes it especially suitable for the making of coloured papers. Under the ownership of the Durham family, the mills were well-known in the polite world around 1800 for fine letter-paper, which the Durhams imported from Holland while continuing to manufacture the traditional lines. Under the Adlards, the firm was kept up-to-date and expanded. They became famous for the manufacture of blotting paper and coloured packaging papers, and for fine writing paper made in the smaller Sudeley mill. Since World War I the mill has become a major producer of filter paper of every kind, used in laboratories, hospitals, factories and power stations, and a number of specialized papers for industrial use. Memorial tablets to both families are to be found in the parish church, but their true memorials are the almshouses built for their retired workers, the many cottages built, repaired and improved in the town, and the mill itself, rebuilt in 1877 on the site of the old Upper Mill. The mill reservoir also remains, relic of the days of water power, a tranquil natural-seeming lake with water-fowl nesting it its withy-beds, which were grown to provide raw material for the great baskets used in the mills principally for draining the soaked rags, and were made on the spot by travelling craftsmen. In the nineteenth century the Dandy Rolls (wire rollers which produce the water-marks) were made in Winchcombe itself by George Tovey, a local character equally renowned for his skill and his potations, and his descendants. One of the latter, between the wars, kept the best bookshop in the Cotswolds in a side street of this unpretentious, well-kept little town. George Tovey's workshop later became the Catholic church, and now has a comely modern extension. By the end of the nineteenth century there was also a flourishing brickworks on the outskirts, but the new cottages built for workers in these two industries are happily of stone. There is one handsome inn, the George, built originally by the abbots as a hospice, which before the coming of the motor car must have depended very much on the mill for its business.

William Gates Adlard, under whose auspices the Victorian mill was built, was not only an enlightened employer. In the closing years of his life he supported his friend and neighbour, Mrs Malleson of Dixton (about three miles north-west on the very edge of the limestone hills), in her struggle for the Married Women's Property Act, and for the establishment of the District Nursing service, both regarded at the time as almost equally dangerous measures.

13

Recovery and Change

'Without some form of Protection . . . or war . . . in a hundred years' time these old villages will contain scarcely a single inhabitant. . . . If only the capitalist or wealthy man of business would take up his abode in these places all might yet be well,' wrote J. Arthur Gibbs in 1898, but he did not think this was likely to happen. Wrapped up in his village and in his sporting activities, he was probably unaware of the attraction which the empty landscape, and farms and cottages going for a song, were exercising upon the rising generation of architects and artists.

In the spring of 1871, Kelmscot Manor was advertised for sale by a London house-agent. William Morris, who was looking for a holiday retreat, visited this fine Cotswold house on the bank of a Thames backwater a few miles from Lechlade and was captivated by everything he saw, calling it a 'heaven on earth'. He bought it at once, in partnership with his friend Rossetti, and departed for Iceland, leaving Rossetti with his wife and children to enjoy a Cotswold summer in the delicious garden, in the meadows and on the river.

Rossetti's interest was Jane Morris, but the impression made on him by that summer is recorded in one of his sonnets in which the Kelmscot scene is easily recognizable.

> Your hands lie open in the long, fresh grass,
> The finger points look through like rosy blooms,
> Your eyes smile peace. The pasture gleams and glooms
> 'Neath billowing clouds that scatter and amass.
> All round our nest, far as the eye can pass,

Are golden king-cup fields with silver edge,
Where the cow-parsley skirts the hawthorn hedge.
'Tis visible silence, still as the hour-glass. . . .

When Morris returned, Rossetti readily relinquished his share in the house; to Morris it remained a lasting joy. The architecture of the Cotswold villages he explored, often in long summer outings in a pony-trap with his family, and the apparently unchanging routine of husbandry around him, seemed to him a happy exemplification of all that he believed about the dignity of labour and craftsmanship. Sometimes, while the friend who had taken over Rossetti's share was in occupation of the house, he established himself for a while in Broadway Tower. This folly, built in 1796 by Lady Coventry, is a lonely landmark on the crest of the northern Edge, within easy cycling and walking distance of Chipping Campden, Broadway and another string of beautiful villages in the neighbourhood of Stow-on-the-Wold. He visited Blockley and toyed with the idea of setting up his workshops in one of its abandoned silk mills. About 1880 he bought a house at Hammersmith and renamed it Kelmscott House, and there were joyous journeys up the Thames from London to the original Kelmscot with his friends.

Morris died at Kelmscot and is buried in the churchyard under a stone slab designed by his friend Philip Webb. The house belongs to the Society of Antiquaries of London, and is open once a week in summer. It has been carefully restored and kept as far as possible as Morris left it, with examples of furniture, wallpaper and fabrics made in his own workshops, tiles by William de Morgan, embroidered hangings, and some of the many pictures of Jane Morris by Rossetti. The attics are devoted to the productions of the Kelmscott Press. The surrounding meadows and the village are unspoilt, and the latter contains a hall and several cottages built by his friends and followers.

Morris had already begun the revival of handicrafts before he found Kelmscot, and London remained the centre of his working life; but he discovered in the Cotswolds, and introduced to his disciples, a world where craftsmanship in stone, wood and iron was still very much alive, where the prevailing depression held up the advance of mass-produced and shoddy goods, and where labour was plentiful and property cheap. For the younger generation in the Arts and Crafts movement, having neither his resources nor his wider interests, a move into such a country was both desirable and practical. A stream of disciples followed him into the Cotswolds, forerunners of the multitude of weavers, potters, silversmiths, furniture-makers and painters now to be found sprinkled over the small towns and villages of England.

The first and greatest of these was Ernest Gimson (1865–1919). He came to

London from Leicester as a young man just out of his apprenticeship to work in the office of J. D. Sedding, a popular church architect to whom Morris had introduced him. He became an active member of Morris's new Society for the Protection of Ancient Buildings, whose object was then to preserve churches from over-zealous restorers – the members called themselves 'the anti-scrapers' in allusion to the current disastrous fashion for removing plaster and leaving interior walls bare. The younger members of Morris's circle were nearly all budding architects. W. R. Lethaby, Reginald Blomfield, Detmar Blow and Edward Barnsley went on to establish themselves in this profession, but Gimson rapidly developed an overriding interest in furniture. In 1890 he set up a workshop with the Barnsley brothers, Blomfield, and one or two others, and began to design exquisite and highly wrought pieces of furniture and metalwork for customers and friends. (To this period belong the stalls of ebony inlaid with bone in St Andrew's chapel in Westminster Cathedral.) His ambition, however, was to produce cheap furniture, well-made of English wood without veneer or fussy detail, and he soon decided to move into the country, where he hoped to find experienced craftsmen to work for him.

In 1892 he came into Gloucestershire with Edward and Sidney Barnsley and obtained a lease of Pinbury Park on easy terms from Lord Bathurst. This is a seventeenth-century house in a glorious position in the Stroudwater Hills, a mile or so above Sapperton, once the home of the local historian Sir Robert Atkyns. Both house and gardens were dilapidated, and they immediately set about putting them in order. The outbuildings were altered to make cottages and workshops, to which after a short time Gimson brought four highly skilled cabinet-makers from London. He was also able to train some local men and boys, and in Alfred Bucknell, a wheelwright of Sapperton, he found one of the craftsmen he had dreamed of, able to carry out his designs in gold, silver, copper, brass and iron.

About 1900 the friends added a new wing to Pinbury, which contains a fine plaster ceiling and chimney-piece by Gimson. Three years later Lord Bathurst, delighted with all they had done, offered them in exchange for Pinbury a choice of sites on his estate on which to build their own cottages at his expense, and he entrusted the restoration of Daneway House to Edward Barnsley, allowing the friends to set up new workshops in the outbuildings and to use the house as showrooms.

The last permanent member of this happy community, Norman Jewson, also trained as an architect, began work with Gimson as improver in 1907. At first he lived in what had been a handloom weaver's cottage at Oakridge, which he rented for a shilling a week, but before his marriage with one of Edward Barnsley's daughters moved into the cottage in Sapperton where he died recently. His autobiography, *By Chance I did Rove*, presents a most delightful picture of the people of Sapperton and the neighbouring villages, and the activities of Gimson and his associates, in the early years of this century. Jewson worked principally with Edward Barnsley. They carried out many domestic alterations and restorations for the Society for the Protection of Ancient Buildings. They worked together on the parish hall at Kelmscot, and on Barnsley's most important commission, Rodmarton Manor, the last 'great house' to be built in the Cotswolds. The principles of the Arts and Crafts movement were more fully realized in this building than in any other enterprise. Barnsley designed it in the traditional Cotswold style, the stone and wood came from the estate, and all the work was done by local masons and carpenters; the furniture and fittings came from Gimson's workshops. They are still there, but the public seldom gets the chance to view these treasures.

Rodmarton's other claim to fame is as the home of the Lyson brothers, topographers and antiquaries. Daniel was rector and died there in 1834, and there is also a tablet to his brother Samuel in the church.

The Stroudwater Hills, after several generations of clothiers had made their fortunes in the valleys, were especially full of fine houses of moderate size in singularly beautiful settings, requiring only the addition of modern conveniences to make them comfortable and gracious habitations. Among the most distinguished of the artists who now began to move into them was William Rothenstein, who bought Iles Farm in Far Oakridge, and commissioned Jewson to turn one of its find barns into a studio and make the necessary alterations to the house. Another architect engaged on this type of work was Detmar Blow. He built himself a house at Hilles near Harescomb, which is a good example of Cotswold-revival architecture. Another who settled in the Stroudwater Hills was William Symons, a carver of genius in wood and stone, and puppet-master. Gloucester City Museum has some of his puppets on display, and the Tate Gallery owns some exquisite carvings. Most of the fittings in Chalford church are by Jewson, Symons and Sidney Barnsley, who concentrated mainly on furniture, and Peter Waals, Gimson's foreman cabinet-maker.

Meanwhile a parallel settlement was taking place in and around Campden. In 1888 C. R. Ashbee, another architect-disciple of Ruskin and Morris, had been the leading spirit in the formation of a Guild of Handicrafts intended to be an industrial partnership. Its declared aims included 'to produce honest craftsmanship with or without machinery [a new compromise with the contemporary world] in such a way as to conduce to the welfare of the workman'. For ten years the Guild operated in the east end of London, mostly in Essex House, an old mansion in Mile End, which was adapted to house dormitories for students, library, lecture-rooms and workshops in which members worked and taught cabinet-making and joinery, gold-, silver- and copper-smithing, printing, book-binding and so on. After Morris's death, the Kelmscott presses were transferred to Essex House and some of Morris's staff came with them. In 1901 Ashbee brought the whole enterprise to Campden, an influx of fifty working members, some with families. Braithwaite House in the High Street was converted into a hostel for unmarried members. Ashbee occupied the ancient hall of the Woolstaplers (now a museum), and a derelict silk mill in Sheep Street became the main premises of the Guild, with its own generator producing the first electric light Campden had ever seen.

Ashbee's impact on a rather moribund town was immediate, lasting and far-reaching in its consequences. The Guild had already established relations with the Board of Education through its work for London schools, and it received a grant when it set up a school of arts and crafts in a disused barn behind Elm Tree House. There were special vacation courses for school-teachers, and the members taught woodwork and other suitable craft-subjects to Campden school-children. They made a swimming pool in a disused mill-dam and taught the children to swim. They also opened a social club, encouraged choral singing, provided new uniforms for the brass band and revived the Morris dancers and the Mummers Play.

The townspeople extended only a very cautious welcome to these dynamic outsiders, but for a few years things went well. The general slump which began in 1905, however, soon put the Guild into liquidation, and many members drifted back to London in search of work. In 1907 the presses were sold off to an Indian admirer, Dr A. K. Coomeraswamy, who moved them to the long-desecrated Norman chapel at Broad Campden, where for a few years he concentrated on the production of oriental texts. Meanwhile Ashbee succeeded in securing from an American admirer financial support for his long-dreamed-of plan to bend his members' backs to till the soil in addition to their normal creative work. A trust was formed to buy a farm and to hold the premises in Sheep Street, in which members now rented their workshops and worked independently. Only one of them, however, would have anything to do with the farm, and two of the fields were laid out as allotment gardens available to all townspeople.

The trust closed down in 1920. The Guild premises are now mainly occupied by a firm of builders founded by J. W. Pyment, who had come to Campden as a member of the Guild and stayed on to become the town's principal builder. Another member, Alfred Downer, remained in business and provided many of the handsome wrought-iron hanging signs in the high street. Campden, Broadway and Painswick, previously sunk in depression, had gained a continuing vitalizing influx of craftsmen, artists, literary people and other idealists with a common desire to support and protect their adopted communities, and the Cotswold School became a small but distinct entity in the artistic world. A Guild founded in Painswick in 1933 still flourishes.

In the same period a group of a very different complexion was establishing itself in the south Cotswolds. 'It is hard to say whether it was horror of industrial cities, or the degradation of the workers, or shame in my participation in an evil system that gave me a passionate desire to escape to some spot where I and my friends could settle and cultivate the land,' wrote Joseph Burtt forty years later. He had been a bank-clerk in Cheltenham, and it was through him that the Brotherhood Church of Croydon came to hear in 1898 of a small farm called Whiteway, forty-two acres of high, poor downland in the Stroudwater Hills. The Brotherhood Church was a loosely-knit socialist society, humanist in outlook. At first 'every kind of "anti" had a welcome hearing', but presently the ideals of the most dedicated members more or less crystallized in accordance with the principles of Tolstoy – to hold everything in common, without the use of money, without vows or oaths and without government of any kind in a self-supporting community – and they were looking for a place in which to begin. Three members were with difficulty persuaded to allow their names to appear on the deed of sale by which the community acquired Whiteway, but within two months the title deeds had been consigned to a bonfire. One or two moneyed sympathizers settled in nearby Sheepscombe, and a heroic half-dozen began a life of extreme rigour on the farm – 'miles of apparently idle land . . . not a single tree . . . a bare stone house'. Two very severe winters in which they were reduced to a diet of potatoes until the County Council distrained on these for the rates and forced them to fall back on the generosity of the family at Sheepscombe, followed by two summers in which sympathetic visitors and would-be members often failed to contribute their share of the work, at last convinced them that total communism without sanctions was beyond their reach. The land was then divided, each man taking what he thought he could manage to hold during occupancy only, and they began to aim for a marketable surplus. One man took to brick-making, another made sandals, a third turned baker and produced wholemeal bread which was soon in great demand among neighbouring artists; the women engaged in dress-making and weaving and took their share in the routine of cultivation. In this way, with the aid of harvest work and other seasonal labour outside the community, they managed to establish themselves, and to build with the cheapest materials available a bungalow on each holding and a tiny community centre. That once-bare and bleak farmstead is now a leafy spot, its abundant vegetation amply concealing the shortcomings of the architecture.

The newcomers in the Cotswolds during these years were for the most part middle-class people, and they were sufficiently numerous before 1914 to effect that subtle alteration in the social life of the area which was not felt in most English rural communities until after the Second World War.

In 1914 the exigencies of war brought about a rapid though temporary revival of agriculture. The industrial depression caused by the shrinking of the woollen manufacture had been quickly relieved by a steady trickle of new industries. By 1860 a number of old mills had been taken over by silk-throwers and makers of shoddy, and others for the manufacture of pins. Messrs Watkins and Oakey were established at Kings Mill and one or two others in the Painswick valley. Wimberley Mill near Chalford, after a brief period as a saw mill, was taken over by the Critchley brothers for the same purpose. One of the old buildings still survives on the premises of the firm, which now manufactures electric cables and wiring accessories on a large scale.

All the big engineering firms had similar origins. Messrs Daniels, blacksmiths and millwrights, came to Stroud as early as 1840 from Nympsfield. This was probably the same family-firm one of whose handloom weavers we saw in trouble with his fellow-workers fifty years earlier, for many clothiers ran a grinding shop in connection with their mills. In 1880 Daniels opened a foundry with pattern-making and machine shops, and manufactured corn-milling as well as textile machinery. Later this firm developed gas-producing plant and oil engines, notably those with the brand name 'Trusty' which were the fore-runners of Diesel engines, which were sold in great quantity for driving pumps in mines and railway workshops. Daniels produced the first steam and oil engines for ships' propellers, and became the licencees for high-speed pumps developed in Germany. The firm has now been taken over by an international group, but retains the name. It manufactures a famous chain-saw, but pumps and presses for plastics are the mainstay of the business, a branch developed just after the First World War, when a rubber company engaged in the manufacture of car tyres arrived in the valley.

It was in 1860 that Robert Ashton Lister, a Yorkshireman, opened a foundry at Dursley. He must have had his eye on the cloth industry, but he soon turned his attention to agricultural machinery. One of his first ventures was the Beaufort

Hunt Corn Crusher, followed by a chain harrow which is still in production, an elevator and other farming aids. These were followed by a petrol engine for driving light machinery of all kinds which had an enormous success, and in 1909 the firm patented a generating plant powered by this engine which found an insatiable demand all over the world. The firm is now a member of the Hawker-Siddeley group, but the Lister family is still connected with it. Messrs Mawdsley, another important Dursley firm now part of the Adwest group, began in 1907 in the old Rivers Mill, used since 1783 as a wire mill manufacturing pins and leather articles used in the clothing mills; they also were concerned in the development of electric generators.

1879 saw the first important new arrival in the Nailsworth valley. A brass-founder named Brice, whose foundry at Bristol had been crippled by a strike, established himself in a disused dye-house alongside the railway at Inchbrook. The firm now belongs to the Newman Hender Group and employs two thousand people. It manufactures specialized brass parts, many of them used by oil companies, and has a number of foreign subsidiaries. In the same year E. A. Chamberlain took over the premises of the British Board Mills, a former cloth mill in the heart of Nailsworth. This firm is now the second largest manufacturer of cardboard and fibreboard in Europe.

These are only some of the most substantial and lasting among the new industries which have been coming into the south Cotswolds since the cloth trade declined. Around the turn of the century the valleys must have been dirty with the smoke of their engines, and a great many cottages and villas were scattered over the upper slopes near Stroud, but the area as a whole remains astonishingly unspoilt, and villages higher up the valleys, such as Horsley and Chalford, are far quieter now than they were a hundred and fifty years ago.

The south Cotswold industries naturally did well during the First World War, and they continued to thrive afterwards, whereas many of the cornfields of the wolds soon reverted to pasture. Nevertheless, the sights and sounds of the countryside and the pattern of rural life was beginning to change: mechanical reapers had everywhere superseded the scythe, and though the hay was still turned and cocked, and corn sheaves set up by hand, Lister's elevators were becoming a common sight in the rick-yard. Tractors had hardly begun to displace horses in the fields, but the steam traction-engine bringing and driving a great wooden threshing machine, and the steam trucks from the corn, seed and cattle-feed merchants, and from the brewery, were regular visitors in the remotest villages. The steam roller lumbered in to lay for ever the white dust on the main roads with a coat of tarmac, though the lanes remained untouched for another decade, interrupted by a gate at every field boundary. In the little market towns the fine lias pavements began to give place to concrete and asphalt; the cattle market was moved to concrete pens near the railway station.

In districts blessed with a better railway service, the intense isolation of village communities had begun to crumble at the turn of the century; over most of the Cotswolds it lasted until the arrival of the motor bus in the 'twenties. Laurie Lee has given us in *Cider with Rosie* a poetic account of the Slad valley in the Stroudwater Hills in this period of transition.

By no means every squire and very few farmers had a car in 1920, but the possession of this beloved monster spread rapidly down the social scale, and more and more retired people and refugees from city life began to settle in the fringe villages. The north Cotswolds, with their severer climate, were less attractive to the elderly, but Campden and the villages on the northern Edge began to receive a few commuters who could now drive daily to Honeybourne to catch a train for Birmingham or Stratford. The Lygon Arms at Broadway, which had gone to seed in the railway age, was bought in 1912 by George Russell, restored and turned into a smart hotel. His son Gordon (now Sir Gordon) joined in the enterprise, and when he returned from the war the workshops which had been set up to repair antique furniture and fittings for the hotel became under his direction the scene of the first attempt to adapt the ideas and standards of the Gimson school to mass-production. Russell and Heal carried the message of simple design, good material and sound construction into the commercial field. Meanwhile Peter Waals was still making choice pieces for rich connoisseurs.

In 1930 the Cotswolds were beginning to experience the pains and profits of tourism, with an influx every Saturday and Sunday in summer of dwellers in Oxford, Bristol, Birmingham and Coventry, and by the end of the decade Bourton-on-the-Water had been butchered to make a playground for them to linger in. During the 'thirties, buses from Cheltenham, Gloucester, Stroud, Bristol and Bath plied frequently in the south Cotswolds. The north Cotswolds found themselves at the limit of services from Evesham, Oxford and Banbury, and were for the most part badly served by all three. They relied mainly on local garage proprietors who had a coach or two for hire which they ran as a bus once or twice a week to Cheltenham or Cirencester for shoppers, and once a week to the nearest cinema in the evening. Some of these are still running.

Tentative efforts were being made to revive agriculture. Tractors had almost replaced horses on Cotswold farms, stables were being turned into hygienic milking parlours, and some farmers were beginning to introduce hay-bailers and even grain-drying equipment. All this, together with Council houses and cut-price repairs to old buildings, threatened to destroy the immemorial symphonies of stone. In the Cotswolds red brick is a jarring element, corrugated iron an affront, and both were being widely used. Nor was there any control over unsightly sporadic development.

There was one doughty fighter against such things among the artists. F. L. Griggs was a native of Hertfordshire. As a young man he was employed to illustrate several volumes of the *Highways and Byways* series, and in the course of this work he fell under the spell of the Cotswolds. He settled in Campden, which he immortalized in a series of woodcuts published as a volume in 1940. He entered with zest into the life of the town and struggled to preserve it from ugly intrusions, scoring a notable victory when in 1923 he persuaded the Post Office to lay the telephone cables underground, and in 1926 when at his own cost he secured Dovers Hill against property speculators and gathered the necessary support to buy it for the National Trust. Under his leadership the houses in the marvellous high street were lovingly restored, and long before most rural communities had begun to think of preserving their amenities, Campden was showing the world how to do it.

The Second World War produced a very different effect on the Cotswolds from that of the First. Once again the wolds were ploughed up, the great woods were decimated, the War Office's hold on the Corsham quarries was intensified, and the engineering firms worked at full stretch. Three stories of the historic Stanley Mill were commandeered by the Admiralty for stores; a NAAFI bakery was established at Cirencester: a Polish refugee camp was set up on the hills above Broadway. The outstanding difference was that this time people were brought into far closer contact with the fighting. By 1942 there was an airfield roughly every ten miles, and local people were making the acquaintance of airmen from all the nations involved, as well as foreign refugees and evacuees from English cities whose ways were almost as strange to them. Bus loads of men and women went off day by day from the villages to work on the airfields and in the factories. Nor was there a parallel recession when the war was over. European refugees willing to work a night shift made a substantial contribution to Messrs Marling and Evans' recovery; the NAAFI bakery continued at Cirencester; and many of the airfields remained in the hands of the RAF, others now being used for peaceful activities. Colerne, South Cerney, Brize Norton and Rissington are RAF stations still; Fairford, formerly a USAAF base, is notorious as the home of the Concorde; Frampton Mansell is a Mintech depot; Moreton-in-Marsh the

Fire Service Training College. Of those abandoned, at Daglingworth the land has been reinstated and virtually every trace of the airfield obliterated.

The modern pattern of life, dependant on the electric grid and the internal combustion engine, has transformed the ghost towns of the wolds, which were already reviving before the war. They are now nearly all cheerful and busy places. Trading estates for light industry have been established in several of them, notably at Cirencester, Tetbury and Witney, a useful source of jobs for local people, for none of the Cotswold towns has been artificially expanded by a large influx of strangers planned out of the cities, though commuting has, of course, greatly increased. Cirencester has received the most drastic treatment, but the attractive streets west of the market-place have been preserved. Part of Dyer Street, the eastern approach to the market, has been rebuilt as an arcaded shopping street, and the gardens and warehouses behind, roughly over the site of the Forum, have been replaced by a large car park and modern buildings of moderate height. Considering that this must have been a largely open, paved place in Roman times, it may be said to have been tactfully done. The Monday and Friday markets are still happily held in the market square. The Corinium museum is an admirable example of its kind. The Bingham Library has fared less well; the County Council has taken it over and removed its excellent local collection and other books to Gloucester. The town has plenty of good shops, including an excellent book shop in Dollar Street.

The planning committees do not allow the use of incongruous materials either for repairs or new developments, so that the advance of brick and corrugated iron in the Cotswolds has been mercifully halted, but traditional materials and methods have no chance now of revival except for specialized and costly work. The materials most frequently used are a stone composition made of crushed oolite and a sober-coloured tile which does seem sometimes to attract the mosses and lichens which add so much to the natural beauty of Cotswold slates. Most towns and villages now have closes built of these materials, which are eagerly sought after by local people. A high proportion of old labourer's cottages and small farmsteads, many of which would undoubtedly otherwise have fallen down, are now occupied by urban newcomers. Some local people complain, however, that the price of even the smallest cottage is now beyond their reach.

There has been no collapse of agriculture this time. The area under plough is as great now as it was in the golden years of Queen Victoria, or the lean years of two world wars. Barley is still the favourite crop, but the acreage of wheat has increased above the national average, and yields have doubled; in so notable a hunting country there is still a good demand for oats. Kale is still a popular

33. *A modern house built of traditional materials.*

34. *A modern house built of the new materials.*

fodder-crop in the Cotswolds, and go-ahead farmers are beginning to introduce the brilliant yellow rape in response to its popularity as cattle-feed in the Common Market. The region has some highly successful breeders of cattle, sheep and pigs. The fine stone farmsteads at the centre of these flourishing enterprises are often beautifully maintained and embellished, with their heated swimming pools, grain-handling equipment and orderly yards uncannily recalling the great villas of Roman times. One such is Starveall Farm near Northleach, whose name betrays what our English ancestors thought of it.

The paddocks are full of hunters, for the sporting character of the region is fully maintained. If some of the race-meetings have disappeared, their place is taken by the International Horse Trials at Badminton and lesser events of similar kind, pony-club meetings and local gymkhanas. Cirencester Park has become a centre for polo, and Lord Bathurst also lets it be used for public events of a less traditional flavour. A hot-air balloon rally was held there, for example, in 1974.

The Cotswold Water Park is a notable new development. Gravel pits between Swindon and Cirencester were opened during the war and have been continually extended. Some are rented by coarse-fishing clubs who jealously preserve them from invasion by the public, but a large stretch of water between Fairford and Lechlade and another close to South Cerney are being developed commercially with marinas for sailing, speed-boats, water-skiing and bathing.

The Ramblers Association has two active branches in Gloucestershire and one in Oxfordshire. With the active support of the Gloucestershire County Council, a Cotswold Way has been devised along the Edge from Chipping Campden down to Bath. It has not yet received the coveted designation of the Countryside Commission, but it is fully signposted and a little guide has been published. It offers miles of unspoilt country walking, with marvellous views, punctuated by delightful villages, and requires no special equipment or outstanding toughness. Apart from the Edge, the region cannot be described as ideal for walkers, so much of the land being under the plough. It is well worthwhile to obtain the various walkers' guides which have been published in booklet form and are readily available in the region.

The Cotswolds are sufficiently well supplied with country-house hotels and pleasant inns, but Cirencester is perhaps the best starting-point for exploring the central plateau. The following itineraries would each supply material for more than one outing.

Leaving Cirencester on A417, and passing through Ampney St Mary (p. 100) and Poulton (p. 156), we come to Fairford, a quiet little town with a wonderful church, a centre for fishermen. Take a minor road passing north of the church and turning right to drive up the Coln valley. First comes Quenington, with a notable church (p. 93); the village has been well looked after by the family firm of Godwin, which has had an unobtrusive engineering works here for about a hundred years. The next village is Coln St Aldwyn, perhaps settled by a remnant of the population of a Roman township on Akeman Street (p. 67) (St Aldwyn is said to have been a member of the Saxon monastic community at Cirencester). We cross the wold to reach the river again at Bibury, the most famous of the valley villages, to be visited preferably in spring or autumn. Church and manor house hug the river bank; from the clapper bridge a little below the churchyard large trout may be seen lurking among the weeds; beyond it a footpath passes a row of sixteenth-century cottages to climb into the lovely twin village of Arlington. This was the original crossing, but a spring close by made the water too cold for drovers' herds, and in the eighteenth century the present bridge was built downstream. Cottages on the right of the road are built into an old quarry. On the Arlington side of the bridge stands a great corn mill now used as a museum. It contains mill machinery and usually an exhibition of some works of the Cotswold school (p. 192). Upstream from the bridge is a trout hatchery.

The chief beauties of the valley begin at Bibury. Above it comes first Ablington, a hamlet containing a few cottages and barns grouped with a gem of a manor house built in 1580 and formerly the home of J. Arthur Gibbs; then comes Winson, notable for magnificent barns and a pretty millhouse; then, after another mile through the meadows, Coln Roger with its Saxon church. Here the road climbs a little and looks across the valley to Calcot, which seems to grow out of the further bank, before coming to Coln St Denis, another pretty group about the church's solid Norman tower. We reach the Fosse Way and plunge down to Fosse Bridge with a handsome hotel beside it. The first turning on the left over the bridge leads to Chedworth Roman villa (p. 64) and Withington (pp. 64, 74, 92), another large and attractive village. Beyond Withington, a straight two miles made across the village's open fields when they were enclosed brings us to A436. Turn right here and then left through the Shiptons (p. 74) to Syreford, Sevenhampton and Brockhampton in the upper valley where the river is a mere brook. The Coln rises a mile above Brockhampton, within half a mile of the source of the Isburne which flows north into the Warwickshire Avon. Here stands Charlton Abbots, one of the highest, saddest villages on the wolds, formerly belonging to the abbots of Winchcombe who kept a hospice for lepers there. The road now begins to descend towards Winchcombe and passes beneath Belas Knap (p. 49). It reaches A46 midway between Postlip (p. 185) and Winchcombe.

The minor road leaving Winchcombe opposite the church serves Sudeley Castle (p. 78), then climbs steeply up the Edge and meets an ancient saltway

(p. 76). Turn right along this through Hawling (p. 73) and Salperton, too tiny lonely villages, and continuing on the saltway cross A40 and drop down into Compton Abdale, attractively set in a little side valley of the Coln (p. 29). Turning right to pass the church, we leave the saltway and join an even older road known as the White Way. This leads down to the Coln which we cross at Cassey Compton, a noble but somewhat run-down manor house. Cross the valley road and continue on the White Way, perhaps making a detour to visit Chedworth village (pp. 65, 76, 81, 99); the White Way passes through another picturesque hamlet, Calmsden, to enter Cirencester by the Spital Gate.

Another route begins on A417. A mile beyond Fairford, make a detour to visit the outstanding Norman church at Kempsford; the towpath of the Thames and Severn canal (p. 139) may be followed for three miles through the fields to the round house where the canal joins the Coln as it flows into the Thames. A track from the round house leads into the outskirts of Lechlade. The motorist must return to A417.

Lechlade (p. 132) is a pretty little town with a fine church and a busy marina occupying old wharves close to Halfpenny Bridge on the Swindon exit (A361). Kelmscot is only three miles beyond the town, and reached by continuing along A417 to St John's Bridge and taking B4449. Returning on A417 through Lechlade, the first turning on the left leads through Southrop (p. 93) to the pretty twin villages of Eastleach Martin, or Bouthrop, and Eastleach Turville, divided by the sparkling little Leach. They are best viewed in early spring when St Martin's churchyard is full of snowdrops. Thence by another minor road we reach Filkins. In this attractive village there is an interesting little private museum of country things, the miscellaneous collection of the owner, Mr George Swinford, who began his working life as a mason in the Barrington quarry. Filkins is on the ancient road from Southampton (p. 132). The return might be made by taking a minor road on the left through Westwell onto A433, and turning left to pass through Aldsworth, Bibury, Arlington and Barnsley, another outstanding village, on the way to Cirencester.

A third route takes us northwards. Leaving Cirencester on Ermine Street, the first turning on the left signposted Daglingworth is a quiet valley road, leading through Daglingworth (p. 71) and the Duntisbournes (pp. 71, 95); at Middle Duntisbourne the stream occupies the village street. Beyond Duntisbourne Abbots, the hills close in; turn left and climb onto the ridge at Jack Barrow (from which the slab was taken to carve a cross for the skeletons from another barrow [p. 50]). Beyond this narrow ridge, the lane plunges down dramatically through the woods into the head of the Frome valley. The next turning on the right climbs up again into little Syde (tiny church with saddle-back tower) but the valley should be followed to its end before climbing up to Brimpsfield (pp. 77, 92). From Brimpsfield take the road eastward through Cowley and Coberley to Seven Springs, where beneath the intersection of A435 and A436 the Church rises in a basin which claims to be the source of the Thames. (The true source is behind the Thames Head Inn on A433 west of Cirencester; a statue of Father Thames brought from the Great Exhibition of 1851 formerly marked the spot, but has recently been removed to protect it from vandals.) The return from Seven Springs may be made through Elkstone (p. 93), Rendcomb (p. 99), North Cerney and Bagendon (pp. 57–8, 90).

Sapperton (pp. 27, 154) is only seven miles west of Cirencester. It is a gateway to the lovely valleys of the Stroudwater Hills, where many of the lanes are still quiet enough to make pleasant walks, and it is an especially attractive village in itself. The canal towpath (p. 140) begins a mile below the village at the Daneway Inn and leads down to Chalford. An alternative either for walking or driving skirts the beech-fringed edge of the valley to Frampton Mansell before descending beneath the railway viaduct onto the valley-floor at Twizzells Mill. Walkers can cross the Frome Valley by the old road (p. 138) to Oakridge and Bisley (pp. 68, 173). Another attractive drive into the clothing district may be made through Todmarton to Cherington, and thence by a secret valley to Avening (pp. 92, 159), following A434 past Longford Mill (p. 168) down to Nailsworth (pp. 119, 167), and thence up B4058 past the Midland Fish Hatchery to Horsley (p. 156); returning through Chavanage (p. 126), and Tetbury (pp. 136, 153) or Beverstone (p. 78) and Westonbirt (p. 153). Painswick is an almost equally good starting point for exploring the Stroudwater Hills as well as the Edge from Randwick up to Leckhampton (pp. 29, 142).

Burford (pp. 32, 95, 133) is the natural centre for exploring the lovely Windrush valley. Eastward a minor road runs past Widford (p. 67), Swinbrook (pp. 123, 225), Asthall (p. 67), and via Asthall Leigh to Minster Lovell (pp. 80, 181). North Leigh (pp. 63, 71) is only a few miles beyond, and return could be made through Church Hanborough (pp. 93, 99) and Fulbrook. Westward of Burford lies lovely Taynton (pp. 31, 225), the Barringtons (pp. 32, 89) and on the Sherborne Brook, Windrush (p. 32), Sherborne (pp. 88, 125), Farmington and Turkdean (p. 89). To reach the upper waters of the Windrush, take a right turn at the end of Great Barrington village and go through Great Rissington to Bourton-on-the-Water (pp. 25, 57, 153). The crystal Windrush runs along the main street spanned at frequent intervals by elegant low bridges. Although it now contains many gift shops, cafés, a model railway, a vast car park and other tourist attractions, Bourton remains a masterpiece of the Cotswold tradition worth visiting, especially in spring or autumn.

The upper waters of the Windrush basin can equally well be visited from Stow, Campden, Moreton or Broadway. The river rises high in the wolds behind Stanway, and flows past Cutsdean, once a centre of the bishop of Worcester's Cotswold estates (p. 207); thence into a narrow valley past Ford, Temple Guiting, Barton (p. 90), Lower Guiting or Guiting Power, all worth a brief visit. The second turning on the left a mile south-east of Guiting Power follows the alignment of the Jurassic Way (p. 21) and after two miles crosses the prehistoric Buckle Street (p. 209); at the crossroads turn left along this for the Cotswold Farm Park, a fascinating visit for both adults and children (p. 179). East of Buckle Street the ancient Huntsman Quarry is still working. Return to the Windrush Valley and turn left, left again on A436, and immediately fork left for Naunton, another characteristic village. From Harford Bridge below Naunton a minor road on the right (left fork immediately) leads to Upper Slaughter (pp. 77, 112), nicely perched above a little brook called the Eye. The Eye runs down the village street at Lower Slaughter, spanned by a few bridges. Make a detour through Stow, or cross the Fosse Way and go up through Wyck Rissington to Wyck Beacon on A424, the Stow-Burford road. A detour may be made to see the remaining open field at Westcot (p. 26) and the derelict Milton quarry (p. 32) on the way back to Burford.

14

The North Cotswolds

The road between Stow-on-the-Wold and Stanway (B4077) may be taken as the southern limit of this district. From the neighbourhood of Stanway, the Edge runs north-north-east to Meon Hill. Beyond this tree-capped promontory, the Stour cuts back into the Jurassic formation, rising near Barton-on-the-Heath on the low watershed which separates it from the Evenlode. Between the high scarp of this valley and the Edge lies a wedge-shaped plateau fretted on the east by an insignificant stream called the Knee Brook and its feeders. The Knee Brook rises three miles above Campden, and flows in a gentle broadening valley eastward to the Stour. This valley forms a sort of annex to the market-gardening country of the Vale of Evesham; around Campden, Ebrington and Charingworth orchards abound, and the slopes are green with brassicas and peas. Before the advent of mechanical harvesting, the arrival of the 'travellers' for the pea-picking was something of an event in the Campden diary, and harvesting the sprouts offered welcome winter employment during the agricultural depression. Above and beyond this valley as far as the eye can see flow the Stonebrash cornfields.

The Fosse Way plunges down along the eastern edge of this plateau between Stow-on-the-Wold and Moreton-in-Marsh. Although it lies in a soggy plain (the name is really Moreton Henmarsh), Moreton is a true Cotswold town, with an elegant main street lined with trees, in the centre of which stands a handsome market hall given by Lord Redesdale in 1887 and designed by Sir Ernest George. There was probably an immemorial settlement of fishermen and fowlers where the church now stands, but as a town, Moreton was founded by the abbot of Westminster in the thirteenth century to take advantage of the intersection of two trunk roads, the Fosse Way and the Great Road to Worcester. The oldest building in the town is the tower at this crossroads from which the curfew was rung until 1860. The abbot laid out his market-place at a slight angle with the Roman road, which until the nineteenth century was still called the Old Road. It afforded a convenient back entrance for the burgages on the east side of the market-place.

Moreton is now a cheerful, busy little town, but until the last twenty years, in spite of its favourable situation and since the nineteenth century the only worthwhile train service in the north Cotswolds, it never was able to overtake Stow-on-the-Wold, the pre-Conquest centre of the district. Stow was better placed to make a living out of the Cotswold flocks. By 1381 there were two annual fairs of five days' duration, and the town guild was prosperous enough to establish a school. There must have been something of a recession in the fifteenth century, for St Edward's has none of the perpendicular splendour of the great 'wool' churches, but the grammar school was re-founded soon after the Reformation in a new building (the Masonic Hall in Church Street). The church was badly damaged in the Civil War and has been repeatedly, and not happily restored. In the eighteenth century about 50,000 sheep were said to change hands at each of the two fairs, and the horse fair is still an important local event today. In the same period there was also a manufacture of boots and shoes. Stow has the best market square in the Cotswolds, very large and well-enclosed, and almost completely unspoilt by the intrusion of incongruous shop-fronts. It is lined with sixteenth- and seventeenth-century houses, in traditional style with the exception of the pilastered façade of the seventeenth-century St Edward's House. The Kings Arms was allowed by some people in the seventeenth century to be the best inn between London and Worcester.

Leaving the square in the south-western corner, we pass a small public house which offers the local Donnington Ales. We may take the Tewkesbury road (B4077) as far as pretty Upper Swell, where the church, small manor house, water mill and few cottages are hemmed in between the mill-pond and the hillside in the narrow valley of the Dikler. Dikler is a Celtic name; the English may have christened it the Swell, for that name is derived from the word used to describe a stream which behaves in an unpredictable or violent manner. The Dikler is the only stream on this limestone range to run underground. It rises on Bourton Down (p. 137) at the junction of the Inferior Oolite with the Upper Lias sands, about five miles north-west of Bourton-on-the-Hill, and flows down into a wooded gully at Hinchwick, where it forms a pond and disappears, to emerge again in the artificial pool at Donnington brewery, an enchanting group of buildings about a mile from Upper Swell. The pool, made to drive the brewery machinery, now acts as a reservoir for Moreton-in-Marsh. Hinchwick is reached

35. *View from Corndean Hill near Winchcombe.*

through Condicote, the loneliest village on the wolds, and perhaps one of the oldest. It bestrides Ryknield Street, an immemorial track improved by the Romans, and has a Bronze Age 'henge' earthwork alongside the green. Beyond Hinchwick a road climbs up on to 144 on Bourton Down, formerly the abbot of Westminster's sheep-walk, administered from his manor of Bourton-on-the-Hill, to which for centuries the church at Moreton was merely a chapel-of-ease. Bourton-on-the-Hill, climbing up A44, is an outstandingly well-built and pretty village. Above it the road passes through a once-famous quarry, probably first opened to build the church and the monastic farmhouse.

From Bourton quarries a minor road on the left offers an interesting detour through Batsford and Blockley. Batsford makes its first appearance in written record as early as the eighth century, when King Ethelbald of Mercia gave a large upland estate, ideal for sheep-rearing, to the bishop of Worcester. By 855, a clearing lower on the hillside, Blockley, had become the site of a minster, the mother church of a wide area in the north Cotswolds, and was the centre of the bishop's sheep-rearing enterprise.

The bishops were robbed of Batsford by one of Ethelred the Unready's over-powerful magnates and they never recovered it. It remained an obscure village perched on the scarp above Moreton, and was later obliterated by the park. In the eighteenth century it passed into the hands of the first Baron Redesdale, who is buried in the church. It was another Baron Redesdale who in 1888 commissioned Sir Ernest George to build for him the existing large and elaborate neo-Elizabethan creation, and who laid out the famous gardens, embellished with buddhas and Chinese temples. The building of the house was supervised by the young Guy Dawber, who spent most of his life thereafter working in, and writing about, the Cotswold style. His most imposing design was that of Eyford Park, near Stow-on-the-Wold. Batsford may be taken to be the scene of Nancy Mitford's most amusing novels.

Blockley is the more interesting village. When England was divided into shires (about 1002), the bishop managed to get his Cotswold estates centred on Blockley and Cutsdean included in Worcestershire, in which they remained until the rationalization of the boundaries in 1931. The manor house probably stands on the site of the episcopal residence, inhabited perhaps by one or two of his chaplains. Late in the Norman period he gave the village a church of which the chief decorative features are the unusual corbel table and a finely worked chancel arch. The vestry, formerly a two-storied chapel, was added about a hundred years later. The church has been almost continuously tinkered with throughout the ages. The south porch has the date 1620, the clerestory 1636, the tower was rebuilt by Thomas Woodward of Campden in 1725–7, and the flat ceiling of the nave was probably put in in 1838. The whole was fully restored in 1873. Within are two brasses of priests, one, unusually, showing a kneeling figure vested for mass. There is also a fine series of monuments to the Rushout family of Northwick Park. This mansion (built in 1686) lies north of the village; it was remodelled in 1733 on designs made by Lord Burlington. The interior was ruined during the last war, and Lord Northwick's famous collection of pictures is now dispersed.

Blockley village lies in a small, steep valley called Dovedale. Eighteenth-century romantics are said to have given it this name. The stream rises about a mile above the parish church at the base of the Inferior Oolite, and flows down the valley with considerable force – a fine stream for washing the bishop's flocks, and no doubt one of the twelve mills on the bishop's estate recorded in Domesday Book was within sight of the parish church. In due course fulling stocks made their appearance in the village, for by the end of the seventeenth century some cloth mills had been taken over by silk-throwers from Coventry, and Blockley was becoming an industrial village engaged in the manufacture of ribbons. In 1780 there were five mills at work. Of these, two remain, both built around 1700, and charmingly converted into houses. In 1884 there were still six mills and six hundred people at work, but the industry was collapsing under pressure of French competition.

The cottages of Blockley are stone-built but very plain – no squire here anxious to prettify his surroundings – but the Crown is a handsome inn fit to entertain commercial gentlemen, and there are several good houses built for the masters. The Baptist chapel has an imposing façade with Ionic pilasters and a Roman-Doric door-frame; it was built in the nineteenth century to replace a smaller one now used as a parish hall. This pleasing scene began to attract commuters and pensioners from Oxford in the 1930s, but Blockley was still able to send quite a large contingent to work in the factories and airfields during the last war. Since then incomers have taken over a much larger number of dwellings.

Three settlements – Ditchford, Dorn and Upton – on the bishop's estate perished in the Middle Ages, and are now represented in each case by a single farm and a few mounds in the neighbouring fields. These include at Dorn the traces of a considerable Roman settlement (see p. 167), and the farmstead contains the remains of a chapel. Excavations at Upton have also yielded traces of Roman occupation, but did not reveal why the village was abandoned; it may have been to make room for the bishop's expanding flocks, for it does not seem to have lasted until the Black Death which wiped out many settlements in England. A minor road out of Blockley leads back to A44 passing close to Upton Wold Farm, a superb example of the smaller Cotswold manor house.

Turning right on to the A44, a mile or so farther on comes a quaint signpost with metal arms, with a spike above said to have been intended for the heads of sheep stealers. At the next crossroads, Ryknild Street and another track known as Buckle Street meet before passing over the Edge on a minor road signposted to Saintbury. The Five Mile Drive reaches the Edge at the Fish Inn. This building was designed as a summer-house by the squire of Weston-sub-Edge, from which to enjoy the majestic prospect of the Severn plain flanked by Cleeve Cloud and Bredon. In full view of this spectacular panorama, Fish Hill descends over 400 feet in a series of dog-leg bends to Broadway.

Broadway, says Nicklaus Pevsner, is *the* show village of England, and in summer is thronged with tourists. It deserves, however, a careful perambulation on a sunny day in autumn or winter. From the seventeenth-century Court Farm which we pass on the right as we enter, down to the admirable group about the green, there is an uninterrupted succession of houses built of golden Guiting stone, a sort of dictionary of Cotswold building skill in a succession of styles forming a marvellously harmonious whole. The village was one of the first in the north Cotswolds to become popular with people of taste, and most of the houses received tactful alteration and enlargement at the beginning of the present century. The Lygon Arms was originally the manor house; it bears the date 1620 over the door, but has a wing behind perhaps a hundred years older. A dining-room and gabled wings perfectly in keeping were added in 1910 by C. E. Bateman of Birmingham. St Michael's church on the green is a nice example of early Victorian gothic. From the green, Church Street leads to the old church at Bury End more than a mile from the village. Here are more fine houses, including Abbots Grange, an important fourteenth-century building with Elizabethan alterations. This was the summer house of the abbot of Evesham who, like the bishop of Worcester, secured the inclusion of his Cotswold estate in his own county where it still remains. St Eadburga's is basically a Norman church, with much alteration.

Behind St Eadburga's begins the long drive of Middle Hill House. This was the home in the last century of Sir Thomas Phillipps, one of England's greatest book and manuscript collectors, and a notable eccentric. Towards the end of his life he wrote to a friend, 'I wish to have one copy of every Book in the world,' yet books had been only a sideline. Manuscripts were his principal interest and he amassed a priceless collection several thousand strong. He was far ahead of his time in his concern for the preservation of valuable manuscripts and humbler historical records. He made numerous catalogues and transcripts, and to publish them employed his own printer, whom he installed for some years in Broadway Tower, and later in Middle Hill itself, where he delighted to entertain fellow scholars and collectors, as well as taking part in some of the normal sporting pastimes of his peers. These amiable activities were unfortunately counterbalanced by a violent and cantankerous disposition, rabid religious prejudice and an unbridled facility in writing libellous and wounding letters.

To his lust for books everything was sacrificed. His first wife took refuge in the bottle and died young. His second managed to survive the unpaid bills, the frequent threats of distraint, the occasional appearance of the bailiffs and her husband's rough and inconsiderate treatment of herself by taking refuge from the discomforts of his house in ill-health requiring frequent visits to the spas. 'You will find great alterations to the comforts of Middle Hill,' wrote Sir Thomas to a friend in 1857, 'you could then move from room to room readily, but now nearly all are blocked up with Books in Boxes. The Drawing Room is the only room we live in, and three bedrooms for ourselves and friends. . . .' There were three daughters.

In order to save his son from the total ruin his bibliomania (which set in before he had left Oxford) seemed destined to bring on, Philipp's father, a Manchester cotton king, had entailed his estate on Thomas's heirs. The eldest girl, Henrietta, was therefore the heir. The three girls, until they escaped into marriage, spent their time compiling lists and making transcripts for their father. Their opportunities of acquiring likely suitors were further restricted by his debts. Henrietta consequently fell in love with the first personable young man among the scholars her father used to invite to visit his library. This was a rival collector, Edward Halliday, who later made his name in Shakespearian scholarship. Sir Thomas was too much in debt to give his daughter the customary dowry, but insisted that the young man's father should provide the two with a very handsome income. When his arbitrary demands were not met, he withdrew his consent in a fury, and as his daughter continued with her plans, he finally locked up her clothes. The next day Henrietta packed up what remained of her belongings while her father and sisters were dining at Northwick Park, and the following morning very early she stole out of the house with her sister and was married in Broadway church, with the support of two friends and a crowd from the village to throw bouquets into the carriage as she drove away.

Perhaps Sir Thomas would eventually have been reconciled, but within a matter of months Halliday came under suspicion of stealing some manuscripts from the library of Trinity College Cambridge! The academic world eventually passed a verdict of not-proven, but Sir Thomas pursued his daughter and her husband with implacable hatred to the end of his life, doing all he could to ruin them. Failing of this, he left Middle Hill untenanted and unmaintained, and sought to leave his library to the nation. The various public bodies he approached however, were chary of accepting a bequest likely to have quirky strings attached. The only one of his daughters who had to some extent shared his interests died young, and in the end the priceless collection passed to his second daughter and her husband, who had no interest in it nor means of maintaining it, and it was ultimately dispersed.

Beyond St Eadburga's the road climbs up to Snowshill, a small grey upland village lying beneath the crest of the Edge which reaches 1042 O.D. between here and Broadway Tower. The church is over-restored, but the cottages are ancient and the manor house is an example of the Cotswold style at its best, built *c.* 1600 and modernized perhaps a hundred years later, with an enchanting terraced garden laid out in 1919. It is open to the public and contains a collection of toys, clocks, musical instruments and domestic and farm implements made by a former owner, Charles Wade, who divided his time between Snowshill and his West Indian estate and was himself something of twentieth-century eccentric, with a repertory of ghost stories and psychic happenings.

The scarp between Broadway and Cheltenham is so steep that very few minor roads make the ascent, none between Broadway and Stanway. There is a delightful walk of about eight miles from Snowshill via Shenberrow Fort to Stanton clearly marked on the one-inch Ordnance map, returning through Stanway and by a track up Lidcombe Hill, past Paper Mill Farm. The turnpike descent of Stanway Hill (B4077) offers another superb panorama through gaps in the hanging beechwood, which here is fringed by laburnum trees cascading over the road in spring.

Four villages lying along the lower slopes of the scarp between Broadway and Ilmington – Weston-sub-Edge, Willersey, Saintbury and Aston-sub-Edge – belong rather to the wold than to the Vale, being largely stone-built, with parishes running up into the hills. Saintbury on Buckle Street, clinging to the steep hillside, is the most attractive, and boasts a connection with Robert Dover (1575–1652), the founder of the celebrated Cotswold Games. This pleasure-loving gentleman, a successful lawyer with aristocratic connections, founded his 'Olympic Games' early in James I's reign as a way of keeping up the sport and carnival of the traditional Whitsun Ales in despite of the puritan temper of the times. He had the enthusiastic support of very many of the local gentry, and especially of Endymion Porter of Aston-sub-Edge, courtier-diplomat and patron of the Arts, who was tutor to Prince Charles and later helped him as king to form his collection of pictures. Porter provided the site, assisted in securing King James's approval, and publicized the enterprise among his literary friends: Ben Jonson, Decker, Heywood and Drayton all contributed to a little volume published in 1612 under the title *Annalia Dubrensia.*

36. *Cottages at Stanton.*

The games lasted for three days in Whitsun week, and continued almost without intermission for over 300 years. They were held on the summit known since they were founded as Dover's Hill. The scarp here forms a natural amphitheatre; the steep edge of the oolite declines to a much gentler slope on the Upper Lias sands, the Middle Lias terrace forming a wooded back-drop. A wood-cut frontispiece in the *Annalia* shows the wooden castle or pavilion which was set up, according to tradition, on the two low mounds just west of the National Trust's topograph; the gentry are seen feasting round a low board and various contests are in progress. There was hawking, coursing and swordplay;

for strapping young countrymen, tumbling, wrestling, bouts of singlestick or shin-kicking, and every other kind of rough play; the girls had their own less painful games, and there was dancing in the evening until it got dark enough to slip away into the woods. A minor road runs along this part of the Edge from Fish Hill, and less than a mile west of Dover's Hill passes the Kiftsgate Stone, marking the meeting place of the hundred of Kiftsgate, at which the kings of England used once to be proclaimed. At Dover's Hill crossroads a right turn brings us down into Chipping Campden.

Campden's curving high street must be the most lovely in England. By moonlight it is pure magic; in daylight it reveals a succession of beauties too numerous to record here. It has been most carefully preserved, but not reduced to the status of an historical showpiece, though one may suspect that a high proportion of the genuinely Cotswold families now lives in the new quarter skilfully tucked away at the west end. The handsomest merchants' houses are for the most part occupied as hotels, but the smaller ones, no less elegant, are largely taken by commuters and well-to-do pensioners from the Midlands. Few artists and craftsmen such as delighted to live there fifty years ago can afford the prices even the smallest cottages have commanded since the last war. Moreover it cannot be denied that so large an influx of 'foreigners' has somewhat modified its former quiet, almost rustic character.

Campden has been the home of a number of interesting characters. First must come William Grevel, though we do not know much about him, nor whether he was born here. His fourteenth-century house stands at the upper end of the high street, and there he died in 1401. On his memorial brass 'the flower of the wool merchants of all England' is depicted in the style of a rich merchant, forked beard, short hair, a fitting tunic reaching to the ankles girdled with a highly ornamented belt from which hangs a dagger, over all a loose cloak. He left 100 marks for 'the new work' in Campden church, and had probably already contributed to it, but little of the work done about that time remains, for it was later in the century following his death that extensive alterations and additions gave the ancient building its noble perpendicular form.

The town itself, as we see it today, owes more to Baptist Hicks, a financier to whom James I and his court were nearly all deeply in debt before ever the king came to the throne. The Hicks were an ancient Gloucestershire family, whose descendant is Earl St Aldwyn, grandson of a Victorian Lord Chancellor (Sir Michael Hicks Beech). Baptist's father was a London mercer, dealing in silks and velvets; his mother is said to have invested in Drake's round-the-world voyage. Baptist became enormously wealthy, and early in the new king's reign established

37. *The High Street, Chipping Campden.*

himself in Campden as a landed gentleman. To the church he gave a new pulpit and a beautiful fifteenth-century brass lectern, presumably a piece of monastic spoil perhaps acquired as a pledge.

His first gift to the town (1612) was a terrace of almshouses finely executed in traditional style, which form with the church a singularly perfect group, and one of the most famous of Cotswold scenes. He repaired the town hall and built the noble market hall. In 1919 these two buildings were most happily linked by a terrace with a graceful cross designed by F. L. Griggs as a war memorial. Hicks rescued the grammar school from dishonest trustees and built new premises, of which the main schoolroom is incorporated in the Victorian building opposite the market hall. These are only his most notable benefactions. For himself he built an ostentatious mansion of which only the two small lodges next to the churchyard and a summer-house at the end of his terrace remain intact. He died in 1629 and his house did not long survive him. During the Civil War it was garrisoned by a troup of freebooting cavaliers, who must have made many converts to the parliamentary cause before they departed setting fire to the house as they went. Even royalists were not convinced that this was a piece of strategic prudence; the townsfolk were in no doubt that it had been the result of a final drunken carouse.

Sir Baptist Hicks was made Viscount Campden a year before he died. His title and estates descended by special licence to his daughter Juliana and her husband Sir Andrew Noel of Rutlandshire. It was a steward of hers, William Harrison, who was the hero of the famous mystery known as the Campden Wonder.

This discreet and elderly rogue went out one August day in 1660 to collect his lady's rents. When night came and he had not returned, his family sent a servant to look for him. This John Perry hung about gossiping and waiting for the moon to rise before setting off. In the morning Harrison's son Edward joined in the search, and presently an old woman came forward with a bloodied hatband and comb of the steward's, but no signs of struggle or further evidence were found in the place to which she led them. The Harrisons accused John Perry, and though several witnesses confirmed his story as far as it went, he was kept in custody for a week during which he made several contradictory and incriminating statements. When he next appeared before the magistrate he told a new story, declaring that the old man had been robbed and murdered with his own connivance by his mother and brother, who had thrown the body into a cess pool. Joan and Richard Perry steadily denied the accusation, and the pool was dragged without result, but all three were committed for trial.

At the autumn assizes the judge prudently refused to try the case because no body had been found, but the following spring before a different judge the jury without hesitation found the Perrys guilty, although John had sufficiently recovered his wits to deny his incriminating statements. Unfortunately Richard Perry had been persuaded to admit to another theft from Harrison, and the neighbourhood had become convinced that Joan Perry was a witch. At the special request of Edward Harrison, who stood at the gallows' foot, all three were hanged on Broadway Hill, Joan and Richard still protesting their innocence. John Perry watched them die before he too solemnly declared he knew nothing of his master's death and prophesied his return. His body was left to rot in chains.

Two years later William Harrison turned up. He said he had been wounded and robbed, secretly nursed back to health, transported to Deal, and put aboard a vessel which had been captured by Turkish pirates. He recounted with picturesque detail how he had been sold into slavery, befriended by one master, escaped from another, and had persuaded some sailors to carry him to Lisbon, where a friendly merchant had paid his passage home. Such adventures were the stock-in-trade of contemporary story-tellers, and his unlikely story does not seem to have been accepted without reserve by everybody; nevertheless he lived a few more years and died well-respected in Campden. Afterwards it was rumoured that guilty knowledge had induced his wife to take her own life, and that relatives going through her papers had found a letter from her husband written between the time of his disappearance and the execution of the Perrys. The truth has never been established.

Dame Juliana lived to be ninety-five, and she and her husband were buried at Campden. They are commemorated by a superb monument by Joshua Marshall showing the couple in their shrouds standing in the doorway of an open tomb. No doubt this macabre and powerful conception worked on the minds of the townsfolk, for when Norman Jewson as architect superintending repairs to the church caused the vault to be opened, the sexton warned him that according to local belief one of the party going down would be dead within a week. As it happened Lord Gainsborough's agent took ill and died suddenly two days later, and the tenants of the gatehouse cottages soon began saying that Dame Juliana was walking every night, 'and she'd been quiet ever since her coffin was resealed in 1881'.

Juliana's grandson was created earl of Gainsborough in 1682, and the eldest son was known thereafter as Viscount Campden. In the middle of the nineteenth century the earl spent much of his time at Campden. He became a Roman Catholic, and as a consequence by 1881 the Catholic community in the town was large enough to require a church and school, for which the earl gave a site. St Catherine's is easily the most handsome Catholic parish church in the Cotswolds, and fits in well at the end of Lower High Street. It used to be an impressive experience to hear this vigorous congregation of countryfolk roar out *Adeste Fideles* after the midnight mass of Christmas.

We have already met George Ballard (1707–55), the stay-maker's apprentice whose passionate pursuit of learning and antiquities led him to become the friend of many of the great antiquaries of his day. Too poor to buy the first Anglo-Saxon dictionary, recently published, he made a manuscript copy of the volume and was subsequently able to enrich it with a number of additional words identified by himself. He wrote one book, no doubt inspired by his friendship with Elizabeth Elstob and Sally Chapone (p. 127), Memoirs of *Several Ladies of Great Britain who have been Celebrated for their Writings and Skill in Learned Languages and Sciences*. He might be called Campden's first conservationist, for he made strenuous efforts to save the Norman font at Broad Campden, and the fine table tomb with recumbent effigy of Sir Thomas Smyth in Campden church, as well as recording the inscriptions of several now-vanished brasses. He was buried in the parish church, and his friends planned a worthy monument for him, but apparently it was never erected.

A more famous contemporary was Jonathan Hulls, a pioneer of steam. His father was a weaver, farming in a small way at Broad Campden but prosperous enough to send his son to the grammar school. It was a custom in Gloucestershire to test the aptitude of a boy by putting a book under his pillow just before the school year began in January; if in the morning he expressed a wish for it he was sent to school, if not he was destined for the plough. Jonathan grew up passionately interested in what were then called the natural sciences, and found two friends in Campden who shared his enthusiasms – William Bradford, the writing master, and Richard Darby, malster and carrier. The three became known in the town as the Lovers of Mathematics. Darby's house in the High Street is still called after him. Hulls became interested in Newcomen's engine, used for driving mining pumps, and conceived the idea of a boat propelled by steam, which with the aid of the squire of Batsford he patented in 1736, publishing a description of his invention illustrated with drawings the following year. This was still thought worth reprinting in 1860, but the experimental boat Hulls had built and tried on the Avon at Evesham was a failure, and he was never able to raise the money to try again. After this disaster he devoted himself to evolving various small practical instruments, including a slide rule which continued in use for a century at least. He died in 1758.

Frederick Landseer Griggs, R.A., who did so much for the town, was a Campden man by adoption only. Born in 1876 and trained as an architect in

Hertfordshire, he became an etcher with a beautiful technique, a highly individual style, and a visionary theme. In many of his etchings, notably Ex Anglia Perdita, Sarras and Lanterns of Sarras, he depicts a golden age created by craftsmen and tradition working hand-in-hand, in which ugliness and shams found no place. Campden seemed to him almost an embodiment of this idea, a rare survival, living but threatened. The Cotswold style dominates many of his imaginary scenes, which glow with a dying radiance. Campden he did all he could to save, and he built himself a house, Dovers Court, behind the upper end of the High Street, in keeping with his ideals. He died there in 1938, and his grave in the Catholic cemetery is marked by a fine headstone carved by his friend Gordon Russell.

Beyond Campden and the valley of the Knee Brook the land rises to a considerable height, reaching 851 O.D. on Ilmington Down. This is the northernmost extremity of the north Cotswold spur. High on the western slope lie Hidcote Boyce and Hidcote Bartram, two typical Cotswold villages with two famous gardens, that of Hidcote Bartram belonging to a most beautiful manor house.

15

Wychwood and the Ironstone Country

By A.D. 1000 little remained east of Ermine Street of the natural covering of woodland which clothed the wolds in prehistoric times. There was only one forest in the whole region visited regularly by Saxon kings for the purpose of hunting. This was Wychwood, occupying much of the 50,000 acres between the Windrush and the Glyme, most of it high ground such as had elsewhere been reduced to hill pasture or arable. Large areas of Oxford clay overlie the stonebrash here, producing a cold, ill-drained soil better suited to forest trees than primitive farming enterprise, though the presence of barrows and long-stones indicates some prehistoric clearance, probably temporary, in the remote past.

A charter of 994 shows that the bishop of Winchester's Witney estate, extending northward into the forest as far as Akeman Street, included several small scattered settlements colonized outwards from valleys cleared and more or less continuously inhabited since Roman times. At Widford, Asthall, City Farm in Hailey, Wilcote and Shakenoke Farm, Saxon settlement and Roman remains appear to coincide. Such names as Spoonley and Hailey denote woodland clearings originally visited only seasonally for certain harvests, which were already permanent settlements, probably with a few arable acres surrounded by a larger area of rough grazing. During the course of the next two centuries the great Benedictine abbey of Eynsham brought the villages of Church Hanborough, Northleigh and Combe into existence at the expense of the forest.

Already by A.D. 1000 one of the Saxon kings had made a hedge enclosing a part of the forest nearest to the royal manor of Wootton (the wood-tun) as a game preserve, and had built a hall in it. This was called Woodstock (= the woodland enclosure) and was known thereafter as Woodstock Park until it was given to the first duke of Marlborough and became Blenheim Park.

The Norman kings imposed their ruthless Forest Law on the whole forest, but the precise dimensions of Wychwood in the eleventh century are unknown.

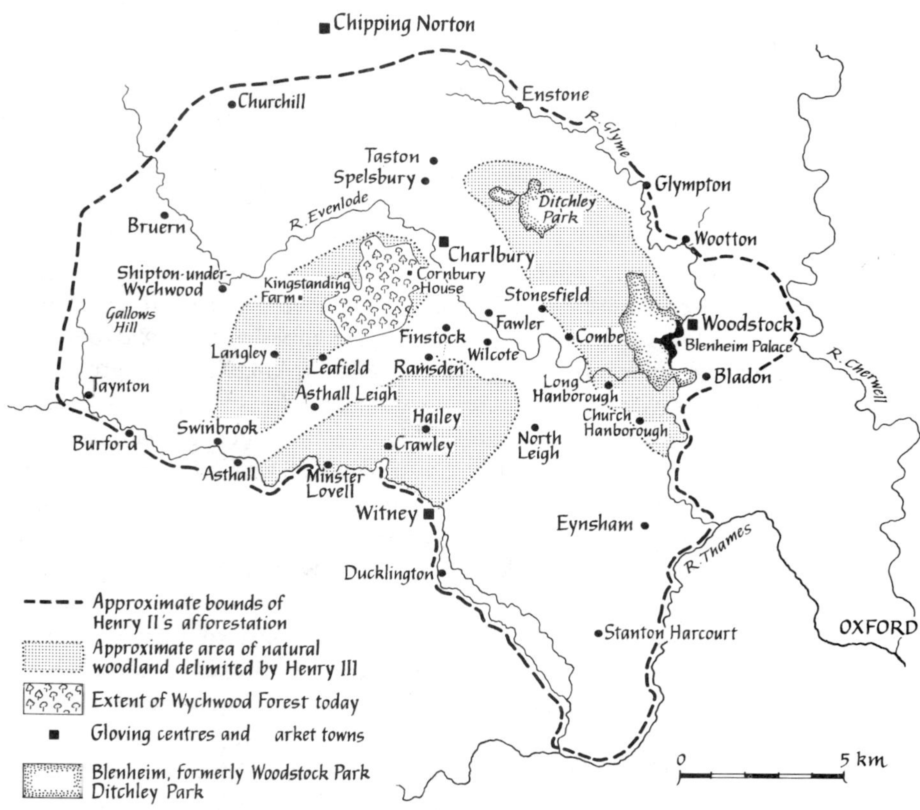

Map 11 *Wychwood.*

Henry I loved this hunting ground and used Woodstock Park to keep and hunt his collection of exotic animals, including leopard, lynx, camel and porcupine. He replaced the Saxon hedge with a stone wall seven miles in circumference, and the wooden hall with a palace of stone. He also built a lodge deep in the forest at Cornbury, and possibly another at High Lodge in the Park. The palace stood roughly a hundred yards east of Blenheim; its ruins were destroyed by the first duchess Sarah, who resisted her architect's desire to treat it as a picturesque feature on the ground that it would be occupied by thieves. Here Henry often kept his court, and was visited by foreign princes; in the chapel his daughter Matilda, who afterwards claimed the throne from Stephen, was married to the emperor of Germany. To supply the needs of the court and house the king's followers, a settlement grew up on the east bank of the Glyme which is now known as Old Woodstock, and until 1837 remained in the parish of Wootton. Meanwhile colonization of the forest went on; felling trees to create grazing or arable (assarting in Norman terms) could be licensed or pardoned on payment of a fine. Taking a deer was punishable by death or mutilation, but there were plenty of poachers ready to risk life and limb, and it is recorded that in 1421 scholars and clerks of Oxford 'armed and arrayed as though for war' came hunting in the forest in despite of the keepers.

Henry II was quite as fond of Woodstock as was his grandfather. He installed his mistress Rosamund Clifford (Fair Rosamund) in a separate lodging adjacent to the palace. An officer on leave who visited it in 1634 recorded his impressions of Woodstock Palace. He saw the 'strange winding walls and turnings' of the ruined Bower, the maze which features in the romantic story. Lurid legend describes the jealous queen attaching a thread of silk to the king's spur, and thus finding her way in to force her rival to drink from a poisoned cup; another more probable story says the king tired of Rosamund, who then retired to the nunnery at Godstow where she was certainly buried and held in honour. A paved pool known as Rosamund's Well close to the bridge in the park marks the site of her bower to this day.

The people of Woodstock believed they owed much to this romance. A hundred years later they declared in evidence that Henry had 'often resided at this manor for the love of a certain woman named Rosamund . . . and because the men of the king were lodged too far from his manor aforesaid [in Old Woodstock] the same lord the king granted divers portions of land of the demesne to divers men for the purpose of building hostelries thereon . . .'. At the same time the king granted them their Tuesday market, and thus the present town centre came into existence.

It was from Woodstock that Henry promulgated a revised code for all the royal forests, and he greatly enlarged the bounds of Wychwood, taking in a large number of old-established villages such as Charlbury, Spelsbury, Shipton- and Ascot-under-Wychwood, Fawler and Stonesfield, and new clearings such as Asthall Leigh, South Leigh, Finstock and Ramsden. Leafield may have been in the making at this time. It was established by 1213, but had no parish church until 1862. Two of the village's ancient fields were still called Long Sart and Broad Sart in the eighteenth century. The village stands on a high, bare down at the foot of a round barrow. Its people used to be dark-complexioned, and were thought of by their neighbours as strangers, possibly even an enclave of Britons.

The inclusion of so many established settlements enabled the king to increase his revenue from the Forest by granting landowners licence to make assarts. The abbot of Eynsham obtained such a licence about 1153, which was used so vigorously around Finstock, Stonesfield and Charlbury that there were frequent disputes with the king's Forester over the cutting of timber. Thirteenth-century abbots sold large quantities of grain from Finstock, and today these villages stand in an ocean of cornfields. The arbitrary exactions, rigid controls on expansion and new building, and fearful punishments of the Forest Law must have been extremely vexatious both to landlords and villagers, and in 1298 Henry III redefined the bounds to include only those areas still covered with natural woodland. The Forest was thus divided into three parts: Woodstock Park and a broad strip running northward between the Evenlode and the Glyme to Enstone, another broad strip running from Cornbury down to the outskirts of Swinbrook, and a third area of almost equal size from the Windrush between Asthall and Witney extending almost as far north as Ramsden. This last was separated from the royal Forest in the fifteenth century to become the private chace of the Lovels. Cornbury Park, the area around High Lodge in Blenheim Park and perhaps Hensgrove Wood contain the last of the true forest, but the lower ground remains noticeably well-wooded, and no new villages have been planted since Henry III's time.

Nathaniel Plot in his *Natural History of Oxfordshire* published in 1688 claimed that King Alfred made his translation of the *Consolations of Boethius* at Woodstock. Every English king from Ethelred the Unready to James I stayed there. Even Richard I, who spent so little time in his kingdom, visited it. The burgesses obtained the right to hold a four-day fair from King John, who is also said to have endowed a chantry which provided the town, still subject to the parish of Bladon, with a priest of its own. The church retains traces of work of about this date. John also built a lodge at Langley of which earthworks there are thought to be a remnant.

From the time of Henry III the Forest was often part of the dowry of the reigning queen. Edward III's queen, Philippa, loved the place, and several of her children, including the Black Prince, were born there. The Prince is said to have lived in the house called Manor Farm in Old Woodstock, formerly known as

Praunces Place. The tudor house contains some older work at the back, and especially a chimney hollowed out of a single huge block of carved oolite. Chaucer's wife is said to have been one of the queen's waiting women, and the house in Park Street known as Chaucer's House seems to have belonged to the poet's son.

From Henry VI the town obtained its first charter of incorporation, confirming the rights the burgesses had long enjoyed. Local tradition claims that Elizabeth Woodville waylaid Edward IV while he was hunting in the Forest, and thus became his queen. Edward alienated the local gentry by extending the limits of the Forest. This was put right by Richard III. Henry VII repaired and enlarged the crumbling palace and built a gatehouse; he also largely rebuilt the lodge at Langley, of which remain the north and west walls with a fine bay. A nearby farm called Kingstanding is supposed to be the site of a butt towards which game was driven during the royal hunts.

It was in Henry VII's gatehouse at Woodstock that the Princess Elizabeth spent a winter in custody after Wyatt's rebellion. In recognition of the loyalty shown her by the townspeople during this distressing episode, she gave them a second market and two more fairs. For herself she had had enough of the palace, which was left to decay, but she visited a favoured courtier, Sir Henry Lee, at Ditchley more than once, and gave him leave to enclose part of the forest to create a park. In her reign also the bounds of Woodstock park were enlarged, eliminating the fields of Old Woodstock; the existing wall, however, was built by the first duke of Marlborough.

James I, an enthusiastic hunter, repaired quarters for himself in the palace, but expected his courtiers to live under canvas in the park. Later he stayed at Ditchley, as did Charles I, who made many enemies by another attempt to reimpose Henry II's bounds in order to raise money. He began the building of a wall round the whole Forest which was completed by Cromwell in 1655; only fragments of this remain. The palace sustained a catastrophic siege in the Civil War which sealed its fate as a royal residence.

Cut off by the Forest with its unprofitable soil and repressed economy, Woodstock had remained a poor town very dependent on the palace. This dependence had one curious result. The court naturally brought with it hundreds of horses and a demand for skilled smiths' work. From this grew, at least as early as the sixteenth century, a manufacture of highly wrought and polished steelwork, for which discarded horse nails provided a suitably tempered raw material. By Elizabethan times Woodstock buttons, buckles, chains, scissors and chaced boxes were famous for their elaboration. In the eighteenth century a Woodstock chain of two ounces fetched as much as £170 in Paris. The new turnpike had from 1736 produced the necessary supply of road-tempered horse nails, but this industry perished in the nineteenth century, perhaps with the decline of traffic on the Great Road.

The presence of the court, and still more the proximity of an ample supply of deer and sheep skins, for centuries provided ideal conditions for glovers. The industry increased rapidly in the seventeenth and eighteenth centuries. By the early nineteenth century the town was producing 360–400 dozen pairs annually, and 60–70 'grounders' were employed in cutting out the skins which were distributed in packs at respectable inns in the town and in the Forest villages (for example at the Fox in Leafield) to the 1400–1500 women and girls who sewed them at home. By 1850 the output had increased to 500 dozen pairs a week. Witney, Charlbury and Chipping Norton were only slightly less involved. Traditionally only Forest women were employed. 'At the right time of year the hedges are still covered with sheep and goat skins bleaching in the sun, while at the cottage doors the women may be seen plying their needles . . . especially in the Stonesfield district.' Many of the skins were dressed at Witney, for which hundreds of thousands of locally-produced eggs were employed. By 1900, however, ready-tanned sheep skins were being imported from South Africa, and 'buckskin' gloves were made of imported reindeer. Machine sewing was first introduced at Witney, but in 1904, 2,000 women were still employed. Thereafter the industry declined rapidly in Oxfordshire; by 1967 Woodstock had only five glove manufacturers, Charlbury but two, and Chipping Norton and Witney none.

The organization of the Forest, essentially dating from the remote past, is revealed in a report of the Commissioners of Woods and Forests made in 1792. The Forest was then divided into five Walks, and there were nine officers: a ranger, two verderers, a launder, four bailiffs or keepers, and a woodward.

The chief officer was the ranger. For about two hundred years the Langleys held this office, and it may have been hereditary. By the sixteenth century it was normally held by a royal favourite, under Elizabeth the earl of Leicester was followed by Sir Henry Lee of Ditchley, under Charles II the office went first to the earl of Clarendon and then to the king's witty and dissolute friend the earl of Rochester, author of a famous lampoon on his master ('Here lies our sovereign lord the king', etc.), and verse which even today is not readily available in any library. It was at High Lodge in Blenheim Park that he made a startling but sincere death-bed repentance. This lodge was gothicized in the eighteenth century, but it still survives, and its battlemented roof gives a fine view over

Wychwood and the Oxford plain. The rangership was ultimately made hereditary in the Churchill family, and the Marquis of Blandford takes his title from an alternative name for Cornbury Hall.

Next in importance were the two verderers, elected by the freeholders of the county. They had charge of the game, prepared for the royal hunts and supervised the hunting of others who were entitled to it. On a mandate from the Crown they also sold deer to gentlemen intending to set up a private deer park; one of the last of these was Cromwell's friend Dutton, who had two brace for his new herd at Sherborne. The keepers worked under the verderers, were the scourge of poachers, and also provided browse for the deer in winter, fenced the preserves, etc. In 1792 sixty-one bucks and forty-two does were being killed annually, six of each for the royal larders. The verderers received as salary annually two bucks and two does each.

Under the verderers' control came the annual hunt allowed to the people of the surrounding townships. This was associated with the Whitsun festival, to which in the Cotswolds many of the folk-customs of May-day were attached, no doubt on account of the region's cold late springs. The people of Ducklington were roused at midnight by the blowing of a horn made for the occasion of peeled green willow, and at daybreak on Monday they went to the forest gate in Hayley, where they were joined by groups from Stanton Harcourt, Witney, Bampton, Brize Norton, Charlbury, Leafield and the other hamlets. The hunt were entitled to kill three deer (a small allowance, one would think, for so large a gathering), which were divided and brought home in triumph, the man first in at the death taking the head and antlers. There followed the Youth Ale, a week's revelry presided over by two children, elected Lord and Lady of Whitsun; every lad gave his lass a favour, the Morris dancers went round the villages, and a mummers' play was often performed. The end came with a feast on Saturday when the deer was eaten. This ceremony continued until 1827. An outbreak of plague in 1593 had brought Burford's hunt to an untimely end; thereafter the Lord and Lady of Whitsun led a procession to the edge of the Forest to receive the gift of two bucks and a fawn.

The launder (in medieval times the *agister*) had charge of the grazing on the lawns or clearings in the forest, and the many acres of rough heath (*bruaria*, hence Bruerne) such as may still be seen in the New Forest. Edward I's brood mares always ran in Wychwood. The villagers of Ascot, Shipton, Asthall, Fulbrook, Swinbrook, Minster Lovell, Taynton and Widford, as well as the forest hamlets, were entitled to graze horses and horned cattle (except oxen). Leafield, Langley and Shorthampton could also pasture sheep. No swine were allowed in

1792. In the Middle Ages the swine pastures would have been farmed for profit, farmers paying an agistment fee to send in their herds.

The woodward (forester) was responsible for the timber and his salary came from the profits of sale. Coppice wood was managed on an eighteen-year rotation. When it was cut, the Officers of the Forest took what they needed for fencing. They and other privileged people had certain rights (the abbot of Bruerne, for example, had been entitled to 'the third load'); the rest was sold. In 1535 wholesale dealings were forbidden and poor folk could purchase the small wood at an easy rate. In 1778 123 oaks had been felled for the navy, but the Commission found that there were so few good oaks still standing that the Forest could no longer be regarded as a reservoir of naval timber. Thereafter the agitation for enclosure soon began.

Propaganda was based on moral as well as economic grounds. The forest was said, apparently with justice, to be the nursery and hideaway of murderers, thieves and poachers. The forest folk were naturally as fond of evading what seemed to them an unjust law as any modern highlander. The bolster tombs in Burford churchyard were well-known to be good places for concealing the booty; in the forest inns, poaching stories were told with gusto, and more terrifying tales with an awed relish. Opinion was divided about the well-attested spirit which caused accidents in Worsham Bottom. Some thought it was an imp known as Black Stockings who brought down horses, others declared it to be a shrieking boy who had been skinned alive by sheep stealers to prevent his betraying them. A similar fate was said to have overtaken a shepherd of Bruerne.

The eponymous Tom, Dick and Harry were Forest brigands, sprung from a respectable family called Dunsdon of Swinbrook. They operated from Icomb, storing their booty and concealing their horses in a quarry-mine which ran under their cottage. They are credited with taking £500 from the Gloucester Mail, and boasted of their exploits in the forest inns. It was thus that the butler of Tangley got wind of an intended attack, and with the constable and others awaited it in the darkened house. At midnight a hand came through the Judas shutter reaching for the key, and the butler got a rope round it and held fast. Then they heard muttered oaths and the words 'Cut, cut', and after a groan-filled pause the arm dropped inside. Dick Dunsdon was never seen again, and yet it was similar boasting which did for Tom and Harry, who were hanged at Gloucester in 1785, and afterwards left in chains on the Gibbet Oak in Swinbrook parish.

The grave in Leafield churchyard of an unknown man is that of a stranger who arrived by train at Shipton and was robbed and beaten up by the guides who undertook to show him the way through the Forest to Witney. He was probably the rich uncle from Canada of a family who were expecting his arrival at that time, and waited in vain for any further news of him.

In 1854 the Act for the enclosure of the Forest was passed. It applied to 7,000 acres of which 2,000 were allotted to the Crown. Two years later the whole of these had been thoroughly cleared, seven new farms had been laid out, good farmsteads built of local stone, and ten miles of fenced road provided. In 1864 the whole remaining forest was enclosed in Cornbury Park, in which part the

38. *The Shaven Crown Inn, Shipton-under-Wychwood, traditionally built by the abbey of Bruerne.*

Forest fair, a highly popular event of comparatively recent origin, with hundreds of stalls and every kind of noisy entertainment, had hitherto been held. In 1806 it was attended by an estimated 10,000 people, and soon that number had doubled. In those days a procession of aristocratic coaches headed by the duke of Marlborough as hereditary ranger opened the proceedings, but after enclosure the attitude of Authority changed, and after repeated attempts to suppress the fair had failed, in 1888 Lord Churchill, the deputy ranger, settled the matter by ploughing up the fairground. With the fair and the useful grazing rights went the annual visit to Wussell's or Worts Well on Palm Sunday, to get water for a drink known as Spanish Liquor, made by infusing a stick of liquorice and held to be of great therapeutic value. Originally it was probably made with the wild liquorice (*Astragallus glycyphyllus*) which grows in Wychwood. Only rarely and by express permission is this visit now allowed.

A large part of the Forest belonged in the parish of Witney until the nineteenth century, when Hailey and Curbridge were made independent. A civil parish of Wychwood was created after the enclosure. Forest creatures, goat, coney, boar and staghound are portrayed on the corbel table above the church's north porch. Unlike Woodstock, Witney was a thriving market town very early, and manufactured woollen cloth besides. When Henry III visited the bishop of Winchester there, he laid out the then great sum of £20 for his wardrobe. The town expanded, therefore, from the higher ground round the churh, the *ey* (= island) from which it takes its name, towards the fulling and tanning mills on the Windrush in a long sloping main street. The butter cross (*c.* 1600) stands at the top, presumably on the site of the bishop's original market-place, and the Blanket Hall (1721) near the bridge. As in so many other towns, a twin settlement developed over the bridge, which was made a separate borough (Newland) by the landlord of nearby Cogges, and this became the industrial quarter of the town.

By the seventeenth century blankets had become the principal product. The loose weave and high nap of the traditional blanket, produced from the first by wires instead of teazels, is supposed to have been introduced by Thomas Blanket of Bristol, presumably a white-clothier, in the fifteenth century. By the end of the seventeenth century Witney blankets were being exported in large quantities to the American colonies, and according to Plot, red and blue blankets were eagerly bought by the native Indians. The increase in this trade must have underlined the need for the grammar school which was founded in 1660; it has a fine contemporary building next to the church approached by an avenue of elms.

The Blanket Hall was built for the newly incorporated Company of Blanket Weavers, whose regulations did the trade little good. However, in 1800 the winters' production was customarily sent down the St Lawrence into Canada in summer, the summer production going to America, and blankets of the highest quality were being sold to Spain and Portugal. Sensible cooperation between the principal masters, Early, Marriot and Collier, all Quakers, enabled the industry to weather the introduction of power-looms etc. with ease and a notable revival followed. The manufacture is still flourishing today, using partly man-made fibres. The large stone-built factories of the blanket-makers dominate the outskirts of the town. Witney's essential character is to some extent preserved, but the high street has been roughly handled by the multiple stores. There has been more new development, less carefully managed, than in most Cotswold towns.

Charlbury has no such problem, having lost most of its industrial and commercial reasons for existence. It was founded by the abbot of Eynsham as a market for the villages of the Evenlode valley hemmed in by the Forest, but in this capacity prosperous Witney was always a competitor; as the roads improved, Woodstock and Chipping Norton also became serious rivals. Mail coaches did not even call at Charlbury; the post was fetched down from Enstone in a little cart drawn by a pair of dogs. Cut off first by the Forest, and later by Cornbury Park on the west and Ditchley Park on the east, the market could hardly have survived without the glovers, though the coming of the railway must have injected new life. The company lost no time in advertising special trains to Charlbury for the Forest fair, and an attempt was made to transfer it to the town. In 1852 Charlbury glovers employed over a thousand people, and several small factories had been built. In due course the outworkers bought sewing machines from their masters, and were able to make about £1 a week, at a time when farm labourers were lucky to get twelve shillings, and quarrymen not much more. By 1905 Messrs Fownes had absorbed most of the small manufacturers. The market and fair survived until the present century; now the handsome houses and pretty cottages are largely occupied by retired people and commuters, and the little factories as warehouses by firms from Witney and elsewhere.

Chipping Norton has been more fortunate. Founded before 1300, its fine wide market-place was laid out along the road on an awkward slope which has been terraced in modern times. Its situation at an important intersection has always been in its favour. No. 20 in the High Street was most probably an inn in the fourteenth century; the cellar, formerly at ground level, contains some nice stonework of that date. The great 'wool' church testifies to its prosperity in the fifteenth century. Several handsome houses on the south side show the influence of the Baroque style to which Heythrop and Blenheim introduced local builders, and the comfortable circumstances of the principal townsfolk in the eighteenth century. In 1800 about twenty-two coaches passed each way through the town; there were well-established manufactures of gloves and horse-cloths and the manufacture of tweed had recently been introduced. Many of the older houses were being re-faced with stone. By the latter part of the nineteenth century the town was extending along the western exit, and many of the cottagers found employment in the new mill in the valley below. Bliss's Valley Tweed Mill, built in 1872, is a remarkably handsome structure very much in the Lancashire style, crowned by a tall chimney of the Tuscan order mounted on a flat dome. It was designed by George Woodhouse, a specialist in mill-building in the north-west. It is still in production, and the town retains its character as a busy local centre.

Two more villages in the Wychwood district deserve mention. Churchill owes its outstanding church, built in 1826, to its good squire James Langton. This worthy did much to improve the agriculture of his parish and the lives of his labourers. He died in 1863 and is commemorated by a grandiose drinking fountain, which must have been a most welcome convenience in the days when most villagers got their water from wells, streams and dubious stand-pipes. A huge monolith of local stone appropriately commemorates William Smith, the pioneer geologist. The chancel of the old church survives in the valley west of the village. Close by runs the brook beside which Warren Hastings, another native of the place, used to dream of recovering Daylesford for his family.

Hardly a trace remains in Ascot and Milton-under-Wychwood of the single heroic episode in their history. Soon after founding the National Agricultural Labourers' Union in 1872, Joseph Arch addressed a candlelight meeting of 2,000 men at Milton and held further meetings at Stonesfield and Combe. The following May a Milton farmer dismissed all his workers for striking in protest against his treatment of a carter, and engaged four labourers from Ramsden on the other side of Wychwood. Then sixteen women of Milton formed a picket armed with sticks, and went out to meet the Ramsden men, whom they easily stopped by explaining their case. The women were arrested and taken before the magistrates in Chipping Norton, who sent them to prison for a week or ten days with hard labour. A fine had been expected, and this harsh sentence was greeted with such vociferous anger that the military were called in. The villagers of Milton dared for some time afterwards to annoy the local farmers by calling 'ba-ba-blackleg' after them, and there is no doubt that the very existence of the union, however feeble, forced farmers to grant slightly better wages and conditions, although emigration agents from the colonies moved about the villages meanwhile gathering recruits. On the village green at Shipton stands a memorial to 17 men, women and children who perished at sea off Tristan da Cunha with 400 others on their way to New Zealand in 1874.

Woodstock has an excellent museum of local life, with a useful bookshop offering pamphlet information and itineraries for walkers and motorists. There is a plan on foot to establish an Oxford Way, beginning at Henley and crossing Wychwood from Woodstock to Shipton.

. . . . . .

Beyond Wychwood and Chipping Norton lie the Redlands, the glory of Oxfordshire according to Arthur Young. The reddish-brown soil is intensely fertile, some of the best corn land in the country. It belongs to the Middle Lias, with rare patches of Oolite capping a few heights towards the northern Edge. Its intense fertility is mainly due to the presence of iron. 'I have seen fields covered with flints and pebbles produce better corn than where there is none,' says Plot in his *Natural History of Oxfordshire*. The insignificant streams which drain the area, the Sor, the Swere and the Swale, have deep precipitous valleys cut down to the Lower Lias, which broaden towards the Cherwell in fruitful meadowland. The district has long been famous both for corn and cattle and is thus still devoted to mixed farming. Already by 1086 most of the natural woodland had been eliminated, and some upland villages had hay-cutting rights in the Cherwell valley. Until the nineteenth century the people of Duns Tew made a happy annual pilgrimage to North Aston for the hay harvest, those of Wootton to Steeple Aston.

The three Tews make a single appearance in Domesday Book, but these ancient rights probably identify the parent settlement as Duns Tew. Great Tew, however, is the show village. The ironstone cottages, though built in the nineteenth century, are perfectly traditional in style, with moulded door-frames and drip-moulds over the windows, and most of them are roofed with Stonesfield slate. The village is approached through deep tunnels of woodland interspersed with beautiful evergreen trees and shrubs. This lush and picturesque scene owes much to the Scottish architect and agriculturalist J. C. Loudu n whose designs for villas and farmsteads inspired many a Victorian suburban architect. He managed the estate here early in the nineteenth century, taking over old enclosed pasture which he reorganized for arable farming, laying out rectangular fields with their hedges running north and south to provide shelter from the prevailing wind, and accommodation lanes of generous width, open on one side to the drying sun and following the contours instead of defying the gradients of this hilly parish. The pretty little Falkland Arms on the village green commemorates Lucius Cary, Viscount Falkland, the philosopher-hero of the royalist cause, killed in the battle of Newbury (1643), who in happier times kept open house at Tew for poets and scholars.

Great Tew is the only one of the ironstone villages on the tourist circuit, but anyone fond of solitude, to whom the gentle elegance of the oolite villages is already familiar, would find they well repay exploration. I drove through the Redland on the blazing August Bank Holiday of 1975 hardly meeting a single car. Public conveniences and expensively decorated inns, those badges of tourist approval, are almost non-existent. The inevitable influx of commuters has produced for each village a new quarter, and cottage gardens shrill with the marigolds, petunias and salvias townsfolk use to better advantage to brighten their window-boxes, but the incomers have no doubt exercised an unobtrusive conserving hand.

Drive northward from Sandford St Martin. This is a typical 'closed' village where building and settlement were rigorously controlled by one or more substantial landlords to keep down the Poor Rate. No straggling here, and the handsome cottages built 1859–80 are completely traditional in style. A lovely manor house standing behind an imposing gate opposite the church completes the scene. B4022 is joined at Great Tew; turn left on A361 and take a minor road to Swerford, perching dramatically in the narrow valley of the Swere.

We come next to Hook Norton, the largest of these villages, filling its valley and spreading along it, with the church and main street high on the hillside above. This is the original Hog's Norton, 'where the pigs play the organs' as the local rhyme has it, with a reputation for rudeness dating back to the sixteenth century, but today full of notably polite and friendly people. The brewery at Scotland End (continue past the church and turn right up Brewery Lane) is a sturdy set of ironstone buildings picked out with red brick in the window architraves and diversified by a 'half-timber' and cast-iron hoist. It is still an independent company and produces an excellent beer.

The Brymbo Iron Company had their works about a mile east of the village alongside the railway. Freight charges to South Wales were from the first so high that it was found necessary to calcine the ore to reduce its bulk before dispatch. Two of the company's stone-built kilns are still in a yard on the left of the road. The line has been taken up, but the oolite pillars which carried it over Hook Norton remain standing white in the intensely green fields. Two miles farther east along this minor road comes Wigginton, a small attractive village on the north side of the Swere valley. There was a Roman villa within half a mile of the church.

Returning to Hook Norton, we take the first lane leading northward to the Sibfords, formerly hamlets in the parish of Swallcliffe. They are poised high on either side of a feeder draining north-westward into the Stour, and look out over the vast midland plain with the great bulk of Ilmington Down and Meon Hill shouldering in on the west. We come first to an excellent modern quarter leading into the dignified main street of Sibford Ferris, one side of which is almost totally occupied by Home Close (1911), a most successful exercise in the Cotswold style, a Griggs etching realized; on the other side are substantial farmsteads. At the end, screened by trees on the right, stands the early-nineteenth-century manor house, which since 1842 has been a boarding school of the Society of Friends. Banbury's famous sectarian zeal spread independents over the surrounding country, and here, as we turn left to cross the deep valley, is a pretty little Quaker cemetery. Sibford Gower is less distinguished. The manor house, now called Old Court House, is a rambling thatched fantasy grafted on to a seventeenth-century house by Frank Lascelles, the pageant king, who made his home here, and used to drive up from Banbury behind a pair of Arab ponies. He was a man of wide sympathies, anxious to promote international understanding, especially between peoples of different colour. He left the house for this purpose, but his bequest never took effect.

Next comes Shutford, built round the head of a stream and filling another precipitous little valley. From 1747, Shutford was a centre of the plush industry, an offshoot from Coventry, for which the district west of Banbury was famous. The material was woven on primitive looms as a part-time activity by agricultural workers on the Redlands. In 1811 Samuel Wrench of Shutford employed twenty-three men in his finishing shop. Plush is a kind of open shaggy velvet, formerly extensively used in horse clothing; it became very popular for interior decoration in nineteenth-century homes, and was also much used in the many pre-war courts of Europe as a substitute for velvet. About 1880 machinery was introduced, and thereafter Shutford and Banbury had the monopoly. The firm of Wrench continued in business here until 1948. It is easy to understand why, by then, it was impossible to persuade workers to live in so quiet a spot, rural from its duckpond at the bottom to the church and manor house at the top. The latter is rendered singularly tall by a long gallery under the roof, in which Colonel Fiennes is said to have drilled recruits in the Civil War.

From Shutford we must turn westward to visit Epwell, a tiny gem set round a spring which has cut for itself another steep little valley; then eastward again to Shenington's high green, beneath which the church is admirably placed looking across another deep valley to Alkerton church and rectory, buried in tall trees. From Alkerton eastward again to Swallcliffe, with medieval tithe barn and noble church perched above a little combe leading into the Sor Brook valley. After leaving Swallciffe and turning left at Lower Tadmarton Mill, we get a view of Swallcliffe Lea, where lay a considerable Roman township; the undulating skyline is broken by the clump of trees lying within the Iron Age fort on Madmarston Hill, and by other round eminences. Between all these villages minor roads drive across the high bare cornfields, dotted by substantial stone farmsteads, the product of late-eighteenth-century enclosure. Here and there opencast ironworking uncovers the orange-brown soil, or an area of unproductive grass shows the site of older mines; nowadays the land is immediately reinstated. A422 between Wroxton and the Edge runs with pleasant effect on a kind of causeway, the fields on either side four or five feet below the natural level.

A visit to Upton House would provide a good climax for this drive. The house is owned by the National Trust, and contains an outstanding collection of paintings and porcelain belonging to Lord Bearsted. The garden front gives on to a great lawn, and beyond terraced flower and vegetable gardens lead down to a deep dell occupied by bog gardens and ornamental ponds – one of the district's wild steep valleys transformed into a garden of delight.

Hornton village should not be missed. It stands at the head of the Sor Brook valley. The famous quarries were formerly within this attractive village behind the church, and are now occupied by cottages and gardens. The same stone is now extracted on the heights above, within a quarter of a mile of Edgehill tower. The church has a good Norman font and fourteenth-century frescoes.

The next village down the valley, Horley, has a characteristic site. The church has a good deal of Norman work, and a fresco of St Christopher against a charming background of fishermen in a flowery meadow, well-preserved. The return journey must be made through Adderbury and Bloxham, or South Newington (beautiful tracery and outstanding wall-paintings) and Barford St Michael. The church here has a notable north door, unusually high and surrounded by beak-head ornament; it stands perched on a mound. This remote village contains a number of exceptionally well-designed modern stone terraces.

Adderbury and Bloxham's glorious churches have been described in an earlier chapter (p. 96). Bloxham was formerly a borough and market town; the thatched court-house in the churchyard contains medieval features and adjacent to it stands the old grammar school. The town was built on either side of a steepish little valley, the main street consisting of two narrow winding lanes containing some substantial houses and inns. About 1800 a new road was driven across the market-place on a causeway, and the commercial centre, if such it can be called, shifted to the east bank, on the crest of which rises the over-tall building of All Saints School, a typical example of public-school gothic by G. E. Street. The school was founded in 1854 as a private enterprise by the Rev. John Hewitt, and is now attached to the Woodward foundation.

Three miles west lie East and West Adderbury, a single large village divided by the Sor Brook. It is the finest of all the ironstone villages, full of good houses, farms and cottages, with a fine tithe barn and a sixteenth-century grammar school (Rawlins House). Though he was educated at Burford grammar school, Adderbury House was the earl of Rochester's birthplace, and the home through-

39. *Medieval tithe barn at Adderbury.*

out her life of his spirited and long-suffering countess, a great heiress, who in the days when girls were expected to conform, declared her intention of marrying to please herself; the marriage, however, cannot have brought her much happiness. The house, altered out of recognition by the dukes of Argyle and Buccleugh in the eighteenth and nineteenth centuries, is now an Old People's Home.

Bloxham dogs
Come to Adderbury to buy their togs.

Adderbury was another centre of the plush-weaving industry. About 1850 open-cast ironworking began in the parish, and was carried on until the end of the century.

At Adderbury we join A423, the Oxford–Banbury road, and three miles south come to Deddington ('Drunken Deddington' according to a local rhyme). This is almost a ghost town now, its wide market-place empty, though with inns and houses worthy of its former condition. Here is another fine church, which once had a steeple to compete with its great neighbours. In its shadow, the Bull Ring is now a quiet court. The massive earthworks of the castle lie behind the south side of the market, to the right of B4031. After the decline of the market the town depended on the plush industry, the brewery, and perhaps the ironworks for its living, all of which have now forsaken it. A423 passes down New Street, already partly built in the fourteenth century; Leadenporch House is a fine hall-house of that date. Continuing southward, a minor road running along the side of the Cherwell valley through the Astons would make a pleasant diversion.

Banbury is the natural market centre of the ironstone district, easily overwhelming such small markets as Deddington and Bloxham as soon as the condition of the roads permitted. Today its cattle market is the most important in the country, visited by buyers from Europe and beyond. Though public buildings are of ironstone, the general impression is of red brick. A modern manufacturing town with an old industrial quarter next to the canal and with a big new industrial extension along the northern exit, it is in process of restructuring at the centre with an up-to-date system of streets, car-parks and concrete office blocks. It has a population of over 20,000 and is growing fast.

All this, however, is as out of keeping with the Cotswold scene as its historic iconoclasm is with the Cotswold tradition, within which the bounty of nature is exploited, but not to the point of abuse, and economic opportunity is seized, but never made the excuse for vandalism. Here are neither uncultivated deserts nor industrial wastelands, but a beautifully productive landscape. It is the special charm of the region to have moved with the times without surrendering its ancient graces.

Select Bibliography

Select Bibliography

Physical character

PAYNE, GORDON E., *A Physical, Social and Economic Survey of Gloucestershire* (1945).

MARTIN, A. F. and STEEL, R. W. (eds), *The Oxford Region* (1954).

DREGHORN, WILLIAM, *Geology Explained in the Severn Vale and the Cotswold Region* (1957).

RIDDLESDELL, E. J., *The Flora of Gloucestershire* (revised edn, 1975).

PLOT, NATHANIEL, *The Natural History of Oxfordshire* (1677).

Prehistory and early history to 1066

GRACIE, H. S., 'Mesolithic Gloucestershire', *Bristol and Gloucestershire Archaeological Society* (*BGAS*), AS. 89 (1970–5).

CLIFFORD, ELSIE M., 'The Cotswold Megalithic Culture', *Current Archaeology*, XXIV (1971).

CRAWFORD, O. G. S., *The Long Barrows of the Cotswolds* (1925).

O'NEILL, ST J. and GRINSELL, L. V., 'Gloucestershire Barrows', *BGAS*, LXXIX (1960).

SMITH, I., 'Ring Ditches in East and Central Gloucestershire', in P. Fowler (ed.), *Archaeology in the Landscape* (1972).

BRISTOL ARCHAEOLOGICAL RESEARCH GROUP, Field Guide 1: *Prehistoric Sites in the Mendips and Cotswolds.*

'Recent Bronze Age Discoveries in Oxfordshire', *Antiquaries Journal*, XIV, p. 264.

'The Earthworks of Rodborough, Amberley and Minchinhampton', *BGAS*, LIX (1937), pp. 287–307.

CLIFFORD, E. W., *Bagendon* (1949).

O'NEILL, ST J. and H. E., 'The Roman Conquest of the Cotswolds', *Archaeological Journal*, CIX (1963), pp. 23–58.

'Wycomb', *Gentleman's Magazine*, XVI, Pt I (1964), XVII, Pt II.
'Woodchester', *BGAS*, XLVIII, p. 75.
DONOVAN, HELEN, 'Roman Finds at Bourton-on-the-Water', *BGAS* (1935), pp. 234–9.
'Romano-British Stations on Ermine Street', *BGAS*, XLV, pp. 294–5.
FINBERG, H. P. R., 'Roman and Saxon Withington', *Lucerna* (1964).
The Agrarian History of England, I, Pt II, p. 159.
SMITH, A. H., *The Place-Names of Gloucestershire.*
STENTON, F. M. and GELLING, M., *The Place-Names of Oxfordshire.*
HILTON, R. H. and RATZ, P., 'Upton, Gloucestershire 1959–64', *BGAS*, LXXXV.
FINBERG, H. P. R., 'Some Early Gloucestershire Estates', *Gloucestershire Studies* (1957).
FINBERG, H. P. R., 'A Cotswold Boundary Dispute', *Gloucestershire Studies* (1957).
TAYLOR, C. S., 'The Origin of the Mercian Shires', in H. P. R. Finberg (ed.), *Gloucestershire Studies* (1957).
HOUGHTON, F. T. S., 'Saltways', *Transactions of the Birmingham Archaeological Society*, LIV (1929–30).
DARBY, H. C. and TERRET, I. B., *The Domesday Geography of Midland England.*
DARBY, H. C. and CAMPBELL, E. M., *The Domesday Geography of S. E. England.*

Architecture

DOBSON, D. P., 'Anglo-Saxon Buildings and Sculpture in Gloucestershire', *BGAS*, LV (1933).
VEREY, DAVID, *The Buildings of England: Gloucestershire, The Cotswolds*, I (1970).
PEVSNER, NIKLAUS and SHERWOOD, JENNIFER, *The Buildings of England: Oxfordshire* (1975).
PEVSNER, NICKLAUS, *The Buildings of England: Wiltshire* (revised Bridget Cherry) (1975).
REECE, RICHARD and CATLIN, CHRISTOPHER, 'Cirencester. Development and Buildings', *British Archaeological Report 12* (1975).
LAITHWAITE, M., 'The Buildings of Burford', in A. Everitt (ed.), *Perspectives in English Urban History* (1975).
VEREY, DAVID, *Cotswold Churches* (1976).

Agriculture

HILTON, R. H., 'Winchcombe Abbey and Sherborne', in H. P. R. Finberg, *Gloucestershire Studies* (1957).
THIRSK, JOAN, 'New Crops and their Diffusion: Tobacco Growing in seventeenth-century England', in C. Chalklin and M. Havinden (eds), *Rural Change and Urban Growth* (1975).

MARSHALL, W., *The Rural Economy of Gloucestershire* (1779).

YOUNG, A., *The Rural Economy of Oxfordshire* (1804).

GARNER, F. H., 'Farming', in C. and A. M. Hadfield (eds), *The Cotswolds: a New Study* (1973).

BRILL, E., *Life and Tradition on the Cotswolds* (1974).

Industry

AWDRY, W. (ed.), *Industrial Archaeology of Gloucestershire* (Gloucestershire Society of Industrial Archaeology, 1971).

1. The Quarries

VELLICOTT, C. H. and HEWITT, ETHEL M., 'Building Stones', *Victoria County History of Somerset*, II, p. 393.

SAUNDERSON, MARGARET, 'Stone Quarrying', *Victoria County History of Wiltshire*, IV, p. 247.

HOSKINS, W. G., 'The Middle Ages', *The Oxford Region* (1954).

ARKELL, W. J., *Oxford Stone* (reprint 1970).

BRILL, E., 'Two Cotswold Quarries', *Old Cotswold* (1968).

JEFFREY, R., 'Quarrying and Iron Ore', *Victoria County History of Oxfordshire*, II, pp. 268, 265.

2. The Woollen Industry

DE MANN, J. and CARUS WILSON, E., 'The Woollen Industry', *Victoria County History of Wiltshire*, IV.

PONTING, K., *The Woollen Industry of the West of England* (1961).

MOIR, E. A. L., 'The Gentlemen Clothiers: a study of the Organization of the Gloucestershire Cloth Industry 1750–1835', in H. P. R. Finberg, *Gloucestershire Studies* (1957).

MOIR, E. A. L., 'Sir George Onesiphorus Paul', in H. P. R. Finberg, *Gloucestershire Studies* (1957).

BRILL, E., *Old Cotswold* (1968).

WALROND, L. J., 'Wool, Woolmen and Weavers', in C. and Q. M. Hadfield (eds), *The Cotswolds: a New Study* (1973).

TANN, JENNIFER, *Gloucestershire Woollen Mills* (1967).

JEFFREY, R., 'Blankets', *Victoria County History of Oxfordshire*, II, p. 247.

MINCHINTON, W., 'Early trade unions in Gloucestershire', *BGAS*, LXX, p. 134.

3. Paper

ADLARD, E., *A Short History of the Postlip Mills* (1949).

BRILL, E., *Old Cotswold* (1968).

4. Forests

BRILL, E., *Old Cotswold* (1968).
WATNEY, V., *Cornbury and the Forest of Wychwood* (1910).

Transport

BRILL, E., 'Burford in the Coaching Era', *Old Cotswold* (1968).
HOUSEHOLD, HUMPHREY, *The Thames and Severn Canal* (1969).
KLEW, KENNETH, *The Kennet and Avon Canal* (1968).
COMPTON, HUGH, *The Oxford Canal* (1975).
MACDERMOTT, E. T., *The History of the Great Western Railway* (1927).

Towns

FINBERG, H. P. R., 'The Genesis of the Gloucestershire Towns', *Gloucestershire Studies* (1957).
JONES, W. H., *A History of Bradford-on-Avon* (1907).
GRETTON, M. STURGE, *Burford Past and Present* (1908).
RUSHEN, P., *A History of Chipping Campden* (1911).
WHITFIELD, C., *Chipping Campden* (1958).
BADDELEY, W. S. ST CLAIR, *Cirencester.*
PLAYNE, A. T., *A History of Minchinhampton and Avening* (1915).
HYETT, F., *Glimpses of the History of Painswick.*
BADDELEY, W. S. ST CLAIR, *A Cotteswold Manor (Painswick)* (1924).
SHELMERDINE, J. M., *Introduction to Woodstock* (1971).
MARSHALL, A., *Woodstock Manor* (1873).
BALLARD, A., *Chronicles of Woodstock* (1896).
LINDLEY, E. S., *Wotton-under-Edge* (1962).

Social and General

HADFIELD, C. and A. M., *The Cotswolds: a New Study* (1973).
DURANT, H., *The Somerset Sequence* (1951).
GIBBS, J. A., *A Cotswold Village* (1898).
JEWSON, N., *By Chance I did Rove* (reprint 1974).
MUNBY, A. J., *Portrait of an Obsession* (1967).
SHAW, NELLIE, *Whiteway* (1924).
GRETTON, M. STURGE, *A Corner of Wychwood* (1913).
GREENE, GRAHAM, *Lord Rochester's Monkey* (1975).
BRIGGS, K., *The Folklore of the Cotswolds* (1975).
GREEN, V. H., *The Young Mr Wesley* (1961).

General Histories

SMITH, BRIAN and RALPH, E., *A History of Gloucestershire* (1972).
ATKYNS, R., *The Ancient and Present State of Gloucestershire* (1776).

RUDDER, SAMUEL, *A New History of Gloucestershire* (1779).
FINBERG, H. P. R., *The Gloucestershire Landscape* (revised edition 1974).
EMERY, F. S., *The Oxfordshire Landscape* (1974).

Guides
Murray's Handbook for Oxfordshire (1913).
RICHARDS, *The Cotswold Way. A Walkers Guide* (1973).
WISE, SARAH E., *What is Wychwood?*
PRICE, PETER, *Walks for Motorists: The Cotswolds* (1976).
DRINKWATER P. and HARGREAVES, H., *Cotswold Rambles* (1975).
DYER, J., *Discovering Archaeology. The Cotswolds and the Upper Thames* (1970).

Index

Index